P9-BHX-083

Romans

Romans

An Exposition of Chapter 6
The New Man

D. M. Lloyd-Jones

15412

ZONDERVAN
PUBLISHING HOUSE
OF THE ZONDERVAN CORPORATION
GRAND RAPIDS, MICHIGAN 49506

ROMANS — THE NEW MAN
© D. M. Lloyd-Jones 1972

First published in the U.S.A. 1973
Second printing 1974
Third printing 1975

Set in 11 on 12 pt Monotype Garamond

Printed in the United States of America

To the faithful and enthusiastic Friday-nighters at
Westminster Chapel 1955-68

Contents

Contents

Contents

[ix]

Preface

One Sunday evening at the close of a service at Westminster Chapel, somewhere about 1943, a certain well-known preacher came into my vestry and said to me: 'When are you going to preach a series of expository sermons on the Epistle to the Romans?' I answered immediately: 'When I have really understood chapter 6.'

Like many others I had struggled with this chapter for several years, and had read, not only the well-known commentaries, but also many sermons and addresses on it. But none had satisfied me; rather they had left me with the feeling that they were all in trouble. Some just skimmed lightly over the surface, using the chapter to prove their particular holiness theory. The more solid commentaries seemed to be contradicting themselves and each other.

In 1954, while preaching a series of sermons on Spiritual Depression, and studying this chapter again, I suddenly felt that I had arrived at a satisfactory understanding, and preached two sermons on Sunday mornings giving what I now regarded as the true exposition of the main argument of the chapter. Having done so, I felt that I was now in a position to preach an extended series on the whole Epistle; and I began to do so in October 1955.

This volume is devoted entirely to the sixth chapter. The Apostle's argument is closely knit, and it is vital that we should carry in our minds all he has already said as we approach each fresh point. Although this involves much repetition, it is essential to a true understanding.

The matter is highly controversial, very largely because of its great importance. My hope is that these sermons will at any rate lead the readers to go back again to the chapter, and work through it carefully and patiently. Personally, I found my new understanding of it to be one of the most liberating experiences in my Christian life. I trust that this may be repeated in the lives of others.

These sermons were preached on Friday nights in Westminster Chapel during the period October 1958-April 1959.

Once more I am deeply grateful to Mrs E. Burney, Mr S. M. Houghton and my wife for their invaluable help.

September 1972

D. M. LLOYD-JONES

One

*

What shall we say then? Shall we continue in sin, that grace may abound?
God forbid. How shall we that are dead to sin live any longer therein?
                                                          Romans 6 : 1, 2

In the Epistle to the Romans, the important section that starts with the sixth chapter, is, I suppose, the best known section in the entire Epistle. It is the one that is most frequently spoken about, and probably it is true to add, the one that is most frequently misunderstood and misinterpreted. It is a familiar one because it is the section that is dealt with and quoted and expounded so frequently in connection with teaching concerning sanctification and holiness. It is generally regarded as the classical passage and statement in the whole of the New Testament on that particular theme. I shall try to show, however, that it is just at that point that this whole section has been so frequently misinterpreted and misunderstood.

A very common and popular way of dividing up the message of this Epistle is the following: Chapters 1 to 5, justification. Chapters 6 to 8, sanctification. Chapters 9, 10, 11, The problem of the Jews and of the last and ultimate things. Chapters 12 to 16, practical exhortations and applications. That kind of division sounds very interesting and attractive; it seems to make the teaching of the Epistle simple; but I shall endeavour to show that it is quite wrong, not only because it is so utterly mechanical, but also because it imposes upon the Epistle something which the Epistle itself does not say.

Certain people like to have everything classified in this fashion very neatly under headings; they feel that it makes everything much simpler; but I suggest that in the end it always makes things much more complicated. In any case it should be an invariable

[1]

rule in the interpretation of Scripture that we should be guided by the words before us, and should not impose upon them a scheme that may be in our mind but not in the words themselves. It is good to have tidy minds, and if you can produce a number of divisions all starting with the same letter of the alphabet it is possibly an aid to memory. But we must never do that at the expense of the words of Scripture themselves. I feel that the trouble with this section, generally, has been that in order to have some such tidy division in our minds we are guilty of forcing the words and imposing upon the text something that is really not there.

It is important therefore that we should look first of all at this section in general before we engage in a detailed analysis and exposition. As we do so I would start with this proposition, that here we are obviously not starting with a new section in a fundamental sense. I mean that the Apostle has not finished with one subject at the end of chapter 5 and now takes up something entirely new. That would be to start a new section in a fundamental sense. I argue that the Apostle is not doing that here; that is where that glib and easy classification and sub-division of the Epistle goes wrong. It insists on starting a new section here, and saying, So far Paul has dealt with justification, now he takes up the theme of sanctification. Some put the beginning of the new section here – chapter 6 verse 1; others put it at chapter 5 verse 12. In dealing with that verse I tried to indicate that I saw no suggestion that he was beginning to deal with sanctification there. I now say the same about this first verse of the sixth chapter.

We have not got an entirely new section here. On what grounds do I say that? Because of the very words that we have before us. 'What shall we say then?' About what? About what he has just been saying. So the Apostle has not finished with what he has just been saying; he is going on with it. What he is going to say now is something that arises directly and obviously from what he has already been saying. Clearly, therefore, we are looking at something which has a very direct and immediate connection with the previous chapter, something which arises directly from it.

What is that? We must remind ourselves at this point of the whole theme of chapter 5. What was the Apostle's teaching there? There is little point in going on to chapter 6 if we have forgotten what the Apostle has been saying in chapter 5. Let us never forget that as Paul wrote this Epistle it was not divided up into chapters. That was only done about the sixteenth century, and at certain points it was not done in a very accurate manner. But it was done for the convenience of readers. Actually it was a continuous letter. What then was the Apostle's theme in chapter 5? It was the theme of assurance and the certainty of salvation. Our argument was, that having worked out his great doctrine of justification by faith alone in the first four chapters, and having dealt with the various arguments that were brought against it, the Apostle then began to deduce the things that result from justification. 'Therefore being' – having been – 'justified by faith, we have peace with God, we have our access into this grace wherein we stand by faith, and we rejoice in hope of the glory of God.' That is the theme of the whole of chapter 5. Paul is asserting that our justification guarantees our final redemption in the fullest sense; that if a man is justified by faith, he can be happy about his ultimate salvation. If you are justified you can be assured that you are going to be sanctified and glorified. If we are justified by faith we 'rejoice in hope of the glory of God'. Or, as we indicated, we find the same leap from justification to glorification as is found in chapter 8, verse 30: 'Moreover whom he did predestinate, them he also called: and whom he called, them he also justified; and whom he justified, them he also glorified.'

That is the Apostle's theme and argument in chapter 5 – that if we are justified we are in a position to know that the whole of redemption is going to be ours. He wants these Romans to realize that, so he works it out and shows how nothing can come between them and this guaranteed end. Tribulations cannot do so, nothing can do so; indeed they all but add to the certainty. We have an absolute proof of that, he says, in this, that if God gave His Son to die for us when we were enemies, 'much more, being reconciled, we shall be saved in his life' [Chapter 5 verse 10].

That in turn led us on to that wonderful section, from verse 12 to the end of the chapter, in which the Apostle introduces the most wonderful of all themes, our union with the Lord Jesus Christ. We were joined to Adam, we are now joined to the Lord Jesus Christ. Paul says that our salvation is as certain as that. We are in Christ, and because we are in Christ all that belongs to Him will become ours, even as all that belonged to Adam has already become ours. Because of that one sin of Adam we have

reaped the appalling consequences. But because of this one act of
the Son of God we are going to reap all the benefits of salvation.
At the end of the chapter the Apostle's argument reaches its
tremendous climax: 'Moreover the law entered, that the offence
might abound. But where sin abounded, grace did much more
abound. That as sin hath reigned unto death, even so might grace
reign through righteousness unto eternal life by Jesus Christ our
Lord.' In Christ we are under the reign of grace, our future is
guaranteed, we have certainty. That is the Apostle's whole point,
that this wonderful act of justification is an initial move which
leads to all the other blessings and guarantees them all. He
deduces them all from justification. That is the theme which he
works up to the stirring climax at the end of chapter 5.

But the Apostle has not finished with the matter, and will not
do so until he reaches the end of chapter 8. For the moment,
however, he pauses. He has not finished with the great theme of
chapter 5, but he feels that it is necessary that he should stop for
a moment, and turn aside to deal with an extremely important
question. At the end of chapter 5 he has made a momentous
statement; he has said that the Law 'came in that the offence might
abound', but he adds that, though the offence did abound, 'grace
did much more abound'. Then comes the further statement, that
as we are under the power and the dominion and the reign of
grace, nothing can prevent our final salvation. But here Paul
anticipates a difficulty, and he wants to make his meaning plain
and clear. He has just said something that can be easily misunderstood; indeed there were many at the time who were
misunderstanding it, and especially the Jews. And not only
unbelieving Jews, but many Jews who had been converted and
had become Christians were in difficulty about the matter. The
Apostle, as always, is anxious to help his readers to understand
his message aright. So in order to prevent false deductions being
drawn from his teaching he takes up this question immediately
in order to make it clear once and for ever.

In other words, the statements made in verses 20 and 21 of
chapter 5 raise two special problems at once, and both are connected with the question of the Law. The first difficulty is this:
will not this sweeping statement about grace, and the apparent
setting aside of the Law, encourage people to sin, and to sin even
more than they did before. In other words, and introducing the

technical term, is not this kind of teaching likely to lead to what is called antinomianism, that is, to lawlessness? Are not people likely to say: 'Very well, if you tell me that where sin abounds grace much more abounds, does it not follow that the more I sin the more I shall know of the grace of God? Therefore, in a sense, the more I sin the happier I shall be, and the more I shall understand these matters; what I do doesn't matter. Isn't this teaching going to encourage people to sin?' That thought arises immediately in the minds of people.

But then there is a second question. If the Apostle speaks like this about the Law, was the Law then altogether useless and valueless? Why did God ever give the Law to the children of Israel? What was it meant to do; what was its place and its function in God's great plan and scheme of redemption? Now a thinking, intelligent Jew, whether unconverted or converted, would be very liable to think along those two lines as he listened to the climax at the end of chapter 5. So the Apostle pauses at once in his tremendous argument about assurance, and about the finality of justification, to deal with these two possible difficulties.

That is exactly what he does in chapters 6 and 7. We can say, therefore, that these two chapters are a kind of parenthesis between chapter 5 and chapter 8. The theme of chapters 5 and 8 is one and the same, and is continuous. Chapter 8, you remember, starts with the words: 'There is therefore now no condemnation to them that are in Christ Jesus.' That is a link with the end of chapter 5, not with the end of chapter 7. Chapter 8 begins where chapter 5 leaves off. Chapters 6 and 7 come in between. They are not a digression, they are a parenthesis; they are an interruption of the main argument in order to clear up subsidiary difficulties that have arisen in connection with particular statements. Chapter 6 deals with that first question, as to whether this sort of teaching is not going to lead to antinomianism, as to whether this tremendous statement about grace 'much more abounding' is not going to incite people to loose living and to sin. The business of chapter 6 is to deal with that difficulty. Then chapter 7 deals with the second matter and is an exposition and an explanation of the whole place and function and purpose of the Law in God's economy of redemption. Then after the Apostle has dealt with these two questions, he is in a position to take up again the great theme of the finality of justification; and he does so, as I say, at the beginning of chapter 8 and continues with it to the end of the chapter.

That is why I claim that it is entirely wrong to think that a new major section begins at verse 1 chapter 6. That is not the case at all, and it does violence to the Apostle's argument to suggest that it is so. In other words I entirely reject the notion that what is happening in chapters 6 and 7 is that the Apostle deals only with the question of the method of sanctification. According to a popular and familiar teaching he is said to open out that subject in chapter 6, and then in chapter 7 to proceed to tell us what his experience used to be when he was a defeated Christian; and then in chapter 8 to tell us how he became a victorious Christian. I am simply suggesting that there is no evidence whatsoever for that kind of division, and that it does violence to the Apostle's teaching to interpret it in that way. Chapters 6 and 7 are a parenthesis dealing with two special difficulties in connection with what the Apostle has been saying at the end of chapter 5. The very words 'What shall we say then? Shall we continue in sin that grace may abound?' of necessity compel us to realize that here we have an explanation, an exposition, of what he has been saying in those verses.

But let us look at this a little more closely. In chapter 6 the Apostle is dealing with the danger of antinomianism, the danger which has so often arisen in the history of the Church, of people saying, 'Ah, this is a wonderful doctrine, this doctrine of salvation, it is the free gift, the free grace of God; it really means that it does not matter at all what you do, you are saved once and for ever'. People have misused the doctrine in that way for the reasons that the Apostle will explain. That is what he deals with in chapter 6.

We can sub-divide this chapter into two sections. This must be obvious because in verse 15 the Apostle virtually repeats what he says in verse 1, where we have, 'What shall we say then? Shall we continue in sin, that grace may abound?' And he answers by saying, 'God forbid'. In verse 15 it is, 'What then? Shall we sin because we are not under the law but under grace?' And 'God forbid' again. Obviously the division therefore is: the first section, verses 1 to 14; the second section, verses 15 to 23. What does he deal with in these two sections? In the first section he deals with the whole question of the danger of antinomianism in a more or less purely doctrinal manner; and it is indeed very wonderful doctrine. It is an elaboration of the doctrine of our union with Christ which he has already introduced in chapter 5. It is pure doctrine with an occasional exhortation thrown in, especially when you come to verses 12, 13 and 14. The second section from verse 15 to the end is more practical, more experimental. Having shown in a doctrinal manner the folly of this wrong deduction that leads to antinomianism, he now shows that it is utterly foolish and unreasonable in an experimental and practical manner. In both he shows the utter absurdity of saying, 'In the light of your teaching let us therefore sin', but he chooses to do it in these two particular ways.

Thus we have taken a comprehensive and a very general view of the argument of this chapter 6. That enables us now to look at section 1. Here again we can still further sub-divide the matter. Verses 1 and 2 do no more than raise the question and give a general answer. In verses 3 to 11 the Apostle gives a more detailed answer, and an exposition of the doctrine of our union with Christ. Then in verses 12, 13 and 14 he makes a general appeal to us in the light of all this. Such is a rough division of this first section; and that enables us to come to a detailed exposition.

We have looked at the matter in general in this way because, as we have often seen before, if we are not clear about the general trend or thrust of the argument we are certain to go wrong in the detailed exposition of the particular statements. It is always good in interpreting Scripture to have the whole in your mind before you come to the parts; and we must never interpret the parts in such a way that they do not correspond to our conception of the whole. So having started with the whole we now turn to verses 1 and 2.

In verse 1 Paul states the question: 'What shall we say then? Shall we continue in sin that grace may abound?' The question is quite simple. I am not going to weary you with a matter that is discussed and debated by the commentators, namely, as to whether this is a purely rhetorical question or whether there was some objector who had actually said this. We do not know. This is a very good way of dealing with difficulties. A wise teacher always anticipates difficulties; and the Apostle was a very wise and experienced teacher. He knew, and he had already had experience of it in his ministry, that certain people would make wrong deductions from what he said; so he anticipates them. So it may well be that he introduces this rhetorical question in order to deal with a difficulty that might arise in people's minds. But, as I say, it may equally well be the case that there were people who were falling to this error in Rome; it is certainly clear that many had done so in various places in the early church. However, here is the question, 'Shall we continue in sin, that grace may abound?' If it is true that where sin abounded grace has much more abounded, well then, 'shall we continue in sin, that grace may abound yet further?'

First of all let me make a comment, to me a very important and vital comment. The true preaching of the gospel of salvation by grace alone always leads to the possibility of this charge being brought against it. There is no better test as to whether a man is really preaching the New Testament gospel of salvation than this, that some people might misunderstand it and misinterpret it to mean that it really amounts to this, that because you are saved by grace alone it does not matter at all what you do; you can go on sinning as much as you like because it will redound all the more to the glory of grace. That is a very good test of gospel preaching. If my preaching and presentation of the gospel of salvation does not expose it to that misunderstanding, then it is not the gospel. Let me show what I mean.

If a man preaches justification by works, no one would ever raise this question. If a man's preaching is, 'If you want to be Christians, and if you want to go to heaven, you must stop committing sins, you must take up good works, and if you do so regularly and constantly, and do not fail to keep on at it, you will make yourselves Christians, you will reconcile yourselves to God, and you will go to heaven'. Obviously a man who preaches in that strain would never be liable to this misunderstanding. Nobody would say to such a man, 'Shall we continue in sin, that grace may abound?', because the man's whole emphasis is just this, that if you go on sinning you are certain to be damned, and only if you stop sinning can you save yourselves. So that misunderstanding could never arise. And you can apply the same test to any other type or kind of preaching. If a man preaches that you are saved by the Church, or by sacraments, and so on, this

[8]

kind of argument does not arise. This particular misunderstanding can only arise when the doctrine of justification by faith only is presented.

Let me put this in another way. You remember what the Apostle says in chapter 4 in the fifth verse: 'But to him that worketh not, but believeth on him that justifieth the ungodly, his faith is counted for righteousness.' It is when a man says a thing like that – that God justifies the ungodly – that the misunderstanding is liable to arise. Or when a man says what we found in chapter 5 verses 9 and 10: 'Much more then, being now justified by his blood, we shall be saved from wrath through him. For if, when we were enemies, we were reconciled to God by the death of his Son, much more, being reconciled, we shall be saved by his life.' It is when we preach things like that, that this misunderstanding tends to occur. So this is a very good test of one's preaching.

There is a sense in which the doctrine of justification by faith only is a very dangerous doctrine; dangerous, I mean, in the sense that it can be misunderstood. It exposes a man to this particular charge. People listening to it may say, 'Ah, there is a man who does not encourage us to live a good life, he seems to say that there is no value in our works, he says that "all our righteousnesses are as filthy rags". Therefore what he is saying is, that it does not matter what you do, sin as much as you like'. There is thus clearly a sense in which the message of 'justification by faith only' can be dangerous, and likewise with the message that salvation is entirely of grace. I say therefore that if our preaching does not expose us to that charge and to that mis-understanding, it is because we are not really preaching the gospel. Nobody has ever brought this charge against the Church of Rome, but it was brought frequently against Martin Luther; indeed that was precisely what the Church of Rome said about the preaching of Martin Luther. They said, 'This man who was a priest has changed the doctrine in order to justify his own marriage and his own lust', and so on. 'This man', they said, 'is an antinomian; and that is heresy.' That is the very charge they brought against him. It was also brought against George Whitefield two hundred years ago. It is the charge that formal dead Christianity – if there is such a thing – has always brought against this startling, staggering message, that God 'justifies the ungodly', and that we are saved, not by anything that we do, but in spite of it, entirely and only by the grace of God through our Lord and Saviour Jesus Christ.

That is my comment; and it is a very important comment for preachers. I would say to all preachers: If your preaching of salvation has not been misunderstood in that way, then you had better examine your sermons again, and you had better make sure that you really are preaching the salvation that is offered in the New Testament to the ungodly, to the sinner, to those who are dead in trespasses and sins, to those who are enemies of God. There is this kind of dangerous element about the true presentation of the doctrine of salvation.

Now let us look at the answer which the Apostle gives in verse 2: 'God forbid', he says. We have already met that expression in the third chapter and have seen that it is not a strictly literal translation. The Apostle did not use the word 'God' at all, but the Authorized Version translators wanted to bring out the emphasis strongly, so they said 'God forbid'. What it really means is 'by no means', 'let it not be', 'it is unthinkable', 'it should never even be suggested'. It is a very strong term, and in a sense the translators were justified in rendering it as 'God forbid'.

Why does the Apostle put it as strongly as that? Clearly for this reason, that to put that question, or to raise that matter at all, simply shows a complete failure to understand everything that he has been saying about justification by faith only. If a man raises this question about continuing in sin, it means that so far he has not grasped what the Apostle has been saying in chapters 1 to 5. That is why it is unthinkable, that is why it should not be mentioned for a moment. Such a man has not only misunderstood justification, he has entirely misunderstood the doctrine of our union with the Lord Jesus Christ. If he had understood that, he would never raise a point like this.

Let me make the same point in another way. A man may say to me, 'You teach that where sin abounded, grace did much more abound; shall we therefore continue in sin that grace may abound?' What this man is really saying is that he has completely failed to understand the whole meaning and purpose of grace. What is that? The Apostle, one would have thought, had put it quite plainly in the last verse of chapter 5, 'That AS sin hath reigned unto death, EVEN so might grace reign through righteousness unto eternal life, by Jesus Christ our Lord'. What is the business of grace? Is it to allow us to continue in sin? No! It is to deliver us from the bondage and the reign of sin, and to put us under the reign of grace. So when a man asks, 'Shall we therefore continue in sin that grace might abound?', he is merely showing that he has failed to understand either the tyranny of the reign of sin, or the whole object and purpose of grace and its marvellous reign over those who are saved. Or, to put it positively, a man who really understands justification, its meaning and its purpose, will never think like that and will never speak like that. But I want to put it even more strongly. A man who is justified, and who is under the reign of grace, cannot think like that, still less act like that.

That is exactly what the Apostle proceeds to say. 'God forbid', he says. 'How shall we that are dead unto sin live any longer therein?' Here, we come face to face with one of the greatest and most important statements of this Epistle. In some shape or form we shall find that the Apostle goes on repeating this one statement. It occurs in verse 2. We shall find it again in verses 6 and 7 and 8. Again we get it in verse 10, and, in a sense, it is in the exhortation of verse 11. Nothing therefore is more important for us than to understand the exact meaning of this statement, 'How shall we that are dead unto sin live any longer therein?'

Here we arrive at the commencement of our detailed verse-by-verse exposition. We have taken note of the context, the setting, and the way in which we have to approach the chapter. And now, at the outset of our detailed exposition we must get clear in our minds the meaning of this great phrase. Unfortunately the Authorized Version, in this instance, has a bad translation. It is what I have been quoting, 'How shall we that are dead to sin live any longer therein?' But it should be, 'How shall we that died to sin . . .' That is what you have in the more modern translations; and here they are undoubtedly right. The Apostle has used the aorist tense, and the aorist tense means this – it is something that has happened once and for ever, it is a reference to a definite fact that belongs to the past. He is not referring so much to something that is true of us now. He says, 'How shall we that died to sin'. It is something that has happened once and for ever, some time or other, in our past history as believers. We died to sin. It does not mean, therefore, 'are dead to sin', and it does not mean 'have died to sin'. If we translated it, 'How shall we that have died to sin?', it might still appear to be a process which had gone on over a period of time, but that now we can say that at last we have reached the end of this process and have died to sin. The Apostle does not say that. He is referring to one act, to one event, to something that has happened at one unique point in our history. 'How shall we that died to sin?' It is the aorist tense. We shall have to be careful to observe this when we come to verses 6, 7, 8, 10 and 11, because he uses this same tense in all those cases also.

As we come to deal with the meaning of this 'key' doctrine we shall see how vital it is to bear this text in mind. Here is something, Paul says, that has happened to you once and for ever. I will anticipate the detailed exposition to this extent, I will tell you when it happened. This is something that happened when we ceased to be 'in Adam' and when we began to be 'in Christ'. I leave it at that for the moment. Here, then, in verses 1 and 2 the Apostle is introducing this possible misunderstanding in terms of antinonianism; and he gives his general answer. Then, having given it in general, he will take it up in verse 3 and will go through it in detail in order to show us the utter absurdity of deducing from the glorious doctrines of justification, and salvation by grace, that it no longer matters how we live as Christians, and that, in a sense, the more we sin the more glory will redound to the reign of grace.

Two

*

What shall we say then? Shall we continue in sin that grace may abound?

God forbid. How shall we that are dead to sin live any longer therein?
                                                    Romans 6 : 1, 2

In this second verse we have one of the fundamental propositions of the Apostle. I maintain that in this answer which he gives to the question in verse 1 he is really giving his complete answer. He then goes on to give it in detail in verse 3 and the following verses. In saying that, I am aware that I am disagreeing with the renowned and redoubtable Charles Hodge in his Commentary on this Epistle. Charles Hodge feels that in verse 2 the Apostle is just making a general statement, but that in verse 3 he begins with his argument. I dissent from that entirely, and suggest rather that the Apostle gives his full argument in verse 2 and then proceeds to divide it up into parts. My reason for saying that, is that verse 3 starts with the words, 'Know ye not?' In effect he is saying, 'Well, I have made my comprehensive statement; let me now establish it, let me prove it to you, let me demonstrate my contention'. Not only that; I trust that as we proceed we shall see that the whole of this section which runs on to the end of verse 14 is nothing but an extended commentary on this statement which the Apostle makes here in verse 2. The other statements are particular aspects of it, but here we have the whole. To prove my contention we now proceed to our exposition.

This statement is one of the Apostle's fundamental propositions; and it is one of the most important statements of Christian doctrine, therefore, in the whole of the Epistle. That is why the Apostle goes on repeating it in various forms in almost every verse up to verse 6. He says here, in verse 2, 'How shall we that are dead to sin live any longer therein?' In verse 3: 'Know ye not that so many of us as were baptized into Jesus Christ were baptized into his death?' That is part of it. In verse 4 there is an extension of this thought: 'Therefore we are buried with him by baptism into death, that like as Christ was raised up from the dead by the glory of the Father, even so we also should walk in newness of life'. Then verse 5: 'If we have been planted together in the likeness of his death,' etc. Verse 6: 'Knowing this, that our old man is crucified with him.' Indeed Paul goes beyond that, for in verse 8 we have, 'Now if we be dead with Christ, we believe that we shall also live with him'. Then in his exhortation in the 11th verse he says, 'Likewise reckon ye also yourselves to be dead unto sin, but alive unto God through our Lord Jesus Christ'.

Now all these are variations of this one fundamental proposition; sometimes parts of it, sometimes the whole of it. It is clearly something which in the mind of the Apostle is altogether crucial, and therefore of vital importance to us. Indeed I do not hesitate to say that to understand the meaning of this phrase is the key to the understanding of the Apostle's whole doctrine of salvation – in its full sense.

It is imperative therefore that we should know exactly what it means. We shall of necessity be in trouble in all the verses I have quoted if we are not clear about this verse; but once we are clear about this the rest will follow comparatively easily.

What then does the Apostle mean? We start with the little word 'we'. Our Authorized Version does not bring out the power and the force that the Apostle put into this word. We read here, 'How shall *we* that are dead to sin live any longer therein?'; but what Paul wrote was this: 'We – how shall we . . . ?' He starts with the word 'We', he puts emphasis upon it. It is vital. Why? Because what he is really saying is this: 'We – being what we are – how is it possible or conceivable that we should continue in sin that grace may abound?' *We* being such as we are – can *we* who are dead to sin live any longer therein?' That is the emphasis, and immediately we are given a key to the interpretation. The whole emphasis is on our uniqueness, our special position, we 'being what we are'. That is what makes the question of verse 1 unthinkable. Paul says, 'If you truly realize who you are and what your position is, this question that has been raised automatically goes out'. In other words, the real trouble with Christian people who do not understand the doctrine of justification by grace through faith is that they do not realize who and what they are; they do not realize their position. We being what we are, and who we are, can such people as we 'live any longer in sin?'

That is the force of the argument, and it is important that we should realize the emphasis he puts upon this little word 'we'. The Apostle is saying that people who raise the kind of question found in the first verse are people who have simply not been able to follow his argument in chapter 5 verse 12 to verse 21. If only they had followed that, and realized who they are and where they stand, and what they are in the light of that doctrine, they would realize how utterly monstrous and ridiculous it is to put such a question. There is the first part of the exposition; and, indeed, as I say, the very prominence that the Apostle gives to the word 'we' virtually tells us everything. Fortunately, however, he goes on and states the matter more fully.

We turn now to what I called the 'key' statement, the 'key' phrase, 'We that are dead to sin'. We have seen that the correct translation of this is, 'We that died to sin', and at once we see the difference this makes. If you read it as 'We that are dead to sin' you might say, Well, it is a description of our present state and condition. We are now dead to sin, that is our present state and condition. But the Apostle was not concerned to say that. Neither does he say, 'We have died to sin', because there again it might suggest a process, that once we were very much alive to sin but that gradually we became more and more dead to it, until we have reached a point at which we can say that after all our effort and struggle and endeavour we have died to sin. But the Apostle did not say that either. He used the aorist tense, and the aorist tense always points to an event or an act that has happened once and been concluded. So we must translate it – and all are really agreed about this; that is why the Authorized Version is most unfortunate at this point – 'How shall we that died to sin . . . ?' It is pointing back to something in the past, a fact, an act, an event which happened once, not a process. The Apostle is not describing a process, he is not describing a present position or condition; he is describing something that has happened to us as a fact, as an act in our own past experience. Now that is of

[15]

crucial importance; it is as crucial as this, that we shall find that
he uses precisely the same tense in verses 6, 7, 8, 10, and 11.
I shall have to keep on repeating this and bringing out this same
point with the same emphasis, that in all these instances it is the
aorist tense. 'We – how shall we that died to sin live any longer
therein?'

What does it mean? what exactly is Paul saying? Here, again,
I must put several possibilities before you, because commentators
have put forward various explanations and answers to the
question. There are some who have not hesitated to say that
it means just this, that as Christians we are dead completely to
the influence, to the power, and to the love of sin. They are what
are called 'Perfectionists'. They teach that they have completely
finished with sin in that sense, that they are entirely dead to its
influence, to its power, and to the love of sin. There is no need
to stay with this because there is only one answer to give to that
teaching, and that is that it is not true. There is no such person.
Not only that, the whole argument of the Apostle makes that
explanation impossible. If it were true then he would never have
written verses 11, 12, and 13: 'Likewise reckon yourselves also
to be dead unto sin, but alive unto God through Jesus Christ
our Lord'. He would never have written, 'Let not sin therefore
reign in your mortal body'. You need not say that to a man who
is completely dead to all the power and the influence and all the
love of sin. It just makes the Apostle's subsequent exposition and
appeal and exhortation quite otiose, and, indeed, ridiculous. So
we reject that immediately.

But there are others who say that it means that the Apostle
teaches that we 'ought' to be dead to sin. He is not saying that
we are dead to it, but that if we were Christians worthy of the
name and really had understanding, we ought to be dead to sin.
'How can you, who ought to be dead to sin, live any longer
therein?' There is only one answer to that also. The Apostle does
not say that we ought to be dead to sin; he says, in the aorist
tense, that 'we died to sin'. There is no 'ought' here; he is telling
us of something that is already true of us.

Then there are others who say that it means, 'How shall we
that are dying more and more to sin, live any longer therein?'
How can we who are dying more and more to sin say, 'Shall we
continue in sin that grace may abound?' That, they say, would be

self-contradictory and ridiculous. Again there is only one answer. The Apostle does not say in the 'continuous present' that we are dying more and more unto sin. The people who put that explanation forward take the Authorized Version as correct and fail to realize that it is the aorist tense. We are not dying more and more unto sin; that is not what Paul says. He says, 'We died unto sin'; we died unto sin in that act, in that fact, in that event in the past. So we must reject those three possible explanations.

We come now to another, and again I confess freely that I am unhappy, because once more I venture to express a criticism of the great Charles Hodge. No one should do that lightly. But we are reminded that no man is infallible; we do not believe in popes. We are entitled to examine the exposition of any man, however great and learned he may have been. Charles Hodge tells us that this statement means, 'How shall we that have *renounced* sin live any longer therein?' He says, Now a man who is a Christian by the very fact that he claims to be a Christian is a man who is saying that he has renounced sin. Why does he say that he believes in the Lord Jesus Christ? He does so because he has come to realize that he is a sinner and that that leads to punishment, eternal punishment; therefore he feels the need to be delivered. He believes the gospel concerning the Lord Jesus Christ as One who can deliver him from sin; therefore when he says, 'I believe on the Lord Jesus Christ', says Hodge, he is saying, 'I want to be delivered from sin. It is because I have come to see what a terrible thing sin is that I want to be delivered from it; I renounce it and all its ways.' Well then, says Hodge, if a man has said that, if he has renounced sin, how can he possibly say, 'Shall we continue in sin that grace may abound?' He is contradicting himself; he is claiming at one moment that he wants to be rid of sin, but then he says, 'Ah well, this wonderful grace allows me to continue in sin', and so he is contradicting himself, says Charles Hodge.

Why do I not accept that interpretation? First and foremost I feel that Hodge is not giving due weight to this 'We', he is not giving sufficient emphasis to the uniqueness of our position. According to Paul that is the thing that makes this suggestion impossible and unthinkable. 'We being what we are' – not something we have done, but our being what we are; that is the vital thing. Of course, when a man claims to believe in Christ he renounces sin, but that is not what the Apostle is saying here.

[17]

He is not talking about something we do, he is telling us about something that has happened to us. He does not say here that we have renounced sin, he says that we died to sin. It is essential that we should reject Hodge's exposition, and indeed go further, and say that at that point he is almost saying something which comes very near to being a direct contradiction of the whole of the Apostle's argument in this section. Charles Hodge leaves it all with us – we have renounced sin. He says that Paul was saying to these Romans, 'When you submitted to baptism, when you came forward as candidates for baptism, what were you doing? Well, you were saying, "I want to finish with that old life of sin; that is why I asked for baptism. I want to be dead to it, I want to have no more to do with it, I renounce it".' But that puts all the emphasis on us, on our activity, on our action, on what we are doing; whereas, as I hope to show, the Apostle's emphasis is on what has been done to us, on our position, our status. Not what we have done but what has been done to us – that great thing that he has been writing about in chapter 5 verses 12 to the end.

I think I understand why Charles Hodge put forward this particular interpretation. Charles Hodge, I believe, was afraid that if he interpreted it as I am proposing to do he would have exposed himself to the charge of antinomianism. But, as I have pointed out, if we do not interpret this phrase in such a way as to expose ourselves to the charge of antinomianism, we are not expounding it correctly. We must be very careful not to allow a spirit of fear to possess us as we seek to expound the truth. So I reject Hodge's explanation.

And now, if I may borrow a statement once made by King David to his wife Michal, 'Let me be yet more vile'. On this occasion I have to disagree somewhat with Robert Haldane also. It is no small thing to disagree with these two giants at one and the same time! What is Haldane's exposition? He sees clearly that what we have just been considering is obviously inadequate, and he rejects the other expositions which I have rejected. He can see that Paul is not talking about something that we are doing but about something that has happened to us. He realizes that there is a very real death to sin here. The Apostle says, 'We died to sin'. Very well, says Haldane rightly, there is some sense in which we must have died to sin. What is it? So he says, 'The

[18]

Apostle means that we have died to the guilt of sin'. And he stops at that. 'We have died to the guilt of sin.' 'What it means,' says Haldane, 'is that as far as the guilt and punishment of sin are concerned we have finished with it, the law cannot touch us.' He virtually says what is expressed in the words of Augustus Toplady –

> *The terrors of law and of God*
> *With me can have nothing to do;*
> *My Saviour's obedience and blood*
> *Hide all my transgressions from view.*

We are dead as far as the guilt of sin is concerned, it cannot touch us. 'There is therefore now no condemnation to them that are in Christ Jesus', and he stops there. Of course, I agree entirely that it does mean that we are dead to the guilt of sin; but I argue that to stop at that is a hopelessly inadequate exposition. The Apostle's argument goes very much further.

I have to reject Haldane's exposition for this reason, that it does not do justice to what the Apostle has been saying at the end of chapter 5, neither does it do justice to what Paul goes on to say in this sixth chapter from verse 3 onwards. What was it that controlled the exposition of Haldane? I feel sure it was the same thing as in the case of Charles Hodge, the fear of being misunderstood, the fear of saying something that might lead some people to say, 'Very well, if that is so, what I do does not matter, I am saved'. So Haldane confines it to the guilt of sin only. He says that the power of sin is still there; and the Apostle does not say that we are dead to that. But I want to suggest that the Apostle does say that, and that the true interpretation, as I see it, and to which I now come, does not stop merely at saying that we are dead to the guilt of sin. I believe that the Apostle is saying here something that is infinitely greater and more thrilling than that, something astonishing. And yet it should not astound those who have been following this exposition so far.

I am suggesting that, if we only allow the context to determine our exposition, there is no problem here at all. In what sense has the believer, the Christian died to sin? The answer is found in verse 21 of chapter 5: 'That as sin hath reigned unto death, even so might grace reign through righteousness unto eternal life by Jesus Christ our Lord.' In what sense have I as a Christian died to sin? I answer, 'I have died to the reign of sin.' Not only to the guilt of sin, I have died to the reign and rule of sin. That is the point the Apostle is making. He is contrasting the reign of sin with the reign of grace, and what he has been saying is that our Lord's death and resurrection have brought the reign of sin to an end in the case of all believers.

That is what the Apostle means by saying, 'Where sin abounded, grace did much more abound'. He has been working it out in detail. 'As by the offence of one, judgment came upon all men to condemnation' – that is the reign of sin – 'even so by the righteousness of one, the free gift came upon all men unto justification of life.' That is the reign of grace. 'For as by one man's disobedience all were made sinners' – that is the reign of sin – 'so by the obedience of one shall many be made righteous.' That is the reign of grace. But he has been putting it in detail. He says, 'For if by one man's offence death reigned by one, much more they which receive abundance of grace and of the gift of righteousness shall reign in life by one, Jesus Christ'. Indeed he had said it all in the twelfth verse of chapter 5: 'Wherefore, as by one man sin entered into the world, and death by sin, and so death passed upon all men, for that all have sinned.' That is the reign of sin. But his whole point is just to say this, that if you are a believer on the Lord Jesus Christ, if you are justified by faith, if you are 'in Christ', you have finished with that, you are dead to the reign of sin, you are under the reign of grace. And that is what he is saying here. So we read, 'How shall we that died to sin' – that died to the reign of sin – 'live any longer therein?' Do not forget that the reign of sin means its rule, its power, its realm. And the reign of grace means exactly the same; it means the power, the influence, the force, the might, the dynamic of grace.

What the Apostle is saying, therefore, is that at the moment we were regenerated, or at the moment of our justification – because it then becomes actual in our experience – the moment we become Christians, we are dead, completely dead, to the reign of sin. We are out of sin's territory altogether. That, I suggest, is what the Apostle is saying in this second verse. In the following verses he works it all out and explains it in detail; he shows us how it happens. But here we have the general statement and proposition, that because we are what we are in Christ, being what we are as the result of what has happened to us, we are dead to the reign and to the rule of sin.

But now I imagine somebody putting forward an objection: 'How can you possibly say such a thing? We still sin, we still feel the power of temptation and the power of sin; how therefore can you say honestly that you are dead to the rule and to the reign and to the whole dominion of sin?' I answer in this way. We must differentiate between what is true of our position as a fact and our experience. There is all the difference in the world between a man's status and position on the one hand and his experience on the other. Now here the Apostle is concerned about our position; and what he says is that every person in the world at this minute is either under the reign and rule of sin or else under the reign and rule of grace. What he says about the Christian is, that whereas once he was under the rule and the reign of sin, he is now under the rule and the reign of grace. It is either one or the other, he cannot have a foot in each position. He is either under sin or else he is under grace. And I repeat, that what Paul says about us as Christians is that we are dead completely to the rule and the reign of sin and of evil. That is no longer true of us; once and for ever we have been taken out of that position.

Now let me substantiate my exposition by quoting parallel statements which are found elsewhere in the Scriptures. Bear in mind what I am proving, that the Apostle is saying here that we have been taken entirely out of the realm, and the rule, and the reign, and the kingdom of sin, and have been brought into this other kingdom of grace and put under its reign. Take Colossians 1 : 13: 'Who hath delivered us from the power of darkness.' Notice what he says! 'Who hath delivered us from the power of darkness and hath translated us into the kingdom of his dear Son.' The Apostle is there telling the Colossians that they who once belonged to the power and the kingdom of darkness and of the devil and of hell, have been translated, transferred from and are no longer in that dominion; they are in this other dominion.

'Translated'. It is not surprising that the Apostle Paul keeps on saying things like this. Was not this the very commission that our Lord gave him when He met him on the road to Damascus? Read the account in Acts, chapter 26 verse 18. The risen Lord gives His commission to the Apostle as a disciple and a preacher and tells him what he is to do. He says, 'To open their eyes, and to turn them from darkness to light, and from the power of Satan unto God'. The people you are going to preach to, says our Lord, are under the power of Satan. He is 'the strong man armed that keepeth his goods at peace'. They are in his kingdom, they are under his power, he is tyrannizing and reigning over them. I am sending you with this message, that you may deliver them from the power of Satan, unto the power of God. There is a transference, there is a translation, there is a moving.

In the same way the Apostle in Philippians, chapter 3 verse 20 says this about Christians: 'Our citizenship is in heaven.' He does not say our citizenship is going to be there, he says our citizenship is in heaven now. We are living on earth but our citizenship is there. 'Ah but', you say, 'how can a man say that our citizenship is in heaven while we are still on earth and are citizens of Great Britain?' But that is the sort of thing the Scriptures say – that if you are a Christian, you really are now a citizen of heaven. We are 'a colony of heaven' in this world, our citizenship is there, not here; this transference of citizenship has taken place. In Ephesians chapter 2 verse 19 you find exactly the same thing. 'Ye are no more strangers and foreigners, but fellow-citizens with the saints, and of the household of God' – again the same transference. In other words there has been a complete change in our position. We have changed our kingdoms once and for ever. We are no longer in the territory of sin, we are no longer under the governing power of sin; sin no longer controls us, sin no longer controls our destiny. Or if you prefer other terms, before becoming Christians we were united to Adam, we belonged to Adam and his fallen race, and all the consequences of his sin and action have come upon us. We were in Adam. But we are no longer in Adam; we are now in Christ. We have been taken out of Adam, we have been put into Christ.

There are only two possibilities for every person alive in this world. He is either 'in Adam' or else he is 'in Christ'. Surely that is the whole message of Romans 5, verses 12 to 21. There are only two heads of humanity, and we are in one or the other, we cannot be in both at the same time. If you are in Christ you are not in Adam. That is what the Apostle is saying here; we are dead to sin, dead to its territory, dead to its rule and reign. But I cannot stop even there. That is all true but it is negative. And I must become positive, because the Apostle's statement is also positive. We are not only dead to the reign of sin, we are under the reign of grace, and all that that means in terms of power. In other words what the Apostle is saying here is that we are not merely forgiven our sins; a Christian is not only a man whose sins have been forgiven, and who has decided to live a better life, and is anxious to live a better life; much more is true of him. He has been transferred to the reign of grace; and the reign of grace is a very powerful reign. It is as powerful as this, says the Apostle, that it is guaranteed to produce certain results. The reign of sin produced results. It caused death to pass upon every one of us, it caused us all to sin, it got us all down. But the reign of grace, says Paul, is infinitely more powerful: 'Where sin abounded, grace did much more abound.' If the power and dominion of sin guarantees certain results, the reign and rule of grace guarantees contrary results still more certainly.

What is guaranteed? Well, what is guaranteed is that my full and final salvation is absolutely certain. I am not merely dead to the reign of sin, I am alive under the reign of grace; and grace is a tremendous power. As a Christian you must not think of yourself merely as a man who has come to a certain decision, and wants to do this and that. No! If you are a Christian what is true of you is that all the dynamic of the reign of grace is upon you, and is working in you, and will bring you to perfection. The Apostle is anxious to bring out the certainty. That is why this suggestion in the first verse is so monstrous – 'Shall we continue in sin that grace may abound'? The whole object of grace is to destroy sin and all its works, and all that belongs to it, so that suggestion is impossible. We are under the power that is destroying sin, so how can we possibly continue in sin? You see the argument? It is inevitable. But none of the other suggested interpretations made it inevitable. This is how the Apostle puts it: 'We being what we are, dead to Adam and dead to sin and its reign and its rule, how can we live any longer therein?'

The word 'live' is obviously important. It means 'continue and abide'. The Apostle is asserting that in view of our position – the fact that we are under the rule and reign of grace – it is impossible that we should continue and abide in sin, or that a life of sin should be our life. This doctrine is not confined to the teaching

[23]

of the Apostle Paul. Our Lord Himself had said it all. 'Whosoever committeth sin' – and by 'committeth' He means 'goes on', 'lives' in that realm – 'is the servant of sin. And the servant abideth not in the house for ever; but the Son abideth ever.' Then the great statement: 'If the Son therefore shall make you free, ye shall be free indeed.' [*John* 8: 34-36.] It is an absolute freedom where the Son is concerned.

Take also the teaching of John in his first Epistle, 'Whosoever is born of God doth not commit sin; for his seed remaineth in him: and he cannot sin, because he is born of God' [1 *John* 3 : 9]. Here is a profound statement! How often have people argued about it! They say, 'What does John mean by "he that is born of God doth not commit sin?" ' Some say,'That is absolute perfection, and you can reach such a degree of perfection in this life that you do not sin at all'. To which there is but one reply – It is not true! What does John mean then? The answer is in the word 'commit', which means 'practise habitually', 'continue in it', 'live in it'; 'be the main tenor of your life'. That is what John says is impossible for a born-again man. 'Whosoever is born of God doth not go on living a life of sin, (he does not practise it habitually), for his seed remaineth in him; and he cannot go on like that, because he is born of God.' He is not saying that a man who is born of God can never commit an individual act of sin, for had he spoken in that way there would never have been a Christian at all in past time, and there would be no Christians now. What he is saying is, that the man who is born of God cannot go on abiding in the realm of sin. In other words he is agreeing with Paul, that the man who is a Christian died to the realm of sin, and does not belong to it any longer. Notice the word he uses. He keeps on repeating the word 'cannot'. 'He cannot', says John, and Paul uses the same 'cannot' here. That is why he drives out the suggestion of verse 1 with 'God forbid! How can we that died to sin live any longer therein?'

Stated otherwise, the Apostle's argument is this, that for a Christian to live in sin is impossible because such a man is under the power of grace. Not only is he out of the power of sin and the realm of sin, he is under the influence and the power of Christ, he is in the realm of this mighty force which Paul personalizes and calls 'grace and its reign'. And because he is under this influence and power he cannot continue where he was before, grace makes it impossible. So in verse 14 at the end of this section he sums up the matter in these triumphant words: 'Sin shall not have dominion over you.' Let it do its worst, it shall not have dominion over you. Why? Because grace is infinitely more powerful – 'Where sin abounded, grace did much more abound'. The Apostle is not merely telling us that we ought not to sin, or that we ought not to continue in sin, and that it is self-contradictory of us, as Charles Hodge puts it, if we do go on sinning in view of the fact that we have renounced sin. What he is saying is, 'You cannot, you shall not go on living in the realm and under the final power of sin'. Why? Well, for the reason that he has already given in verse 16 of the first chapter: 'I am not ashamed of the gospel of Christ.' Why? 'It is the power of God unto salvation to everyone that believeth.'

Such is his argument in chapters 5, 6, 7 and 8. The moment a man has been justified by God, God says to him, in effect: 'I am going to deliver you completely from the power of sin. I will start at once by taking you out of its realm and its kingdom, and by putting you into the kingdom of my dear Son. Then progressively I will deliver you until finally you are perfect and without blemish or spot or wrinkle or any such thing.' That is what Paul is saying; that we died to the reign and the realm and the rule of sin.

'But wait a minute,' says someone, 'I still have a final objection. If what you say is true, if it is true, as you have been emphasizing so much, that in Christ we are really dead and have finished with the rule and the realm of sin once and forever, how is it then that we still can fall into sin? And why does the Apostle have to exhort us to reckon ourselves to be dead unto sin, and not to allow sin to reign in our mortal body, and things like that? How do you answer that?' The answer is clear. Paul is not saying that we are sinless; but he is saying that we are out of the territory, out of the kingdom, out of the realm, out of the rule and the reign of sin. There is all the difference in the world between being in a given position, and realizing that you are in that position. Let me give an illustration or two. Take the case of those poor slaves in the United States of America about a hundred years ago. There they were in a condition of slavery. Then the American Civil War came, and as the result of that war slavery was abolished in the United States. But what had actually happened? All slaves, young and old, were given their freedom, but many of the older ones who had endured long years of servitude found it very difficult to understand their new status. They heard the announcement that slavery was abolished and that they were free: but hundreds, not to say thousands, of times in their after lives and experiences many of them did not realize it, and when they saw their old master coming near them they began to quake and to tremble, and to wonder whether they were going to be sold. They were free, they were no longer slaves; the law had been changed, and their status and their position was entirely different; but it took them a very long time to realize it. You can still be a slave experimentally, even when you are no longer a slave legally. You can be a slave in your feelings when actually in respect of your position you have been emancipated completely. So it is with the Christian.

Or let me put it like this. Many a child is afraid of a servant, a servant employed by his father to look after him. He should not be afraid. If a child only realized that he has been born a member of the family he would not be afraid of the servant in that way. But he does not realize it. He has not got a sufficiently active and lively realization of his position as a son, and so he is afraid of a servant, though he is above the servant in status. It is like that sometimes with the Christian.

Or let me use an illustration that I have often used, and which has helped me, and which I have found in my pastoral work has helped many another. Think again of the problem. How can I say that I am delivered from the rule and the realm and the reign of the devil and of sin, when I still fall to temptation? Look at it in this way. Think of two fields with a road between them. The field on the left represents the dominion, the kingdom, the territory, the empire of sin and of Satan. That is where we all were by our natural birth. But as the result of the work of the Lord Jesus Christ for us and upon us through the Holy Spirit, we have been taken hold of, and transferred to the field on the right of the road – 'Delivered from the power of darkness and translated into the kingdom of his dear son'. I was there on the left, I am now here on the right. Yes, but I spent many a long year in the first field, and the devil is still there with all his powers and his forces.

This is a picture of what often happens. As a Christian I am here in the new field and Satan cannot touch me, as we are told in John's First Epistle, chapter 5, verse 18, 'That evil one toucheth him not'. He cannot touch us because we are no longer in his king-

dom. He cannot touch us; but he can shout across the road at us.
Every Christian who falls into sin is a fool. The devil cannot touch
us; why then do we listen to him? Why do we allow him to fright-
en us? Why do we pay any attention to him? We no longer
belong to him, and he cannot touch us. We know that Scripture
asserts our freedom as an actual fact; but because of the old habit,
the old influence, like the slaves that had been set free, we tend to
forget it, and when he speaks to us we listen to him and fall under
his spell. We should resist him. 'Resist the devil and he will flee
from you' [*James* 4 : 7]; but we fail to realize it. The whole object
of the Apostle in this sixth chapter is to get us to realize it. 'Reckon
yourselves to be dead indeed unto sin'. You are therefore to realize
it, to reckon it. Realize also that you are 'alive unto God
through our Lord Jesus Christ'. It is not true yet, perhaps, in your
experience; but though it is not yet true in your experience it is
true as a matter of fact. We have got to believe it. That is why the
Apostle writes in this way. This is not a matter of experience primarily; he is dealing with a matter of fact. He says, you died to sin
as a matter of historical fact. When you became a Christian you
ceased to be under the rule and the reign and the realm of sin.
That is a fact. He is not talking about your experience; he is telling you something that is true of you, namely, that you have been
translated by the Holy Spirit from one kingdom to another.

'But I cannot believe that', says someone, 'it is too staggering,
it is almost incredible. Here am I on earth, and I listen to that
voice of Satan and fall into sin; and yet you tell me that I am dead
to it.' You are! And I ask you to believe it. I know it is staggering;
but the Apostle has already dealt with your difficulty in chapter
4. Remember what he said about Abraham, at the end of his great
argument about justification by faith alone. He exhorted us to
become children of Abraham, and to do what Abraham did. There
was Abraham, an old man of ninety-nine years, and Sarah a
woman of ninety years, and God came to him and said: 'Abraham,
I am going to give you a child, you are going to have a son, an
heir, the heir of promise.' Abraham ninety-nine and Sarah ninety!
and the deadness of Sarah's womb! It was all entirely contrary to
nature. But God said that to Abraham. It seemed impossible, it
seemed monstrous, it seemed utterly ridiculous; but Abraham
'staggered not through unbelief but was made strong by faith'.
He believed the bare word of God, he believed simply because

God said it. And you and I have to do the same here. Whatever you may feel, whatever your experience may be, God tells us here, through His Word, that if we are in Christ we are no longer in Adam, we are no longer under the reign and the rule of sin. We are in Christ, and we are under the rule and the reign of grace; and 'where sin abounded, grace hath much more abounded' – and will! I died to the realm and the rule of sin when I became a Christian, and I am dead to it now. And if I fall into sin, as I do, it is simply because I do not realize who I am – 'We being what we are'. Realize it, reckon it! You are under the rule and the reign of grace, and therefore you shall not, you cannot, go on living in sin.

That is the great argument; and we can now proceed to consider the way in which the Apostle breaks it up into its relative parts, and then states it again as a mighty whole when we come to the end of verse 24.

Three

*

Know ye not, that so many of us as were baptized into Jesus Christ were baptized into his death? Romans 6 : 3

In this verse the Apostle begins the exposition of the staggering and tremendous statement made in verse 2 which we have considered. Here is the fundamental proposition, that 'we died to sin'. But someone may ask, 'How did we die to sin?' 'How is it true to say of us that we died to sin?' The Apostle in verses 3 to 11 proceeds to answer that question. He has already thrown out a hint with regard to the answer away back in chapter 5 at the end of verse 10. That is why we emphasized that verse so much at the time. 'For if, when we were enemies, we were reconciled to God by the death of his Son, much more, being reconciled, we shall be saved in his life.' It should be 'in his life' rather than 'by his life'. In a sense it comes to the same thing, but if you take it as 'in his life' you have, as we indicated, the first hint of this tremendous doctrine which the Apostle is now going to elaborate. Of course, in verses 12 to 21 of chapter 5 the idea is implicit, because there again we saw that his comparison is this; we were in Adam, we are now in Christ. He does not say it explicitly, but it is implicit in the whole argument. Now he takes that up – and he puts it in this practical way in order to answer this objector – by saying, 'We died to sin'. How did we die to sin? His answer is the doctrine of our union with Christ. This is the doctrine which he expounds and explains in detail, particularly from this third verse to verse eleven, where he winds up his argument in the form of an exhortation which is a logical deduction from what he has been saying. We shall find that he states it negatively and positively, according to his custom.

Here, then, is the doctrine that is before us, the doctrine of our

[29]

union with Christ. Once more we must say that it is one of the most glorious aspects of the Christian truth, one of the most profound, one of the most stimulating, one of the most comforting – indeed I rather like to use the word exhilarating. There is nothing, perhaps, in the whole range and realm of doctrine which, if properly grasped and understood, gives greater assurance, greater comfort, and greater hope than this doctrine of our union with Christ. As we shall see, if we are not clear about this doctrine, we are missing, in a sense, one of the pivotal aspects of the whole doctrine of salvation. We must therefore pay careful attention to it, for undoubtedly, it was in order that we might be clear about it that the Apostle elaborates it in this way.

Unfortunately there are many who have never really grasped this doctrine, indeed they do not seem to realize that it is in the Scripture. People who have read this sixth chapter of Romans many times never seem to have seen it. I believe there is one big explanation of that. It seems to me that many have missed this doctrine at this point because they have been diverted from it by the form of expression which the Apostle uses in presenting it. I mean, that having seen the word 'baptized' in these verses, they never see anything else, and regard these verses as having nothing to teach except a particular doctrine of baptism. That is so regrettable that we must perforce look into this matter.

I would prefer not to do so, but, after all, the business of a teacher is not to do what he likes or what pleases him; it is to help those who listen to his teaching. And as this matter has been so frequently misunderstood and misinterpreted, and, as I say, has so often robbed people of the glorious doctrine that is taught here, we really must rid our minds of any misconceptions or preconceptions. In other words, the best way to understand the doctrine is to be clear as to the meaning of this term 'baptized' as used in this third verse and again in the fourth verse where we read, 'Therefore we are buried with him by baptism into death; that like as Christ was raised up from the dead by the glory of the Father, even so we also should walk in newness of life'.

How has this term been interpreted? Here are some of the common ways in which people have done so. First, there is the Sacramental, or Sacramentarian interpretation which teaches quite openly and plainly that it is the act or rite or performance of baptism that incorporates us into Christ and joins us to Him. That is the doctrine of baptismal regeneration as it is taught by Catholics – Roman, Anglican, Scottish and many others. Whatever the form of Catholicism, that is their teaching. They claim that it is the act of baptizing that, in and of itself, unites the person baptized with the Lord Jesus Christ. It is certainly a clear-cut view, but is it the explanation of these verses? We need not spend much time on it. One over-riding reason for dismissing it at once is this, that according to the New Testament teaching, it clearly (if I may use such an expression) puts the cart before the horse. The teaching of the New Testament is that the people who are to be baptized are those who have already given evidence that they are regencrate; it is believers who are baptized in the New Testament. So it is not the act of baptism that makes them believers, it is because they are believers, or are presumed to be believers, that they are baptized. Take for instance the Ethiopian eunuch; it was because he believed that Philip baptized him. Take the case of Cornelius: 'Can any man forbid water' says Peter, 'that these should not be baptized which have received the Holy Ghost?' He baptized him and his household when he saw that the gift of the Spirit had been given to them as unto himself and others at the beginning. Observe the order. It was the same in the case of the Philippian jailor; it was when he had believed that he was baptized – he and his household. This is, of course, a tremendous argument; it is the Protestant position against that whole Catholic doctrine which teaches that grace is transmitted by and in the very elements. They believe that grace is transmitted in the water, as they believe that grace is transmitted by the wafer that is eaten at the Lord's Supper, that it conveys grace.

There, it seems to me, is the answer to that exposition. The cases given in the New Testament itself clearly show that, far from giving life and union, baptism is rather meant to be something that seals a preceding happening, or is given as an attestation or a seal of an accomplished fact. That is the order, not the other way round. The wrong teaching crept in partly as a misinterpretation of these verses, let us never forget that. The Sacramentarians always go to these verses for their doctrine of baptism, and their doctrine of the Sacraments. That led in turn to an exaltation of the priesthood, and of the Church, and so the tyranny comes in which dominates the life of the individual Christian. Protestantism is a protest against all that; it teaches the universal priesthood of all believers, and asserts particularly that no action on behalf of the Church or by 'priests' can give life, or can produce this union. I leave it at that.

Others, rejecting Sacramentarianism, say that what is taught here is that the baptism referred to means our baptismal vows. It is not anything a priest or a minister does, they say: this is the occasion on which we take certain baptismal vows; we declare our faith, we repudiate the life of sin, and at the same time pledge ourselves to a new way of life. This puts us into the realm and sphere of Christ. This again need not detain us, though I cannot refrain from pointing out that this element of bearing testimony does very frequently tend to be overdone in baptismal services, as if that were the essential thing. In a sense, by submitting to baptism one is making a statement, but that is not the chief thing in baptism. In any case it is not the point here. What is emphasized here is not anything that I do as a believer, it is what has happened to me that incorporates me into Christ and joins me to Christ. The vital doctrine here is the doctrine of my union with Christ, not something that I may or may not do.

Others say that the verse means that we are baptized into the sphere of Christ's influence. There is something to be said for this, because there is a similar teaching in the First Epistle to the Corinthians, chapter 10. 'Moreover, brethren, I would not that ye should be ignorant, how that all our fathers were under the cloud, and all passed through the sea; and were all baptized unto Moses in the cloud and in the sea' [verses 1 and 2]. You notice that they were all baptized unto Moses in the cloud and in the sea. That is an important statement for all people who tend to say dogmatically, 'The word 'baptize' means 'baptize', and it means nothing but 'baptize'. 'The fathers' says Paul, 'were baptized unto Moses' as they were passing through the Red Sea. This obviously means that they were baptized not only into his influence but under his leadership. They were under the leadership of Moses whom God had appointed, and, in that indirect sense, through Moses, they were the people of God. But here in Romans 6 the whole context makes that explanation quite impossible; because what is taught here is not that we have come under the influence of Christ, or into the sphere of His influence; it does teach that, but it goes far beyond that teaching. We are united to Christ, we are 'in Christ', we are parts of Christ. As we were 'in Adam', so we are 'in Christ';

not merely in terms of an influence, but of a union, a spiritual union. So that explanation again is inadequate.

Now we come to the fourth proffered explanation, which says that what baptism means here is that it is a sign of our belief in the redeeming and saving efficacy of the death of Christ as a propitiation for our sins. I believe that water baptism does that; but it is clear that it does not stop at that here. That is why we had to reject Robert Haldane's exposition of verse 2. He confines it to the saving efficacy of our Lord's work in that way, particularly the propitiation resulting from the Lord's death. We believe that; but here we have a doctrine that takes us still further. It is not merely a declaration that we believe in this and subscribe to this; it goes beyond that to our actual union with Christ.

But there is a further reason why we must reject that particular exposition. Verse 4 states quite plainly, 'We are buried with him by (or through) baptism unto death'. Verse 5 takes it further and is still more explicit: 'For . . . we have been planted together', and this 'planting' means the kind of union that results when a shoot is grafted into a parent trunk; it is a grafting, it is a union. To say that it is merely an indication or an attestation of our belief in the saving efficacy of Christ and the virtue of His death falls far short of the rich content of this particular section.

That brings us to a fifth explanation, which says that here the Apostle is teaching that baptism is the symbolic representation, or the pictorial enactment of, a deeper spiritual reality, namely, our union with Christ; our union with Him in His death and in His burial. We go down under the water – a picture of burial – and then we come up again out of the water, which is a picture of resurrection. This is a symbol, a picture, a representation in a dramatic manner of what is happening to us spiritually. And, they emphasize, it is a very remarkable one, and a very appropriate one. First you are buried, and then you rise; your baptism is a pictorial representation of union with our Lord in His burial and in His resurrection.

Let us examine this. To me this expression in verse 4, where we are told that we are 'buried with Him by (or through) baptism', seems to militate very strongly against this exposition. Paul does not say that it is a picture. Paul says that it is accomplished by or through baptism. He does not say that this is a wonderful pictorial or symbolic representation of it. He says that by or through your baptism this happened to you. To that extent the first explanation had a measure of truth in it. Say what you like against the Sacramentarians, but they at any rate have got hold of the idea that this baptism about which the Apostle is writing does achieve something. They go very far wrong in their interpretation of the manner in which it is achieved, or what is achieved by it; but at least they can see that the baptism does something – 'through' baptism, 'by' baptism. This fifth explanation we are looking at, however, does not really leave any room for that at all; it says that it is merely a picture, a symbolical representation, a dramatic enactment only. That is one objection to it. But there are other objections. The doctrine of our union with Christ says that we are united with Him in all that happened to Him; and the first thing that happened to Him in this context was that He was crucified. Paul, introducing this same idea elsewhere, says, 'I have been crucified with Christ'. Where is that represented in this pictorial representation? How does water baptism represent crucifixion? It is simply not there. And yet it is a vital part, perhaps the most vital, of our union with the Lord Jesus Christ. Therefore there should be a doubt at once in our minds as to whether the Apostle uses baptism as a picture. Baptism accomplishes something, and it leads to our union with Christ. So I raise a query against the entire notion of representation.

Indeed I go further and suggest that to argue that the Apostle has water baptism in his mind in any shape or form here is to give a prominence to baptism that the Apostle Paul never gives to it. Take for instance what he says in the First Epistle to the Corinthians in the first chapter verses 13–17: 'Is Christ divided? was Paul crucified for you? or were you baptized in the name of Paul? I thank God that I baptized none of you, but Crispus and Gaius; lest any should say that I had baptized in mine own name. And I baptized also the household of Stephanas; besides, I know not whether I baptized any other, (he is not clear in his memory at this point), 'for Christ sent me not to baptize, but to preach the gospel.' In this statement the Apostle is not depreciating baptism, but he certainly does not give it the central position which this fifth explanation suggests that it has in this sixth chapter of Romans. I argue that it gives an undue prominence to water baptism, whatever the mode.

But there is yet a further objection. The Apostle in several other places deals with this question of our union with Christ. There is for instance Ephesians 2 verses 4–6, where he teaches that, having been quickened, we are risen with Christ, and seated with Him in the heavenly places. But he does not mention baptism at all at that point. Those parallel passages surely throw light on the interpretation of this passage.

'Well', says someone, 'what is the meaning of baptism here? What is the Apostle saying?' Let us approach it in the following manner. All are agreed that the great spiritual truth which is taught here, and in this whole section, is our union with Christ. When I say 'all', I mean all who take an evangelical view of the Scriptures. Indeed we must include the Catholics as they are concerned about this matter. There, then, is an agreement. Those who hold the liberal modernistic view see nothing beyond our making some statement that we believe in Christ, and that we are identifying ourselves with Him. They see nothing beyond that. They do not believe in the doctrine of the union of the believer with Christ. We can forget them. But the others are agreed that union with Christ is the essential doctrine. Let us hold that in our minds. Then take with it the statement that it is by baptism, or through baptism, that this union takes place which leads to all the consequences.

Now, holding those two ideas as being the important ones, the question that arises is, What sort of baptism is this? What kind of baptism is taught in the New Testament which definitely says that it is a baptism that incorporates us into Christ and joins us to Him? The answer is found surely in 1 Corinthians 12 : 13: 'For by (or in) one Spirit we are all baptized into one body, whether we be Jews or Gentiles, whether we be bond or free; and have been all made to drink into one Spirit.' The theme of that great chapter is the Church as the Body of Christ. Christ is the Head, we are the Body. We are all joined to Him, and we are all joined to one another. But how have we thus been joined? The answer is that the Holy Spirit baptizes us into the Body of Christ; it is a baptism by the Holy Spirit. I am not saying baptism *with* the Spirit, I am saying baptism *by* the Spirit. It is the Spirit that baptizes us into the Body, that joins us to Christ; it is the wonderful, mystical action of the Spirit. It can be compared to the action of the Spirit in our regeneration; it is He who does that, who gives us this principle of life. And in exactly the same way it is He who puts us into the Body of Christ; and the expression used is that He 'baptizes' us into Christ, into the body of Christ.

The conclusion therefore at which I arrive is that baptism by water is not in the mind of the Apostle at all in these two verses; instead it is the baptism that is wrought by the Spirit. It is the plain, explicit teaching of 1 Corinthians 12 : 13, and indeed in the whole of that chapter, as it is in other places where the Apostle treats of this particular aspect of truth. And I argue further that the use of this term 'planted together', in verse 5, supports what I am saying. All are agreed that the idea of planting has nothing to do with baptism at all; it is rather the idea of grafting a shoot into a tree. 'Planted together' – in unity, identification – that is the meaning of the term. Paul is not using the figure of baptism in any shape or form there, but is still emphasizing this unity. That also is the work of the Spirit. It can be put in various ways.

Again, take the statement which the Apostle makes in Galatians 2 : 20, which is so frequently misquoted: 'I have been crucified with Christ: nevertheless I live; yet not I, but Christ liveth in me; and the life which I now live in the flesh I live by the faith of the Son of God, who loved me, and gave himself for me'. That is exactly the same teaching. 'I have been crucified with Christ.' 'I live; yet not I, but Christ liveth in me.' Now there you have the identical doctrine, but baptism is not mentioned. That is because water baptism does not achieve union, it does not produce it; indeed at that point it does not even represent it. This is a baptism which is carried out by the Holy Spirit when He incorporates us, plants us into, engrafts us into the Lord Jesus Christ.

It is regrettable that it has been necessary to say all this, because all evangelical believers, even those who talk about the 'pictorial representation,' are agreed in this, that the important and the vital thing is our union with Christ. Let us, then, hold on to the thing that matters, which is this union with Christ. It is because we are united with Him that we derive all these benefits from Him. It is because we are united with Him, (as the Apostle has been arguing from chapter 5 : 10 and onwards) that our final salvation is guaranteed, for everything that happened to Him happens to us. The same held true when we were united to Adam. It was that one sin of Adam that brought all the evil consequences upon us. And it is the action of Christ that brings all blessings upon us. As we were united to Adam, so we are now united to Christ – that is the doctrine. And we must realize that it is the Spirit who unites us to Christ. That is the baptism about which the Apostle is speaking. The great thing in salvation is that we are not only justified, not only forgiven; in a sense the most glorious aspect of salvation is that I am 'in Christ', and Christ is in me, – this vital union! And this we must never fail to realize.

It is sad that preoccupation with modes and forms of baptism should have blinded certain people to this great truth, in the reading of these two verses. Let me ask a simple, practical question. Let everyone answer for himself or herself. As you read these verses at the beginning of Romans 6 what has been the chief impression on your mind? Has it always been our union with Christ, or has it been baptism? It is nothing short of tragic if the main impression left upon our minds is water baptism in any form. Baptism is important, baptism is a command which must be carried out; but do not go to the sixth chapter of Romans for it. There are other places in Scripture which teach it clearly. You can discuss it and argue about it from other texts, but do not bring it in here. 'By one Spirit (or, in one Spirit,) we have all been baptized into one body, whether we are Jews or Gentiles, bond or free; and we have all been made to drink of that one Spirit.' This 'drinking' is comparable to the baptism. It refers to this union and this incorporation.

We can now go on to consider the glorious doctrine of our union with Christ in its various component parts. God forbid that anyone should be stumbled by that word 'baptized', and miss the glories that the Apostle here unfolds. What are they? He starts by saying, 'Know ye not?' 'Don't you know' asks the Apostle, 'haven't you realized, haven't you understood?' What does that tell us? It tells us that the Apostle assumes that this is common knowledge amongst all Christians. He says in effect, 'Need I tell you?', as if to say, I almost feel like apologizing for reminding you. It is common knowledge – this doctrine of our union with Christ, our one-ness with Him. The Apostle had never been in Rome, as he reminds us in the Introduction to the Epistle. He had not taught these people, and yet he says, 'Of course you know this. Don't you know? Don't you realize? Don't you remember?' He says this to people to whom he had never preached in person, and whose Christianity had come to them through some subsidiary teachers; and yet he assumes that every Christian knows

this. But does every Christian know it? Have *we* been thrilled by
this wonderful doctrine of our union with Christ?

Look once more at what I have already quoted from the Epistle
to the Galatians. It is very significant. Everybody is agreed that
the Galatians were a very primitive sort of people, an unstable
people. They lived a primitive kind of life, they were poor in
intellect; but the Apostle had preached to them, and it is quite
clear from his Epistle to them that he had preached this doctrine
of our union with Christ even to them. I draw a very important
deduction from this, namely, that this belongs to the most primitive kind of evangelism. The pity is that so often this doctrine has
been regarded as only applicable to people who reach the higher
heights of the Christian faith, that it is a doctrine for some special
people only. The idea often is that you only teach it in places
where you are no longer evangelizing, but where you are engaged
in deepening the spiritual life and going down into the depths;
in other words, that it is for the advanced scholars, the mature
saints. But that is not Paul's teaching. 'Don't you know?' he
says to these Romans; and he had preached it to the Galatians
among whom he had not spent much time.

I argue, therefore, that we are not evangelizing truly unless
we present this truth – that in salvation we are not merely forgiven and not only justified; the doctrine of salvation includes
the basic truth that we were in Adam but are now in Christ, that
we are taken out of the one position and put into another. That
is primitive evangelism, that is one of the basic elements in the
presentation of the gospel; and therefore if we do not give it due
emphasis we are not evangelizing truly. Evangelism is not simply
saying, 'Come to Christ; He will do this, that, and the other for
you'. No! The glorious thing about salvation is that I am taken
out of Adam, that I have finished with him, and am dead to sin.
I am in Christ, and all the blessings that come to me come because of my union with Christ. I want to emphasize this. 'Know
ye not?' 'Haven't you realized, haven't you grasped, haven't
you understood this?' That is what the Apostle is saying at this
point.

Then take a second point. Take this phrase of his, 'So many of
us'. 'Know ye not that so many of us as were baptized into Jesus
Christ were baptized into His death?' What does 'So many of
us' mean? It means 'all' – nothing less than 'all'. It is just a way of

saying 'All of us who have been baptized into Christ'. He does not say that some Christians have been baptized into Christ but others have not. No, he says, all of us, every individual Christian. Again we see the importance of this matter. The Apostle is not teaching some esoteric doctrine to certain select individuals in the Christian life; he is saying that this is true of every Christian. In chapter 8 verse 9, we find him saying this: 'If any man have not the Spirit of Christ, he is none of his.' It is the same thing. If we are not united to Christ we are not Christians. You cannot be a Christian without being united to Christ; it is true of all Christians. The Holy Spirit who convicts us of sin, the Holy Spirit who gives us the principle of new life, who regenerates us, is the same Spirit who at the same time, joins us to Christ; and this is true of every Christian.

In other words we must never interpret these verses in terms of experience. The Apostle is not dealing with experience at this point; that comes later. What he is dealing with here is something that has happened to us, something that is true of us, something that results from the action of the Holy Spirit upon us. We may not be as well aware of it as we ought to be; the Apostle clearly suggests that there were certain Christians in Rome who were not as clear about this as they should be. And there are people like that today. It does not mean that they are not Christians, thank God for that. If we were saved by our understanding, and experience of truth, well then, God help us! Thank God we are not saved by that, we are saved by this tremendous action of God through the Spirit, who takes us out of Adam, incorporates us, implants us, baptizes us into Christ. That is the thing that saves us; and it happens to all of us, says Paul. He is anxious that we should realize it, and then draw our deductions from it.

So let us be clear in our minds that he is not dealing with experience, but status, condition, position. There are only two positions; we are either every one of us in Adam, or else we are in Christ. There is no middle position. You cannot be a saved man without being joined to Christ, without being in Christ. And as there is no middle position, so also there is no progress or progressing at that point. All of us, every one of us, 'So many of us' have in this way been baptized into Christ.

Then notice that what the Apostle is emphasizing is that we have been baptized 'into Jesus Christ', into Jesus Christ Himself, into the Person. That leads me to say this; we are not baptized into parts of Him, or aspects of the truth concerning Him. We are baptized into Jesus Christ, the whole of Him. Paul states that clearly in the first Epistle to the Corinthians in this way: 'But of him are ye in Christ Jesus, who of God is made unto us wisdom, and righteousness, and sanctification, and redemption' [1 : 30]. You must never say that at one stage you have only taken Christ as your justification, or as your righteousness, and that later on you may take Him as your sanctification. That is dividing Christ: and He cannot be divided. There is nothing so unscriptural, so wrong, as to divide up Christ and to say, 'Ah yes, I am justified, I have received His righteousness, and now I propose to go to meetings which exhort us to take Him as our sanctification by faith, as I have already taken Him as my justification by faith'. You cannot do that. You either take Him or reject Him. You are baptized into Him, not parts of Him – the whole of Christ.

'We', says Paul, 'were baptized into Jesus Christ'; and he says elsewhere, 'We are complete in him' [*Colossians* 2 : 10]. When? Now! Not, we shall be complete later, but we are complete in Him now. We must get rid of the idea of experience at this point. Whatever your experience, whatever your feeling may be, I tell you this; if you are a Christian you are complete in Christ. He is now your 'wisdom, your righteousness, your sanctification, and your redemption'. Now! You may go on to experience these things more and more; and we should do so. That is why we need to be taught, that is why we need to be exhorted to apply what we have learned; but that does not make any difference to the fact. What the Apostle is saying here is this: You are no longer in Adam, you are in Christ; and if you are in Him, what is true of Him is true of you. You realize it progressively, but it is true now. It is the guarantee of your final, complete redemption, of your being delivered from every 'spot or wrinkle or any such thing'. Christ is my sanctification now. If I die at this moment I am sanctified in Him, I am justified in Him. He is all this to me. I am baptized 'into Jesus Christ'.

There is the first big statement. The Apostle will now go on to divide it up. Because I am in Christ, I am in His death, I am in His life, I am in everything that is His. But get hold of this, understand this, that we are baptized into the Lord Jesus Christ

Himself. Everything that was true of Adam became true of me because I was in Adam and came out of him. In exactly the same way – only, as he has argued in chapter 5, 'still more' – grace has 'abounded', 'superabounded'. All that is in Christ, and true of Him in His relationship to the redeemed, is mine because I am 'in Him', and all that He has done and has accomplished becomes mine, as all that Adam did and accomplished became mine. That is the doctrine. We have worked it out in detail and at great length from chapter 5 verse 10 until this point. The Apostle keeps on repeating it because it is vital to what follows. It is because I am in Christ that I am in His death, in His resurrection, in His life, in everything that is His. So I have taken the trouble to emphasize these words, 'All of us', 'So many of us'. All of us are baptized into Christ Himself, the whole of Him as He is, and not particular aspects only of His work at any given point.

Having got hold of this fundamental teaching and doctrine we shall now be in a happy position to face the statements that follow. They should be comparatively simple, in view of what we have already said. If we have not grasped this controlling thought we shall inevitably find everything else difficult. But if you have this 'key', the rest follows as the night the day. We shall go on to follow the way in which the Apostle deduces glorious truths from this primary, central, fundamental statement.

Four

*

*Know ye not, that so many of us as were baptized into Jesus Christ
were baptized into his death?*

*Therefore we are buried with him by baptism into death; that like
as Christ was raised up from the dead by the glory of the Father,
even so we also should walk in newness of life.* Romans 6 : 3, 4

As we come to this detailed outworking of his argument by the
Apostle it is essential that we should hold clearly in our minds
what he is setting out to do. He is refuting the charge brought
against his teaching stated in the first verse, 'Shall we continue in
sin, that grace may abound?' He is not giving an exposition of
the way of holiness and of sanctification, as is commonly suggested; he is simply refuting the charge that is brought against
the doctrine of justification by faith, and against the finality and
certainty of our salvation in Christ. He refutes the charge by
saying, 'God forbid. How shall we that died to sin live any longer
therein?' That is the main proposition, and we have already interpreted what that means. The question that now arises is,
What in particular does this imply? What follows of necessity
from it? What is true of us in the light of this general proposition
that we are joined to the Lord Jesus Christ? In verses 3 to 5
the Apostle works out the results in general; in verses 6 to 10
he expounds it in a more particular manner and in greater
detail. That is our division of the matter: verses 3 to 5, general
deduction; verses 6 to 10, a more detailed and particular exposition.

We start with the more general aspect. Here we are as Christians; we have been baptized into Christ, which means that we
are joined to Him, and thus we are participators in what has
happened to Him. What does that mean? The first result is that

we are joined with Him in His death. 'Know ye not, that so many of us as were baptized into Jesus Christ were baptized into his death?' Note that the emphasis is upon *his* death; we are baptized into 'his death'. He is not talking primarily about a death that we undergo, but about His death, and emphasizing that we derive benefits from His death, because we are united with Him in that death. In chapter 5 verse 12 the Apostle says, 'Wherefore, as by one man sin entered into the world, and death by sin, and so death passed upon all men, for that all have sinned'. Adam committed the actual sin itself but, says Paul, we all did it in him and with him. Now here he says that when our Lord died all Christians died with Him, because we are joined to Him, because we are baptized into Him. What He did we have done; because we have been baptized into His death, we died with Him. As we sinned with Adam, we died with the Lord Jesus Christ.

Let me emphasize this again. This is not something subjective or experimental; the Apostle is not thinking of that here. That is where many go wrong in their exposition of this chapter; they persist in regarding it from the experimental standpoint. It is one of the chapters constantly used in 'holiness meetings' and in addresses on sanctification, for that reason. But that is not what the Apostle is dealing with here; he is dealing with the grand objective fact. It is not something we feel, but something that is true of us, equally true of us as that we sinned in Adam. You do not 'feel' that you sinned in Adam; you believe it because God's Word tells you that it is true. We can see the results and the consequences as they become evident experimentally. In exactly the same way, at this point Paul is simply concerned about the fact, the great objective fact, that because of this union with Him, when Christ died to sin we died to sin with Him.

This is the point, it seems to me, that is missed by so many, not only in this chapter but in so much Christian thinking. Take, for instance, our hymn-books. It is extremely difficult to find appropriate hymns to illustrate this theme we are discussing. Our hymns tend to be so subjective. I went through the entire section of hymns on the Christian Church in *Congregational Praise* and I found that, as is the case with other hymn-books, they simply deal with the fellowship that we enjoy in the Church, the fellowship we enjoy with one another. It is almost impossible to find hymns that bring out this great doctrine of our union with Christ, and our position in Him. We are so subjective that we miss this glorious truth, this objective truth, this great thing that has happened outside us – our position. This is very sad, but nevertheless true.

Let us, then, get rid of all subjective and experimental ideas as regards this matter. They are not here at all; they come later in the chapter. The Apostle is expounding the doctrine at this point; he comes to the application in verse 11, and not until then. That is the thing to grasp. We shall have to keep on emphasizing this. Our death with our Lord is something that is true of us in exactly the same way as it is true to say that we all sinned when Adam sinned. We spent much time on chapter 5 verses 12 to 21 because, if we are not clear about that, we cannot possibly follow the argument here. This is a continuation and application of the theme of the fifth chapter.

We can state this truth in a number of negatives. Our being baptized into Christ's death is not something that is *going* to happen to us; it *has* happened. You cannot be a Christian without its being true of you. It is not something that *ought* to happen to us. How often it is presented like that! 'Ah', they say, 'you have been saved, you are converted, you are justified; you have now to die with Christ if you really want this deepening of your spiritual life, and this further blessing.' But that is not the Apostle's teaching. I repeat that this is not something that *ought* to happen to us; it has happened. Because we are joined to Him, we were baptized and joined in His death. We died with Him – that is the whole case – otherwise we are not Christians. Similarly, it is not a thing that we must try to achieve in some shape or form; it is something that has already taken place. As we saw, the correct translation of verse 2 is, 'How shall we that died to sin?' It has happened. He died to sin, and we died when He died. That is the whole point of the argument. We are baptized into Him, so what has happened to Him has happened to us; and we are baptized into His death. This has happened to all Christians because of their union with Him.

Now let me illustrate it all by turning again to the Epistle to the Galatians. No passage of Scripture is more frequently misinterpreted or misapplied and misunderstood than the statement at the end of chapter 2 of that epistle: 'I am crucified with Christ'

(I was crucified with Christ), 'nevertheless I live; yet not I but Christ liveth in me, and the life that I now live in the flesh I live by the faith of the Son of God, who loved me, and gave himself for me.' This is the statement so frequently used in conventions and meetings concerned to teach sanctification and holiness. And yet if you read the context you find that the Apostle is dealing there with nothing but justification; it is the summing up of his argument about justification, concerning which Peter and Barnabas had gone astray. He deals with nothing but justification in that second chapter of Galatians; yet it is generally used in connection with sanctification. The popular teaching has been, 'You have been saved; that is a matter for thanksgiving, but you are not having victory in your life, you are not experiencing the full blessing of the Christian life; and you never will until you have taken the second step and have become crucified with Christ. Christ has been crucified for you. You understand that; but you have not understood hitherto that before you can become a full Christian you have also to die with Christ.' So they urge upon you to die with Christ as a part of our sanctification. That is surely a complete misrepresentation of what Paul is saying. He is not speaking of some unusual saint, of a man who has reached some second stage, he is talking about justification. He says that every Christian has been crucified with Christ, and that you cannot be a Christian apart from this. It is exactly the same teaching that we have here in the sixth chapter of the Epistle to the Romans.

The Apostle's statement has nothing to do with sanctification as such; it is purely a question of that which is true of every Christian, and, as it were, an aspect of his justification. God justifies those whom He joins to Christ. So it is the first step in the Christian life, not some further step that we should be exhorted to take, and which it is within our capacity and ability to take. The Apostle's assertion, in other words, is that our Lord Himself, when He died, died completely and entirely to His relationship to sin. In verse 10 he states that explicitly, 'For in that he died, he died unto sin once; but in that he liveth, he liveth unto God'. 'He died unto sin.' Christ died unto sin once. Now that cannot possibly mean that He died unto sin that was within Him, because there was no sin in Him. It means that He died to His relationship to sin. He had come into the world to save mankind. That meant that He had to put Himself into a relationship to the Law, and to sin. And He did so. But when He died He ended that relationship.

So what Paul is saying here is that, as the Lord Jesus Christ when He died, died to the realm and the reign and the sphere of sin once and for ever, we also have done the same. We have been joined unto Him, therefore we have been joined with Him in His death. His death means the end of the relationship to the realm and the reign of sin, therefore we have died to the realm and the relationship and the reign of sin. He is proving here how it was that we died unto the reign and the power and the realm of sin. It is, he says, the result of being joined to Christ. We are joined in His death, so what is true of His relationship to sin as a reign and a realm is equally true of ours. It has nothing to do with our subjective experience; it has everything to do with our relationship to this reign of sin.

But in the second place, in verse 4 the Apostle proceeds to say that we are also joined with Christ in His burial: 'Therefore we are buried with him by baptism into death.' This is an odd form of expression, so it has often been misunderstood. It seems to say that it is our being buried with Him that causes our death; which is, of course, ridiculous because death comes before burial. The Apostle's statement is that because we are baptized into Him, and therefore into His death, we are also buried with Him, were buried with Him in the burial that follows the death. We are buried with Him through our baptism into His death. That is the way to read it: 'Through our baptism into His death we also share in His burial.'

What does this mean? Why does he take the trouble to say this? It is clear that it must mean this, that burial, after all, is the final proof of death. It emphasizes the completion, the finality of death. You may look at a body that appears to be inanimate and dead, but if there is any doubt or query you do not bury it until you are absolutely certain that death has taken place. The act of burial is, so to speak, a kind of certificate that the person is really and completely dead. Burial is the final event which proves to a certainty the fact of death. In other words the Apostle is saying, 'You have not only been baptized into Christ's death but also into His burial'. His burial is absolute proof of the fact that He died, in the fullest sense of the term, on the Cross. It was not merely a suspension of life or of animation or of breathing; it was a true death. His burial is proof positive of that.

What does that establish? It is the ultimate proof of the fact that He had really finished with the state and the condition in which He was before. When a person dies, and is buried, he has finished entirely and completely with the life of this world and all that belongs to it. Burial is a proclamation that relationship to this life and to this world has ended. You lower the body into the ground and you put earth over the body; that is the end; the buried person has finished with this life and with this world. So when our Lord was buried, His relationship to life in this world, the life He had entered into at birth, the life that was 'under the law' and within the realm of the power of sin, was finished. That is what the Apostle is arguing. Our Lord's burial was the final proof that He had entirely finished with that peculiar relationship to sin into which He had entered for the purposes of our salvation. That is why he emphasizes the burial. As the man whom you bury has finished with the life of this world, so the Lord Jesus Christ by being buried was stating that the relationship to sin in this world that He had assumed for the purposes of salvation no longer obtained. He moved out altogether from the realm and the reign and the territory of sin into which, and under which, He had deliberately and voluntarily brought Himself in order to save us. That is what is true of His burial.

What of us? He says that we have been buried with Him because we are joined to Him by this baptism. We not only died with Him, we were also buried with Him. Buried with Him from what? Buried from this reign and realm of sin. That is what Paul is saying; nothing else. It is the exposition of the fact that we have died to sin in that sense. So it is true to say of us that, as a man when he dies and is buried has entirely finished with this realm and life in which we live, so when we were buried with Christ it was the final proof of the fact that we also have finished with the reign and the realm and the rule and the power of sin. In a sense this is the exposition of the twenty-first verse of the previous chapter, 'That as sin hath reigned unto death, even so might grace reign through righteousness unto eternal life by Jesus Christ our Lord'. Our being buried with Him marks the end of our being under the reign and the realm and the rule of sin. We are buried in the grave in that respect.

[47]

But thank God it does not stop there. The Apostle goes on to the positive in the second half of verse 4; 'That like as Christ was raised up from the dead by the glory of the Father, even so we also should walk in newness of life'. We are back once more with one of these glorious 'As . . . even so' statements of the Apostle.

I put this, then, as a proposition, my third proposition, in this way. We are not only joined to Him in His death, and in His burial, but also joined to Him in His resurrection. What does this mean? What was true of His resurrection? What did His resurrection mean to Him? That is the question to start with. Get rid of the subjective experimental aspect. What was true of His resurrection? What did His resurrection mean to Him? What does it tell us about Him? Here again, we are not even considering the doctrine of the atonement. We have already done that; we are now considering in particular what the resurrection meant to Him.

The first thing to which the Apostle draws attention is the way in which it was produced, the way in which it came to pass. He says that 'Christ was raised up from the dead by the glory of the Father'. 'The glory of the Father' means 'the power of the Father'. 'The glory' is the essential character of God, His chief attribute. God manifests His glory in different ways. He manifests His glory in forgiving us, in calling us, in all that He does to us. He also manifests His glory by exerting His power. Any manifestation of the being of God is a manifestation of the glory of God, so you will often find in the Scriptures that one term is used for another. Instead, therefore, of saying 'by the power of the Father' he says, 'by the glory of the Father'. If you like you can translate it, that 'Christ was raised up from the dead by the glorious power of the Father', or 'the manifestation of the glory of the Father in power'. It is a particular form of the manifestation of God's glory. This, Paul says, was manifested in a most amazing and extraordinary manner in the resurrection of the Lord Jesus Christ from the dead. The Apostle is very fond of saying this. Let me give another example of the same thing. It is in the Epistle to the Ephesians, chapter 1 verse 19. He is anxious that believers should know what is the exceeding greatness of His power (God's power) to us-ward who believe 'according to the working of his mighty power, which he wrought in Christ when he raised him from the dead, and set him at his own right hand in the heavenly places, far above all principality, and power, and might, and dominion, and every name that is named, not only in this world, but also in that which is to come'. That is another statement of it. So the first thing we have to hold on to is that God raised Him from the dead by His own eternal glorious power. The first thing the resurrection proclaims is the tremendous power of God that was exercised and revealed. But someone may say that we read elsewhere that the Lord Jesus Christ said, 'I have power to lay it down and I have power to take it again'. Certainly! You will find that frequently in the Scriptures. The same action is sometimes ascribed to the Father, sometimes to the Son, sometimes to the Holy Spirit. We have here the doctrine of the Trinity, the three in one and the one in three, so that an action can be ascribed to any one of the divine Persons. But there is a peculiar sense in which God the Father acted in our Lord's resurrection; so Paul refers to the Father.

That is how the resurrection came about. But what does it tell us? The first thing it tells us is that Christ could not be held by the power and the reign of sin and death. Listen to Peter saying this on the Day of Pentecost in Acts chapter 2: 'Whom God hath raised up, having loosed the pains of death, because it was not possible that he should be holden of it' [verse 24]. Death is a tremendous power, it is the ultimate manifestation of the power of sin, as we have seen – 'Sin hath reigned unto death' [chapter 5 : 21]. It is a tremendous power, a gripping, holding power. The power of man is nothing in comparison with this; but as Peter says, God raised Christ up, 'having loosed the pains of death, because it was not possible that He should be holden of it'. Why not? Peter answers by quoting Psalm 16: 'Because thou wilt not leave my soul in hell, neither wilt thou suffer thine Holy One to see corruption' [*Acts* 2 : 27]. Sin and death did their utmost to hold Him, sin and death thought they had conquered Him. He had been buried, the stone was rolled on to the mouth of the grave and sealed. It appeared to be the end. But it was not so. There comes in a power, this glorious power of God, that can even conquer the power of death and of the grave and of hell. Death could not hold Him because He is the Holy One of God, and not only man. The reign of grace and its power was being manifested, and Christ is raised; and the defeat of the reign

[49]

of sin is publicly announced. That is what Peter is saying.

In other words, our Lord's resurrection is the ultimate proof that He has finally and completely conquered sin and its reign, and has entirely finished with it. He has no more to do with it. This other power has done its utmost, it has brought up its every reserve; but it has been defeated and routed; and He is entirely outside it and is no longer in the realm and rule and reign and power of sin. Once more, you see, we go back to chapter 5 verse 21: 'Sin reigned unto death'; but it cannot go further. All sin can do is to kill us and bury us; but it cannot go further. That is the ultimate of its power. Our Lord's resurrection proclaims that, and establishes it. He has finished with it, He is out of it, He has no more to do with it.

Let me put that positively, because the Apostle himself puts it positively. Our Lord has not only come out of the realm into which He had entered, He has risen to another realm, a new sphere, a new set of relationships. It is what the Apostle calls here 'newness of life'. Later on, in verses 9 and 10, he is going to state this much more explicitly. Here, he puts it implicitly, there, explicitly; 'Knowing that Christ being raised from the dead dieth no more; death hath no more dominion over him. For in that he died, he died unto sin once' – its realm, its reign, once and for ever – 'but in that he liveth, he liveth unto God'. This is what gives us liberty and assurance and all that we so sorely need.

Let me show how another writer in the New Testament really says the same thing. Take for instance Hebrews 2:9: 'But we see Jesus, who was made a little lower than the angels for the suffering of death, crowned with glory and honour, that by the grace of God he should taste death for every man,' especially the first part of that verse. What does it mean? Look at Jesus, says the author of the Epistle. He was made 'a little lower than the angels'. He was from eternity altogether above them. He has proved that in chapter 1, where he shows that the Son of God has made the angels, that He was the Creator of the angels. Here He is portrayed, the second Person in the Trinity, the Son of God, far above all creatures, the One by whom all things were made, and without whom was nothing made that was made. He made the angels; but we see Him as Jesus, as a man, 'a little lower than the angels'.

What has happened? The Lord has chosen for a period of time

and for a specific object and purpose, to abase Himself, to humble Himself. He has entered into this life and into this world. He has taken unto Himself human nature. He who is altogether above all the angels has put himself into a lower position. He has entered into our world, He has assumed our nature, He has taken on our whole condition and position in order that He might save us. He has done this temporarily. Yes, says that author, but He has finished completely the work He came to do; there is nothing more to be done. Look at Him now. He is 'crowned with glory and honour'. He is no longer 'a little lower than the angels', He is back where He was before, He is back in His own eternal realm. He has gone out of this realm into which He had entered voluntarily for a while, and for the specific end and object of accomplishing our salvation. That is what the Apostle Paul is saying here.

Again, take the Epistle to the Galatians, chapter 4, verses 4 and 5, and you will find the same message. 'When the fulness of the time was come, God sent forth his Son' – His eternal Son. How did He send Him forth? 'Made of a woman'. He has come down to that; He has entered into a new realm – 'made of a woman', born of the womb of the Virgin Mary. He who is above all creatures in heaven and in eternity, the Maker, Creator, Sustainer of all things is now found in this realm in which it is possible for Him to be born as a babe of a woman. 'Made of a woman'; even more, 'made under the law'. The Lawgiver puts Himself under the Law. He has entered into a realm in which He is now under the Law, and subject to it. Why has He done this? 'To redeem them that were under the law, that we might receive the adoption of sons.' You see what it means? He has deliberately come into this realm in which you and I live, and which is the realm of the reign of sin and the realm of Law. He has entered into it, He has put Himself under it, in order that He might save us. But that was only a temporary relationship; and what the resurrection tells us is that the temporary relationship to sin and the Law which He had assumed, this realm into which He had entered for the purpose of our salvation, has ended. He has gone out of, He is dead to it, He is buried out of it, and He has risen the other side of it. He is no longer in that realm. His relationship to the realm and the rule and the reign of sin has gone once and for ever, as verses 9 and 10 emphasize.

[51]

Christ's resurrection proclaims that all that went before His death is finished; it is over once and for ever. In the resurrection He is no longer 'under the law', He has finished entirely with 'the law of sin and death'. His prayer recorded in John 17 : 5 has been answered. There He is, just before He goes to the Cross, and He prays: 'And now, O Father, glorify thou me with thine own self with the glory which I had with thee before the world was.' What He is saying in effect is this: 'Father, I have humbled myself, I have laid aside the signs of the glory which I had with thee before the foundation of the world and before time. I have done the work which thou didst send me to do, I have finished the work thou gavest me to do. Father, glorify me again with that glory which I have shared with thee from all eternity, the signs of which, for the time being, and for the purpose of my Mediatorship and my Messiahship, I have temporarily laid aside, and entered into this other realm. I have finished the work, so glorify me again with the glory which I had with thee before the foundation of the world.'

There, then, we see something of what His resurrection means and involves and implies. The astonishing statement the Apostle makes is that 'as' that is true of Him, 'even so' it is true of us, 'that like as Christ was raised up from the dead by the glory of the Father, even so we also should walk in newness of life'. He walks in newness of life as the result of His resurrection. So do we. We are baptized into Him, we are joined to Him; what is true of His death is true of us, what is true of His burial is true of us, and what is true of His resurrection is true of us. What does it mean? First, it means this: the same glorious power of the Father that raised Him from the dead has done the same to us. Go back to Ephesians 1 : 19 and 20. Paul prays that 'the eyes of their understanding might be enlightened', that they might know three things. The third is, 'and what is the exceeding greatness of his power (God's power) to us-ward who believe, according to (by the result of) the working of his mighty power, which he wrought in Christ when he raised him from the dead'. The Apostle means that the selfsame power that raised Christ from the dead is the power that raises us from the death of sin into which we had entered as the result of Adam's transgression and the reign of sin. Still more explicitly you find the same teaching in the second chapter of Ephesians verses 5 and 6. Paul says, 'Even when we were dead in sins, he hath quickened us together with Christ, (by grace ye are saved)'; and he continues, 'And hath raised us up together with Christ, and hath made us sit together in heavenly places in Christ Jesus'.

Once more I would emphasize that this is not something that is going to happen to us; it has happened to us already. As we have finished with the reign of sin, we have entered into the reign of grace. We no longer belong to the territory, to the realm of sin; we are in the territory and the realm and the rule of grace. We have been 'delivered from the power of darkness and translated into the kingdom of his dear Son' [*Colossians* 1 : 13]. It was nothing less than the glorious power of God that was revealed and exerted and manifested in raising Christ literally, physically, from the grave that transfers us from the kingdom of darkness into the kingdom of God's dear Son. And it has happened to every one of us who is a Christian.

Another result of this raising up is that we are at this moment in a new life and in a new realm – 'newness of life'. This is not something I am hoping for, it is not something I am striving after, it is true of me because I have been baptized into Christ. I died with Him, I was buried with Him, I rose with Him; I am in the new realm. It is a new life altogether. As He has finished with the rule and the reign and the realm of sin completely and absolutely, so have we also. The Apostle is not saying that we ought to do so, he is not saying that we ought to strive to do so, that we ought to strive to crucify ourselves and to die. No! It has happened already, we are in this position. 'If any man be in Christ, he is a new creature (a new creation); old things are (have) passed away; behold, all things have become new.' 'Our citizenship is in heaven', says Paul in Philippians 3 : 20, It is not 'going to be' – it is! We are strangers here, we are a colony of heaven, we are away from home; 'our citizenship is in heaven'. That is the polity to which we belong, not the old polity of this world. We are no longer 'under the law', we are no longer under the reign of sin; we have finished with that once and for ever; we are 'seated together in heavenly places in Christ Jesus' [*Ephesians* 2 : 6].

In a sense it is but a repetition of what we found in the phrase 'We died to sin'. The Apostle is showing us in these two verses how exactly this came to pass, and why this is of necessity true. He says in effect, 'Does anybody dispute that we died to sin?

Do you not know that you have been baptized into Christ Himself, and therefore if you have been baptized into Christ you have been baptized into His death, you have been baptized into His burial, you have been baptized into His resurrection. You have no more to do with the reign and the rule and the realm of sin'. 'If this is true of us', he says, 'how shall we continue in sin?' With this exceeding great power to 'us-ward that believe', with this power of the resurrection already working in us, the vanquished rule and reign of sin can never possess us again. The devil, that 'evil one', touches us not; while this power is in us he cannot do so; and it will be in us for ever, because 'He who began a good work' in us 'will perform it until the day of Jesus Christ' [*Philippians* 1 : 6]. We shall not be allowed to live a life of sin; it is not only unreasonable as a suggestion, it is in a final sense impossible. 'Sin shall not have dominion over you', the Apostle goes on to say in the 14th verse; and that is because, being joined to Christ as the result of this baptism, we are sharers not only in His death but also in His resurrection. We have entered into newness of life.

Five

*

For if we have been planted together in the likeness of his death, we shall be also in the likeness of his resurrection:
Knowing this, that our old man is crucified with him, that the body of sin might be destroyed, that henceforth we should not serve sin.
                                            Romans 6 : 5, 6

The point at which we have arrived in the Apostle's argument is that the suggestion about continuing in sin is quite monstrous, because we have not only died to sin with Christ but we are also positively in a new life, in a new realm. We have not been baptized only into the death of Christ, we have been baptized also into His resurrection that 'like as he was raised up by the glorious power of the Father, even so we also should walk in newness of life' – in this new life. Now that is the point at which we have arrived, and so we can look at verse 5.

This verse in a sense is a repetition and a summary of what the Apostle has already been saying in verses 3 and 4; but it also goes a little beyond that. It is not mere repetition, it does not stop at being a summary, 'For if', he says, "we have been planted together in the likeness of his death, we shall be also in the likeness of his resurrection.' The Apostle takes the trouble to make this statement because he is anxious to emphasize his last statement in verse 4 – 'even so we also should walk in newness of life'. That is the point he wants to make, that we are walking in this 'newness of life'. This therefore can be regarded as a pivotal statement.

Having worked out the process from step to step in verses 3 and 4, he states it now as a whole. You notice that it consists of two halves, corresponding to the two parts of the sentence: 'If we have been planted together in the likeness of his death, we shall be also in the likeness of his resurrection.' Those are the two sections, and we shall find that he expounds the first half in verses 6 and 7, and the second half in verses 8, 9, and 10. This entire passage is a very closely woven argument; the texture is fine. The Apostle is handling a tremendous theme and it is important that we should keep clear in our minds the exact mechanics of the way in which he does so. He had laid down a proposition in verse 2; he establishes it in verses 3 and 4. He now states it in a slightly different way in verse 5. And then he will work it out again in still greater detail, the first portion in verses 6 and 7, and the second in verses 8, 9, and 10. But what matters above everything else is our union with the Lord Jesus Christ. We are baptized into Him, and it is because we are thus united with Him by this baptism that these things are true of us. And let us never forget that his main purpose in saying this is to answer the false objection which he has mentioned in verse 1.

Let us look then at verse 5: 'For if', Paul says. Let no one be led astray by the word 'if'. It does not mean that there is any doubt or any query about it. It really means 'since' – 'since we have been planted together in the likeness of his death'. This is a common form used in arguing a matter. We say, 'If you agree that that is true, then this must also be true'. That is what Paul means here. 'Since it is a fact that we have been planted together in the likeness of His death', then it must be a fact also that 'we have been planted together in the likeness of His resurrection'.

Then take the word 'planted'. I referred to it previously. It is a word that means 'growing together', growing together in such an intimate way that it means an essential union. That is the meaning of the term 'union by growth', a joined growth becoming one, 'united together'. It expresses therefore a very definite and real union. Then note also that it is in no sense a figure of baptism. We have dealt with that. The point is that we are thus united to Christ as a branch is in the vine; it is a unity in growth and in everything else. Once more the Apostle is emphasizing the intimate nature of the union of the believer with his Lord.

We must also look at the word 'likeness'. 'We have been planted together', says Paul, 'in the likeness of his death.' Why that? For this reason: Our death and resurrection are not identical with the Lord's. Everything that happened to Him, of course, was unique, because of who He was, and because He is the eternal Son of God. Everything that happened to Him, therefore, has a speciality and a uniqueness about it that can never be true of us. So the Apostle uses the term 'likeness' to help us to keep that distinction in our mind. Our death and resurrection are in the 'likeness' of His, but they are not identical with it. We shall never know the suffering He knew, we shall never know many other things which He knew. A parallel in chapter 8 verse 3 will help us to grasp the meaning. We are not told that our Lord came into this world *in* sinful flesh, but we are told that He came *in the likeness* of sinful flesh. That is the same distinction. So it means this, that what has happened to Him literally and actually happens to us spiritually. There is a spiritual sense in which it is true to say that we died with Him. We did not die with Him literally, physically; we shall never know the agony that He knew in His death. But what is important is that, because of our spiritual relationship to Him, the effects, the consequences of His actual literal death become ours, are passed to us. Go back once more to the case of Adam. We were not literally in Adam when he sinned, yet spiritually we were in Adam when he sinned. It is the same parallel still. So this is a very accurate term – in the 'likeness' of His death, and in the 'likeness' of His resurrection. We have all the benefits and the results of that resurrection, so the Apostle calls it 'being planted in the likeness of His death, and in the likeness of His resurrection'.

The next expression we must examine is one which has often been misunderstood. He says, 'We *shall be* also in the likeness of his resurrection'. This expression 'shall be' has led some to think that it refers only to our future literal bodily resurrection. It certainly includes that, but if you say that it means that only, you are rendering the whole argument of the Apostle at this point quite useless, because what he is concerned to show is that we can never continue in sin that grace may abound, in this life and in this world. He is not arguing about what we are going to be like after we have risen from the dead in a literal sense, he is concerned about the life we live as Christian believers in this world in the here and now. He has said at the end of verse 4 that we should walk 'in newness of life'. Where? In the state of glorification? No; but here while we are still left in this world. In exactly the same way this *shall be* refers also to this present life. It is a future tense only from the standpoint of our being dead with Him and buried with Him; it is something that follows, is subsequent to that death. It is not future in the sense that it only means the life in the world to come.

Verse 11 will make this absolutely clear and certain. This is not even a matter of opinion, it seems to me. It is because people take a verse like this on its own, and forget the context, that they go astray. In verse 11 the Apostle says, 'Likewise reckon ye also yourselves to be dead indeed unto sin but alive unto God through Jesus Christ our Lord'. When? Now! We are to reckon ourselves in the here and now to be dead to sin and alive unto God through our Lord Jesus Christ. So when he talks about our having been 'planted together in the likeness of his death', and says, 'we shall be also in the likeness of his resurrection' he is saying that the man who died with Him also rises with Him. It is a continuous action. You cannot take part in the death only. Because you are in Him, you take part in all He has done, death and life. As He died and rose, so you die and rise. So the 'shall be' is not a simple future which has reference only to what shall be beyond life in this world.

What then does the Apostle mean by 'the likeness of His resurrection?' He means the 'newness of life' to which he has referred at the end of chapter 4. We have been raised with Christ into a new life. We are no longer in the old life under the dominion and the tyranny of sin; we have been taken right out of it. We died out of it, we have risen out of it, we are in this new life in this world even here and now. Not only is that said in verse 4, but again in verse 10. 'For in that he (Christ) died, he died unto sin once, but in that he liveth, he liveth unto God.' And if 'he liveth, and liveth unto God' we do also. That is the argument. And the time of the living is the here and now. Hence the appeal and the exhortation in verse 11, 'Reckon ye also yourselves to be dead indeed unto sin, but alive unto God through Jesus Christ our Lord'.

I am emphasizing this for the following reason. I had occasion to criticize the great Robert Haldane in his interpretation of the statement in verse 2 that 'we died to sin'. Haldane, as I explained, says that Paul means that 'we died to the guilt of sin', and he stops at that. I rejected that explanation because Paul is asserting not merely that we died to the 'guilt' of sin, but that we died to the reign of sin altogether. Here we have absolute proof of our contention. We are not left in the grave, we have risen to newness

of life, and we are to walk in newness of life. This is what the
Apostle is concerned about. Not only are we dead to the guilt of
sin, we are dead to the whole reign and realm of sin. And here
is the final proof of his assertion – we are completely out of the
sphere of sin and death, and in this new sphere of life and salvation. We are living in this new life with Christ, because we have
been raised with Him. That is the final proof of the inadequacy
of Haldane's interpretation of verse 2.

The Apostle is really saying that our relationship to sin has
been entirely changed, even as our Lord's relationship to it was
entirely changed when He rose again from the dead. We have
seen that He had come into the realm and territory of sin for a
period of time in order to save us; but the moment He was dead
and buried and rose again He finished with that relationship.
As Paul says in verse 10, 'In that he died, he died unto sin once' –
once and for ever. He had finished with it; and so have we!
That is the whole argument.

But this statement goes even further. I believe that it looks
forward also to the future; for our salvation includes the resurrection of the body and the glorification of the body. During our
earthly life we are only in the 'likeness' of Christ's resurrection,
but there is a day coming when we shall be glorified also in our
bodies, even as He is glorified. That is what the Apostle says in
Philippians 3 : 20: 'We look for the (coming of the) Saviour',
he says, 'who shall change our vile body, that it may be fashioned
like unto his glorious body, according to the mighty working of
his power whereby he is able even to subdue all things unto
himself.' His words to the Romans here, I believe, include this
truth. If we have been planted together in the likeness of His
death, we shall be also in the likeness of His resurrection. This
is already true of us essentially, spiritually; but the day is coming
when it will be true in every respect. We shall be 'without spot
or wrinkle', 'faultless and blameless', we shall be 'perfect' and
'glorified'. We shall stand before Him and see Him as He is, and
'be like Him'. I believe that this statement includes even that,
because the Apostle's great concern here is to bring out the
triumph of grace – its complete triumph. There will be nothing
left undone, all the work will have been completed, and our
redemption will be absolutely perfect and entire. What the Apostle
is emphasizing here is the certainty of this – 'we shall be also'.

It all follows inevitably. If we are in Christ, then we must of necessity share in all that has resulted from His action, because we have been 'baptized' into Him, 'planted' into Him, joined in this intimate manner with Him. It follows of necessity that if we have died with Him – and we have so died – we shall also in this full and final sense be raised with Him.

The Apostle says exactly the same thing in the second Epistle to Timothy: 'It is a faithful saying: If we have died with him, we shall also live with him; if we suffer with him, we shall also reign with him' [2 *Timothy* 2 : 11, 12]. It is precisely the same argument. If we are in Christ all that follows is absolutely certain. Though you are in the flesh at the moment, and are conscious of weakness and frailty and sin and failure, though you are persecuted and buffeted, tried and tempted, all is well, says the Apostle, because 'The Lord knoweth them that are his', and 'the foundation of God standeth sure' [2 *Timothy* 2 : 19]. 'The Lord knoweth them that are his.' Their position is guaranteed; nothing can overthrow it. Though we are now suffering with Him, it is equally certain that we shall reign with Him, and be in glory with Him. This is 'a faithful saying'. Let there be no doubt or hesitation about believing it and living upon it. It is one of the absolute certainties of our Christian faith.

Timothy was a young man who was depressed and unhappy, having problems and difficulties and persecutions. 'Listen, Timothy', says Paul in effect, 'Remember that Jesus Christ of the seed of David was raised from the dead according to my Gospel' [2 *Timothy* 2 : 8]. 'And anybody who is in Him is raised already spiritually, and will finally be raised even in his body and in every other respect. Remember that, hold on to that, and then you will not be overcome by the things that are happening to you. You will then know how to endure hardness as a good soldier of Jesus Christ' [2 *Timothy* 2 : 3]. It is the same argument exactly, only that he puts it there to Timothy in a more pastoral manner than he does here in the sixth chapter of the Epistle to the Romans.

I keep on repeating this, as the Apostle goes on repeating it, because we are all so slow to grasp it. The whole point, he says, is that we are under the reign of grace, we are under the powerful reign of grace, and it is so powerful that sin has been defeated, the devil and hell have been defeated. Christ is victorious. 'We see not yet all things put under him (man), but we see Jesus'

[*Hebrews* 2 : 8, 9]. Well, look at Him, keep looking at Him. Because you are in Him, you are already delivered spiritually, and you will soon be delivered entirely. That is the argument. It is in the light of this that the Apostle says that there can be nothing more monstrous and ridiculous than to suggest that we can 'continue in sin that grace may abound'. Everything that has happened in Jesus Christ was designed to take us out of that realm of sin, and to put us into this new realm. So he ridicules this criticism, plausible as it seems at first, that had been brought against his teaching of justification by faith only, and the reign of grace. 'We died with him.' To what end, for what purpose? In order that we might rise with Him, and having risen with Him, to walk in newness of life. As He has finished with sin, so have we; we have finished with it once and for ever in that sense.

Having laid down this great statement in its two halves the Apostle now proceeds to work it out for us. The first half, 'We have been planted together in the likeness of his death', he works out in verses 6 and 7. Here is verse 6: 'Knowing this, that our old man is crucified with him, that the body of sin might be destroyed, that henceforth we should not serve sin.' Let me suggest a better translation. 'Knowing this, that our old man was crucified with him.' That is what Paul wrote – 'was crucified', not 'is crucified'. It has happened in the past, the verb is in the aorist tense once more. The action is complete, it has happened. We are not being crucified; we have been crucified; the old man was crucified with Him. 'Knowing this, that our old man was crucified with him, that the body of sin might be disannulled (be rendered void, or ineffective), that henceforth we should not be slaves of sin.'

We must first look at the expression, 'Knowing this'. Why does the Apostle put it in that form? It is to remind us that this is something which we should all know, something with which we should be familiar, something concerning which we should have an absolute certainty. He has used a strong term. I am again surprised that the great Charles Hodge says that this is 'experimental knowledge'. My entire exposition asserts the exact opposite and says that it is not experimental; and that to take it experimentally produces utter confusion. This is not experimental knowledge; it is the knowledge of faith, it is knowledge which is revealed in the Scripture, and of which faith is certain. Paul is emphasizing the certainty, but it is not necessarily an experimental certainty. It is the certainty of faith, and it should lead to 'the full assurance' of faith.

He emphasizes, I say, that we should all know this. I therefore make no apology for stopping for a moment to ask a simple question. Do you know this? Do you always live in the light of this knowledge? Is this something of which you are absolutely certain? It is important that I should press the question. If you are familiar with this Epistle to the Romans, had you realized that this is its teaching, and that the Apostle writes to these Romans whom he had never met, saying, 'Knowing this'? This is something that every Christian should know, this is an essential, vital part of our salvation, 'Knowing this . . . '

What is it we know? That our old man was crucified together with Him – 'crucified together with him'. But here we come to this important term, 'our old man'. What does it mean? I suppose there is no term that so frequently troubles Christian people as this term. All who are concerned about sanctification are concerned about this expression, 'our old man'. There are people who have spent their lives in trying to kill their 'old man', to get rid of the 'old man'. It was this striving that, in a sense, took people in ancient times into cells and caves and the tops of mountains and made them become anchorites. It is the basis of the idea of Monasticism in its every shape and form, that which led to mutilations of the flesh, and so forth. It was an attempt to get rid of what was regarded as 'the old man'.

What then is this 'old man?' First, it does not mean the carnal nature and all its propensities. Paul is not teaching that our carnal nature with all its propensities was crucified together with Christ. Neither does it mean our moral being previous to our rebirth. Neither does it mean the flesh with its affections and lusts. Neither does it mean 'old' simply in the sense of 'former', whereas now I am something different. Why am I so concerned with these negatives? It is because I want to show that if you identify the 'old man' with any one of those ideas you will of necessity be in hopeless confusion in the light of other Scriptures which we have to consider. What then does Paul mean by 'old man'? It seems to me to be quite plain if we look at it in the context of the entire passage which begins in chapter 5 verse 12. The 'old man' is the man that I used to be in Adam. That has been the context since chapter 5 verse 12. I was a man in Adam; I am now a man in Christ. What then is the old man? It is the man I once was, but which I am no longer. We have seen many times that the old man that I was in Adam is the one that was crucified with Christ. Our Lord came in and took hold of that man, made it part of Himself in order that He might do away with it and take it out of me. I have ceased to be the man that I was in Adam. As a Christian I am no longer in Adam; I am in Christ. The old man that I can look back upon is that man that I was there in Adam: it is my old humanity. It is not my carnal, sinful nature. That is still here, but the old man has gone, he has been crucified.

'Ah but', says someone, 'crucifixion is a very slow process, it takes a very long time, so what Paul is really saying is that the old man is undergoing this process of crucifixion.' Paul did not say that. Paul used the aorist tense, he said that the crucifixion has happened. As, he says, this happened once and for ever to our Lord, it has happened to us. I shall emphasize this in verse 10: 'In that he died, he died unto sin once.' It is not a process, the crucifixion has ended it. Christ does not go on dying; He was crucified, and He died once and for ever. The crucifixion here points to the death that He accomplished. And I died with Him, that old man died, my old Adamic human nature, the man that I was by my natural birth. That man was joined and united to Adam; he (that is the old man) was crucified together with Christ.

It is important that we should be clear about this because of other statements which the Apostle makes. Take, for instance, Ephesians 4 verses 22 to 24; 'That ye put off concerning the former conversation the old man, which is corrupt according to the deceitful lusts, and be renewed in the spirit of your mind; and that ye put on the new man, which after God is created in righteousness and true holiness.' Then there is a similar statement in Colossians chapter 3 verses 9 and 10: 'Lie not one to another, seeing that ye have put off the old man with his deeds; and have put on the new man, which is renewed in knowledge after the image of him that created him.' There is one more in Galatians chapter 5 verse 24; 'And they that are Christ's have crucified the flesh with the affections and lusts.' I myself am commanded to do something in all these verses. The Galatians are not told that it has been done for them, but that they themselves 'have crucified the flesh with the affections and lusts'. But here we are not told that the old man has crucified himself, but that he was crucified, was crucified together with the Lord Jesus Christ. In other words the only way you can reconcile these statements is to say that the 'old man' is the man that I was in Adam, my old humanity, the man that was born under the law, born in sin, born under condemnation, the man that sinned with Adam and therefore reaped all the consequences of Adam's sin, the man who was under the wrath and condemnation of God. That man died with Christ, was crucified with Him. 'There is therefore now no condemnation to them that are in Christ Jesus.' Why? Because I am no longer that man; I am a new man in Christ Jesus. Christ is 'the first-born among many brethren'; He is the Head of a new race, and I am a member of this new race.

If you realize that that is what the term, 'old man', means you will then understand that when Paul says 'Put off the old man', he means that we must put off the characteristics of the life of the old man. It cannot mean anything else. I cannot be told to 'put off' something that has already been crucified. The difficulty is really one of terms. What the Apostle is saying in effect is, 'Do not go on living as if you still were that old man, because that old man has died; do not go on living as if he was still there; put that off'. That is the meaning of 'putting off the old man' and 'putting on the new man'.

We can expound that statement in Ephesians 4 in this way. The Apostle was saying to the Ephesians, 'Be what you are. You are no longer the old man; therefore do not live like the old man; you are a new man, therefore live like the new man. Be what you are.' I have often used the following illustration. You see a man grown to full age and maturity. You see him almost in tears. He is afraid of someone or of something, and you say to him, 'Don't be a baby'. Why do you say this to him? You do so because he is not a baby. You virtually say to him, 'Be a man, because you are a man'. 'Don't be a baby', you say, 'because you have ceased to be a baby. You are now a man, so be a man, be what you are, and don't be something that you are not.'

There you have the reconciliation of the statement we have here in Romans 6 : 6 with those other statements. Indeed you notice that in Galatians 5 : 24 Paul says quite clearly that it is you and I that have to 'crucify the flesh with its affections and lusts'. That has not been crucified for us; it is the old man that

[64]

has been crucified. So the 'old man' means the old humanity, the man that I was in Adam. I again urge the importance of holding on to the objective character of this statement. It is not experimental; that comes later; this is objective. Paul puts it here in a doctrinal form, so that upon it as a basis he will be able to make his appeal when he comes to verses 11, 12, 13, and indeed all the way from verse 15 to the end of the chapter. We must hold on to the objective character of this statement. The old man is the man that I was in Adam; that is the man that has died once and for ever.

This is, to me, one of the most comforting and assuring and glorious aspects of our faith. We are never called to crucify our old man. Why? Because it has already happened – the old man was crucified with Christ on the Cross. Nowhere does the Scripture call upon you to crucify your old man; nowhere does the Scripture tell you to get rid of your old man, for the obvious reason that he has already gone. Not to realize this is to allow the devil to fool you and to delude you. What you and I are called upon to do is to cease to live as if we were still in Adam. Understand that the 'old man' is not there. The only way to stop living as if he were still there is to realize that he is not there. That is the New Testament method of teaching sanctification. The whole trouble with us, says the New Testament, is that we do not realize what we are, that we still go on thinking we are the old man, and go on trying to do things to the old man. That has been done; the old man was crucified with Christ. He is non-existent, he is no longer there. If you are a Christian, the man that you were in Adam has gone out of existence; he has no reality at all; you are in Christ. If we but saw this as we should, we would really begin to live as Christians in this world. We would all hold up our heads, we would be able to defy sin and Satan, we would rejoice in Christ Jesus as we ought. And Paul says we ought to know this – 'Knowing this . . . '

Let us never again try to get rid of the old man; he has gone. This is something we are to believe, and to receive by faith. This is not something you experience, this is something you believe; and it is only as you believe it that your experience will be triumphant. Let me use an analogy or illustration. With regard to this truth we are called upon, once more, to do what Abraham the father of the faithful did. We were told about that in the fourth

chapter in this way: 'Therefore it is of faith, that it might be by
grace, to the end the promise might be sure to all the seed;
not to that only which is of the law, but to that also which is of
the faith of Abraham, who is the father of us all, (as it is written,
I have made thee a father of many nations), before him whom he
believed, even God, who quickeneth the dead, and calleth those
things which be not as though they were' [*Romans* 4: 16 and 17].
What does Paul mean? He goes on to explain, 'Who against hope
believed in hope, that he might become the father of many
nations, according to that which was spoken, So shall thy seed
be. And being not weak in faith, he considered not his own body
now dead, when he was about an hundred years old, neither
yet the deadness of Sarah's womb. He staggered not at the promise of God through unbelief; but was strong in faith giving
glory to God: And being fully persuaded that what he had promised, he was able also to perform' [verses 18–21].

That is what you and I have to do. God made that statement to
Abraham, and Abraham did not say, 'I am nearly a hundred years
old and Sarah is ninety; what you are saying is therefore impossible'. He did not stagger, he believed God's word. He saw all
the difficulties, and he felt nothing experimentally. There was
Abraham standing under the stars. And God said to him 'Look
at them, can you count them? So shall thy seed be. Can you
count the sand on the seashore? So shall thy seed be'. To a man
aged ninety-nine with a wife of ninety! Abraham felt nothing.
How could he? There was nothing experimental about it, indeed
his natural feelings were all against it. It was just a statement
made by God to the effect that that was what was going to happen. And Abraham on the bare word of God believed it!

You and I have to do the same with this statement. I would not
know that I was in Adam if God had not told me so in His Word.
I would not know that I have been baptized into Christ unless
He had told me. This is an action of the Holy Spirit, which is non-
experimental. The Holy Spirit 'baptizes' me into Christ. It is not
a baptism of or with the Spirit, it is a baptism by the Spirit, He
baptizes me into union with Christ. I know that because I find
it in this Word; and I know that I have died to sin because the
Word tells me so. It is not experimental at this stage at all; it is
the bare statement of God, and I must believe it as Abraham believed that Word. I may feel that I am a sinner, that sin is in me.

That is certainly true. But on the bare Word of God I believe this, that I died with Christ. I am no longer in Adam. 'There is therefore now no condemnation' to me, because I am in Christ. Whatever my feelings may be, whatever the devil may suggest to me, however much the facts may seem to be flying in the face of the statement, faith sees the promise, holds on to it and believes it. And as a result glorious experiences follow. You first believe the Word, then you will have proofs that it is true. But at this stage we must regard it objectively, and take it on the bare Word of God.

That is what the Apostle is concerned about here. If 'we have been planted together in the likeness of his death, we shall be also in the likeness of his resurrection'. Let hell say 'No', let everything within you and without you say 'No', it does not matter. Stand on the foundation of God, plant your feet on this great and glorious promise, because it is true. This is the very essence of the faith position. I am not 'taking' an experience 'by faith', I am taking and believing by faith what God tells me He has done. He tells me that He has put me into Christ, and that because I am in Christ I have died with Him, I have risen with Him, I am walking in newness of life with Him.

In that last phrase you get a hint at experience. I am aware of this, that I am walking in a new life. I can give proofs of new life within me. But at this point that is not what matters. What I must hold on to is this, that I have been put into Christ, and that therefore these things are true of me. It is because of this that my salvation is so sure. It is because God Himself, by the Spirit, has put me into Christ, that nothing can ever take me out of Christ. My future, my eternal future, my final glorification is guaranteed and certain and sure. 'Whom he called, them he also justified, and whom he justified, them he also glorified'. [Romans 8 : 30].

Now we can proceed to work out what the Apostle goes on to show was the object of all this; and the whole time he is answering the false objections which he has mentioned in the first verse. He is still showing the utterly nonsensical character of the suggestion that we should continue in sin that grace may abound. The whole object of all that Christ has done in His grace, he says, is to deliver us finally and completely out of sin and death and to bring us into this new life, which is His own life, which is indeed the life of God.

[67]

Six

*

Knowing this, that our old man is crucified, with him, that the body of sin might be destroyed, that henceforth we should not serve sin. For he that is dead is freed from sin.   Romans 6 : 6, 7

In these two verses, as we have seen, the Apostle is expounding the first part of verse 5 in which he says that 'We were planted together in the likeness of his (Christ's) death'. The first thing this implies is that our old man was crucified with Christ. But he does not leave it at that, he goes on to draw deductions from that fact. Because we were crucified with Christ there are two main results; and he is very much concerned about these because, as I must continue to emphasize, he is still dealing with the false objection to his teaching which he has put before us in the first verse. We must never lose sight of that in interpreting this chapter. He is refuting that, and showing what a monstrous suggestion it is, and for this purpose he draws these two deductions from the fact that our old man was crucified with Christ.

What are his deductions? The word 'that' leads us to them: 'Knowing this, that our old man was crucified with him, *that* . . .' The meaning is 'in order that', 'for the purpose of', 'that it might be to the end'. In other words, this is the object, this is the purpose of the crucifixion of our old man with Christ. It is a double purpose; first, 'that the body of sin might be destroyed'; and second, 'that henceforth we should not serve sin'. Those are the two things that follow inevitably from our being crucified, our having been crucified with Christ.

We look first at the words, 'that the body of sin might be destroyed'. At once we are confronted by the expression, 'the body of sin'. In order to understand its meaning we must get our translation right – 'that the body of sin might be disannulled,

[68]

rendered inert, rendered ineffective'. The term 'destroyed' is not strictly accurate because in English it carries a meaning somewhat foreign to the original text. What Paul is concerned to say is that the 'body of sin' is rendered ineffective, rendered inert, put out of action. But what does this term 'the body of sin' mean?

There are those who teach in their commentaries that this simply means the 'old man' again. They say, 'the body of sin'; in other words 'the old man'. So it amounts to this, that the Apostle's teaching is that 'the old man was crucified with Christ in order that the old man might be rendered ineffective, or null and void, or inert'. This exposition is due to one thing only, namely, that the writers have gone astray in their interpretation of 'the old man'. That was why I was so concerned to emphasize that the old man does not mean the old nature. Here, the Apostle, in this phrase we are looking at, really is dealing with the old nature; and that was why I was concerned to say that the 'old man' does not mean the old nature, because if it does, then the Apostle is just saying that 'our old man is crucified with Him, that the old man might be rendered inert'. Now if he meant that, why did he not say so? Why does he confuse us by bringing in a new term if he is still speaking about the same thing? The Apostle is never guilty of that kind of confusion. He would have said, "Knowing this, that our old man was crucified with him that he might be destroyed, or that he might be rendered ineffective or inert'; and there would have been no difficulty at all.

But here Paul suddenly introduces a new term, 'the body of sin'. Other writers think that 'the body of sin' is a figurative term that is used by the Apostle to represent the 'whole mass' of sin, and to bring out the idea that our problem is not so much particular sins as sin itself. Sin, they teach, is a great mass, and it is so big and so protean in its manifestations, and so varied in its way of dealing with us, that it can be compared very accurately to a body. It has different parts and portions, head and trunk, and hands and feet – the body of sin. The Apostle, they suggest, was just using a figure of speech to bring out this idea of sin as something big and organized and powerful, something that needs to be slain as a body can be slain or crucified. The whole mass of sin must be disannulled or destroyed. Of course there is a sense in which this is right and true. I agree, and I intend to give it emphasis. But what the Apostle is concerned to do in this whole section is to show that under this rule and reign of grace our total connection with sin is to be banished altogether; we are to be delivered entirely from sin, the whole of sin. That undoubtedly is what the Apostle is emphasizing in the section; but that does not mean that this is of necessity the true explanation of the term 'the body of sin'.

I cannot accept it as the true explanation here for the following reasons. Look at the word 'body'. It really does mean 'body'. It is the same word as we shall find the Apostle using in verse 12 where he says, 'Let not sin therefore reign in your mortal body', and so on. In other words, we shall find that the Apostle in this entire section, chapters 6 and 7, has a great deal to say about the 'body'. And I suggest that when he talks about 'the body' he always means the same thing. Unless you have a very good reason for saying that the term 'the body' does not mean the same thing in every case, then you must assume that it does mean the same thing in every case. And I fail to see any good reason for varying the meaning here.

Let us look at some of the verses in which the Apostle uses the term 'body'. Take verse 12: 'Let not sin therefore reign in your mortal body'. In verse 11 he begins to apply the doctrine he has been laying down; he begins making appeals to us. This is the appeal: 'Reckon ye also yourselves therefore to be dead unto sin, but alive unto God through Jesus Christ our Lord.' Then verse 12: 'Let not sin therefore reign.' Where? 'In your mortal body, that ye should obey it in the lusts thereof.' Then go on to verse 13: 'Neither yield ye your members.' He means there the members of our body, the parts and portions of our body. 'Neither yield ye your members as instruments of unrighteousness unto sin, but yield yourselves unto God, as those that are alive from the dead, and your members (parts of your body) as instruments of righteousness unto God.' Then go on to verse 19 and you will find this: 'I speak after the manner of men because of the infirmity of your flesh; for as ye have yielded your members (parts of the body) servants to uncleanness, and to iniquity unto iniquity, even so now yield your members (these same members, parts of your body) servants to righteousness unto holiness.' There you have the uses of the word 'body' in various forms in chapter 6.

Then in chapter 7, starting at verse 17, this is the context: 'If then I do that which I would not, I consent unto the law that it is good. Now then it is no more I that do it, but sin that dwelleth in me'. You notice the distinction? 'It is no longer *I* that do it' – what is it then? – 'it is sin that dwelleth in me'. Go on to verse 18: 'For I know that in me (that is, in my flesh) dwelleth no good thing, for to will is present with me; but how to perform that which is good I find not.' Go on to verse 20: 'Now if I do that I would not, it is no more I that do it.' What is it then? It is 'sin that dwelleth in me'. That is a repetition, more or less, of verse 17. And Paul continues: 'I find then a law, that, when I would do good, evil is present with me. For I delight in the law of God after the inward man: But I see another law.' Where is it? 'In my members' – in parts and portions of my body – 'warring against the law of my mind, and bringing me into captivity to the law of sin which is in my members'. And then, 'O wretched man that I am! who shall deliver me from the body of this death?' – this body, the members of which are doing this to me, and dragging me down. 'Who shall deliver me from this body of death?' Thus we have very striking uses of this word 'body' which we have here in this sixth verse of the sixth chapter.

But we have not yet finished. Go on now to chapter 8 and start at verse 10: 'If Christ be in you, the body is dead because of sin, but the Spirit is life because of righteousness.' The contrast is between the body and the Spirit. Verse 11: 'But if the Spirit of him that raised up Jesus Christ from the dead dwell in you, he that raised up Christ from the dead shall also quicken your mortal bodies by his Spirit that dwelleth in you'. How wonderful, he says, that even your mortal body is going to be quickened and raised eventually! Then in verse 12 he goes on: 'Therefore, brethren, we are debtors, not to the flesh, to live after the flesh'; and in verse 13, 'For if ye live after the flesh, ye shall die; but if ye through the Spirit do mortify the deeds of the body, ye shall live.' He really means 'body' there; he is not talking about sinful flesh, he uses the term 'body' and means 'body'. Go on to verse 23, where he is looking forward to the final consummation, and he says: 'And not only they, but ourselves also, which have the firstfruits of the Spirit, even we ourselves groan within ourselves, waiting for the adoption.' What is that? 'To wit, the redemption of our body'.

You notice that in this great section, chapters 6, 7, and right on to 8, the Apostle is very concerned about the body. My suggestion is that the meaning of the word 'body' in verse 6 is identical with the meaning of the word 'body' in all those other verses. Take one further example, chapter 12 verses 1 and 2. Here we have an example of a great exhortation that follows in the light of all the doctrine he has been expounding. He says, 'I beseech you therefore, brethren, by the mercies of God, that ye present your bodies a living sacrifice, holy, acceptable unto God, which is your reasonable service. And be not conformed to this world, but be ye transformed by the renewing of your mind, that ye may prove what is that good, and acceptable, and perfect will of God'. Again Paul means the literal body. I argue, therefore, that the use of this word 'body' here in chapter 6, where he talks about 'the body of sin' is identical with the use of the term body in all those other verses.

What then does the term 'the body of sin' mean? It means the body, our physical body, of which sin has taken possession. Otherwise stated, 'the body of sin' means 'sin as it dwells in us in our present embodied condition'. We must be quite clear about this. The Apostle is not referring to the body as such, in and of itself, but he is referring to the body as the sphere in which sin and death still reign in us.

Here is the vital distinction as I see it, the distinction between 'I myself as a personality' and 'my body'. The meaning of the term 'the body of sin' is, that sin still reigns and rules, not in me, not over me, but it tends to do so over my body. We are treading here on delicate, not to say dangerous ground; and you will find that some of the great commentators are afraid to say what I have just said. The reason is that they feel that if they say that, they will be exposing themselves to the charge of saying, 'If we say that, are we not saying that sin is something material?'. There are false teachings, Hinduism and similar teachings, which teach that sin is material, and that it dwells in our bodies; and that therefore our bodies are essentially evil. Their teaching is that the body is the source of all sin and evil. Salvation therefore means the liberation of the spirit from the body; and so they regard death as the way of salvation. Some of them talk about 'Reincarnation'. There are people who call themselves Christian who believe that kind of thing in these days. That is what such religions teach, that the body is essentially sinful, that sin is something material which dwells in a man's body, that the whole trouble with our lives is that we have these evil, sinful bodies, and that we should long to be liberated out of them.

That is not what I am saying. It is a false teaching which I utterly reject. What then do I mean? When man sinned, when Adam sinned, sin obtained complete mastery over him. We have seen that clearly in chapter 5 verses 12 to 21. Sin dominated man's life – the whole of him, body, mind and spirit. But, in particular, it had this effect – and this is true still of every man who is not a Christian, this is true of every one who is still in Adam – that his life was dominated by the body, by these powers, these 'instruments', these 'members' that are in the body. They control him whereas he should control them. That is man 'in sin', that is man 'in Adam'. Sin is in control; he is under the dominion of sin, the rule and the reign of sin. Man in sin is, as it were, upside-down. The material, animal part of him is controlling him; his body is supreme and he is governed by it. As this Apostle puts it, in writing to the Ephesians, 'We all had our conversation in times past' in that way, obeying the lusts of the flesh, 'fulfilling the desires of the flesh and of the mind' (Chapter 2: 2, 3). That is the kind of life that is lived by all who are not Christian, all who are in sin, all who are in Adam.

But in Christ that is no longer the case. What is the position of the Christian? It is this. Let me put it in the first person singular. I myself – because of my union with Christ, because I have died with Him, because I have been buried with Him, because I have risen again with Him – I myself am dead to sin as a realm and reign, I have finished with it, it has nothing to do with me. But though that is its relationship to me, it still has a good deal to do with my body. I myself am already in Christ, 'seated in the heavenly places' with Him. That is what I am told about myself. I died with Him, I was buried with Him, I have risen with Him, I have ascended with Him, I am seated with Him in the heavenly places. *I* am. The old man has gone. I am no longer that man; I am a new man in Christ Jesus. That is what is true about me. But though that is the truth about me, it is not yet the truth about my body, my mortal body. Sin is still in my mortal body, in my members, working as 'a law in my members', having its effect upon my 'instruments', 'my members', the parts of my body.

That, I suggest, is what the Apostle means by the term 'the body of sin'. Sin remains in its influence upon the body. I myself as a being, a spiritual being, am entirely and eternally outside the realm of sin's influence; but it has pleased God in His eternal wisdom to leave sin in the body. There is a kind of parallel with this in the Old Testament. God delivered the children of Israel out of Egypt. He took them across the Red Sea, through the wilderness, across Jordan, and gave them the promised land. But He left certain of the nations in that promised land, and His people had to struggle with them. It seems to me that we have a very wonderful parallel there between God's way of dealing with His ancient people on that level, and God's way of dealing with His people now on the spiritual level. The body is not yet delivered from the effects of sin and the Fall – but I am delivered. So the Apostle takes us on from step to step and stage to stage.

I trust that it is clear that I am not teaching that the body is essentially and inherently sinful. That is not what I am saying. What I am asserting is that sin which formerly governed the whole of my personality is now only governing – or trying to govern – the bodily part of me. I in spirit, I as a soul, I as a personality am delivered; I am dead to sin. That was the Apostle's original proposition, you remember: 'How shall we that are dead to sin live any longer therein?' This is a most vital and essential distinction. Let us be clear about the body. The body in and of itself is not sinful. The body has these various parts and portions – Paul calls them its 'members' – the instincts, the propensities, and so on. Now there is nothing sinful in that, in and of itself. Look at the Lord Jesus Christ, He had a body. Let us never forget that the Lord Jesus Christ in His body as a man had the same body as we have, He had the same instincts, every one of them. If it had not been so, He would not have been truly a man. We are told that He 'was tempted in all points like as we are'. In other words, the devil tried to tempt Him along the line of all His natural instincts. We sometimes do not realize that. But I repeat, 'He was tempted in all points like as we are'. And what the devil does is to come to us, and to tempt us along the line of our natural instincts, and the various drives and urges and powers of our body.

We must draw this distinction therefore. There is nothing wrong in the body itself as such; there is nothing wrong with all

[74]

these instincts – nothing! There have been false teachers in the past who have said that some of these natural instincts are sinful. There have been those who have regarded the sex instinct, for instance, as inherently and essentially sinful. It is not so. It is God who put it in us as a vital part of the body. There is nothing wrong in sex. Wrong comes in when sex dominates the whole person, instead of being kept in its right position, and put to its right use. The same is true with regard to the hunger instinct, and all these instincts. If you eat too much it is equally sinful; but do you condemn the fact that you feel the need of food simply because some people eat too much and make gluttons of themselves. It is equally monstrous to do that with respect to sex. Let us not forget that the Lord Jesus Christ was truly a man with a real body, that he had all the powers and propensities and faculties of a male human being, and that 'He was tempted in all points like as we are, yet without sin.' [*Hebrews* 4 : 15].

What then was the difference between the Lord Jesus Christ in the body and every one of us? It was this, that we are born in sin, and 'shapen in iniquity' [*Psalm* 51 : 5]. He was born holy – 'that holy thing which shall be born of thee' [*Luke* 1 : 35]. Every one of the instincts, and all His powers and faculties and propensities, were in the right proportion and kept in their right places; hence the devil could not succeed when he tempted Him to sin. But it is otherwise with us. We are born with a wrong bias, we are born with the bodily elements predominating, tyrannizing over us, running away with us. We therefore have to contend with lust. Our Lord never had to contend with lust, there was no evil lust in Him. The devil tried to tempt Him to lust but he never succeeded. But we are creatures of lust, we are born such; and that is because we are born 'in Adam' and because we inherit his fallen nature.

So I am not teaching that the body is essentially evil, or that sin is something that resides in the body only, and that the body as such is sinful. Not at all! But I am saying that sin still has its power over the body even in the man who is 'in Christ'. The man himself is delivered, but his body is not yet delivered, and that is why the Apostle says, 'We are waiting for the adoption', 'we are longing for the adoption'. What is it? '. . . to wit, the redemption of our body' [*Romans* 8 : 23]. That is yet to come; it has not yet been experienced by us.

[75]

Let me put it in yet another way. I suggest that this term 'the body of sin' means the same as the term 'the flesh' which we shall find the Apostle using later. 'The flesh' does not mean the body in and of itself; but it does mean the body as it is being used and tyrannized over by sin. It means the body as it is possessed by sin and evil; it is the body as sin dwells in it during this earthly life. We can therefore express the Apostle's teaching in this way. 'Knowing this, that our old man, our old humanity, was crucified with him, that – this is one of the results and one of the purposes and the objects – that this hold of sin upon us, even in the body, might be rendered null and void and ineffective.' This is a tremendous conception.

What is the object of salvation? It is that we may be rid entirely and completely of sin and its effects. Adam was once perfect. There was no sin in him at all; and Adam in his state of innocence was able to use all the instincts of his body in a natural and normal manner without being sinful. But as the result of his rebellion and sin he became un-natural, no longer balanced, and the body began to predominate and to tyrannize and to control, so that we, his offspring, do not even think straightly. The mind, after all, is one of the functions of the body. It is through the brain that it works; and all these things have been affected by sin and are governed by it. But the object of salvation is to deliver us from the tyranny of sin – every part of it. The body itself is going to be emancipated and set free. That is what the Apostle is saying – 'that the body of sin might be destroyed', might be made inert, might be annulled, might be rendered ineffective, might be reduced to a condition of impotence. So he does not mean that the body is going to be destroyed. He is saying that this is something that can happen to us now. The object of salvation is that even while we are yet in this world we may more and more approximate to the condition that Adam was in before he fell, to the condition that is to be seen in our blessed Lord and Saviour Himself, that we may live even while still on earth more and more as the Lord Jesus Christ lived in the body while He was here on earth. It does not mean that our bodies are going to be destroyed before we can be fully redeemed. And the Apostle says this should be evident more and more while we are still here. Actually it will not happen to us completely and perfectly until our bodies have been glorified. That is why he says that we look forward to this 'adoption', that is 'the redemption of our body'.

The Apostle was so much concerned about this that he refers to it in other places. Take, for example, the thrilling statement at the end of the third chapter of the Epistle to the Philippians 'Our conversation is in heaven': 'our citizenship is in heaven' [verse 20]. 'I myself', he says, 'though I am still alive in this world, am a citizen of heaven. That is where I belong, that is where my citizenship is. I am a stranger here.' We as Christians are 'a colony of heaven'; this world is not our homeland; and from heaven we also 'look for the Saviour, the Lord Jesus Christ'. Why do we look for Him and await His coming? We are there with Him in spirit, seated with Him in heavenly places; our citizenship is there, but now here on earth we are looking for His coming. Why? For this reason: 'Who shall change our vile body' – and this is not a figurative expression; Paul really does mean the physical body, as is always the case when he uses this term – 'Who shall change our vile body' – or if you prefer the translation, 'Who shall change this, the body of our humiliation' – 'that it may be fashioned like unto his glorious body' – 'like unto the body of His glorification' – 'according to the working whereby he is able even to subdue all things unto himself'. There is a day coming, says the Apostle, when even my body shall have been delivered from the final effects and influences of the reign and the rule of sin. Not yet! but it is coming. Even here and now, as I understand this, the evil effect of sin upon my body should be lessening, but finally I shall have a glorified body. I myself, in Christ, am already glorified – 'Whom he hath called, them he hath also justified, and whom he hath justified, them he hath also glorified' [*Romans* 8 : 30]. I am glorified, and a day is coming when my body shall be glorified. That is the argument.

So in this sixth verse of the sixth chapter the Apostle is really explaining the ultimate objective behind my 'old man' being crucified with Christ. My old man was crucified with Him, that I might be entirely delivered even in the body where sin still reigns. How monstrous it is, therefore, he says, to suggest, as some are doing, that we continue in sin that grace might abound! The whole object of grace and of salvation is to deliver us from sin in every part – in personality, and finally even in the body. How can anyone suggest, therefore, that this is a teaching which says 'Let us continue in sin that grace may abound'?

The Apostle then brings in his second argument, which is, 'that henceforth we should not serve sin'. That is simply another way of saying that 'henceforth we should no longer be the slaves of sin'. He does not just mean that we should no longer commit acts of sin; he says that we should no longer be the slaves of sin. He is looking at the matter in general. Man in Adam is a slave of sin; he has no freedom. The natural man, the sinful man, has no freedom; he is the slave of sin. Man is always a slave; he is either the slave of Adam or he is 'the bond-slave of the Lord Jesus Christ'. The business of redemption is to deliver us from the slavery of sin. The Christian is no longer the slave of sin, but, alas, he still often allows it to rule in his body. It remains in his body, and he allows it far too often to rule him and to govern him. He should not do so, and there is no excuse for his doing so. That is why the Apostle has written this sixth chapter. And that is why he will say in verses 12 and 13, 'Let not sin therefore reign in your mortal body, that ye should obey it in the lusts thereof. Neither yield ye your members as instruments of unrighteousness unto sin; but yield yourselves unto God, as those that are alive from the dead, and your members as instruments of righteousness unto God'.

I trust that the distinction between 'the old man' and 'the body of sin' is clear. It is most important. That is why I have contended so much against the idea that the 'old man' means the 'old nature', and that the 'old man' and 'the body of sin' are one and the same thing. If you believe that, you will still be in bondage. This can be seen clearly in what some of the commentators write. For instance, one says, 'Now that we are Christians we have to oppose the old man'. What nonsense! You do not have to 'oppose' the old man, because the old man was crucified with Christ. Indeed the Apostle goes on to tell us that he not only died with Him but was even buried. Do you go on opposing someone who has been buried in a grave? That is the kind of muddle you get into if you do not keep these terms distinct and separate, and have them clearly in your mind.

Or take another statement, 'We gradually die to the old man'. Again, what nonsense! 'We gradually die to the old man' – the 'old man' who is already dead and who is gone once and for ever!

Another writes about 'Our gradual deliverance from the dy-

[78]

ing man!' But Paul has not only told us that the old man died once and for ever, but that the old man has already been buried. Remember how he emphasized that point. 'Therefore we are buried with him by baptism into death'. It is a very wrong procedure to bury somebody who is only in a state of dying! If the old man is still 'the dying old man' it is a monstrous crime to bury him! Paul says, You do not die to that old man; the old man is not going through a process of dying; he has died, and he has been buried, he has gone once and for ever, he is finished. You are a new man in Christ. How monstrous, therefore, to talk about 'being delivered gradually from the dying old man'!

Even the great Abraham Kuyper could actually write like this, 'God's child remains the old man's grave-digger until the hour of his own departure!' But I repeat, Paul says that the 'old man' was not only crucified with Christ, not only died with Christ, but was buried with Christ. Abraham Kuyper is trying to dig the grave of one who has already been buried! If you are not clear about this, and are still trying to kill the old man, or trying to bury him, you will continue in bondage, and you will be unhappy. The one way to release and deliverance is to realize that we died to sin, that the old man died to sin once and for ever with Christ in His death. The 'old man' does not mean the old nature; it is 'the body of sin' that means that. The old man has not to be killed, you need not dig a grave for him, he has already been buried in it. When Christ was buried in His grave the 'old man' was with Him in it. In verses 8, 9 and 10 Paul will remind us of the same thing again.

Let me close by quoting the Heidelberg Catechism. It asks in the forty-third question, 'What then are further results of the death of Christ?' And here is the answer: 'That by virtue of His death our old man is crucified and buried with Him.' That is better! 'Our old man is crucified and buried with Him, that so the corrupt inclinations of the flesh. . . . ' The Heidelberg Catechism rightly draws a distinction between 'the old man' and 'the flesh'. 'The old man is crucified and buried with Him, that so the corrupt inclinations of the flesh may no more reign in us.' The 'old man' is not 'the flesh', he is not the 'corrupt nature'; the old man is the Adamic nature, the old humanity. The 'flesh' is 'the body of sin', the body in which sin tends to tyrannize still, the body in which sin yet remains. But I am given a guarantee that

under the reign of grace even the body shall be delivered; but
until the day of the glorification of the body I am told this:
'Let not sin therefore reign in your mortal body, that ye should
obey it in the lusts thereof'. In other words, the way to deal with
sin in the body, in the flesh, is to realize the truth about yourself
even now. Realize the truth of what is possible to you in your
body even here and now; but look forward at the same time to
the final glorious truth of your glorification, which will include
the final emancipation of your body also. Then the whole man –
spirit, soul and body – will be entirely and perfectly delivered
from the reign and the tyranny and the rule of sin.

Seven

*

For he that is dead is freed from sin. Romans 6 : 7

To understand this verse properly we must read with it verse 6. The word 'For' at the beginning obviously connects it with what the Apostle has just been saying: 'Knowing this, that our old man was crucified with him, that (in order that) the body of sin might be dis-annulled (put out of operation) that henceforth we should not be slaves to sin (or serve sin as slaves)'. Then comes this statement, 'For he that is dead is freed from sin'.

It must be clear by now that almost every single statement in this vital and all-important chapter is pregnant with thought, and of the greatest possible significance to us from the standpoint of our life and living, and our warfare against sin. As we come therefore to this particular verse which has caused a great deal of perplexity to many people, and a good deal of disagreement, it is essential that we should approach it in its context. No one has ever pretended that this is an easy or a simple chapter; but as it is a crucial chapter we must take our time with it. Moreover the argument is so closely woven that if you do not follow one step you cannot possibly follow the next because each one leads on to the next. So it is important that we should be clear about the Apostle's terms and their meaning, because when he has worked out his argument and laid down his doctrine he will then make a practical appeal to us. Obviously you cannot respond to an appeal if you do not understand the basis of the appeal. As the Apostle Paul himself puts it in writing to the Corinthians, 'If the trumpet yield an uncertain sound, who shall prepare him for the battle?' [1 *Corinthians* 14 : 8]. If we are not clear about the terms with which we are dealing we shall not be able to follow him when he appeals to us in verse 11 and says, 'Likewise reckon ye also yourselves to be dead indeed unto sin, but alive unto God'. The same applies to the exhortations in verses 12 and 13.

The only serious problem or difficulty which is worthy of consideration at this point is often expressed as a query in this way: 'In the light of your exposition, how do you explain Ephesians 4, verses 22–24 where we read, "That ye put off concerning the former conversation the old man, which is corrupt according to the deceitful lusts; and be renewed in the spirit of your mind; and that ye put on the new man, which after God is created in righteousness and true holiness." How do you reconcile that with your exposition of Romans 6 : 6? For in the Ephesian statement we are exhorted to "put off the old man" and to "put on the new man"; but you tell us that "the old man" was crucified with Christ once and for ever.' That is a good question, because the same term is used in both places, namely 'the old man'.

How do we approach this? Let me repeat what I have said before. A good rule with regard to exposition is this; when you find the same word or the same term in different parts of the Bible, always give it the same meaning unless there is some special, overwhelming reason found in the context for not doing so, or unless doing so leads to what is clearly a false theological result. But there are times when there is some such overwhelming reason for not giving a word or a term the usual meaning; and this is one of them. The Apostle in Romans 6 : 6 says that our old man was crucified; it is something that has happened to him, was done to him, and it was done once and for ever. But in Ephesians 4 : 22–24 we are exhorted to 'put off the old man'. Obviously therefore the term cannot mean the same thing in both cases, otherwise the Apostle is contradicting himself. He cannot exhort us to put off something that has been crucified once and for ever, and put away. It is clear that when he says in Ephesians 4 : 22, 'That ye put off concerning the former conversation the old man', the 'old man' is used as a term to cover the conversation, conduct or behaviour that was characteristic of the old man. What we have to put off is the 'conversation' or mode of behaviour of the old man, rather than the old man himself. He says in effect, 'You have been born again, your old man was crucified with Christ. Do not go on behaving as if the old man was still there. Be what you are, do not be what you no longer are.' In other words, there is no contradiction between Romans 6 : 6 and Ephesians 4 : 22–24. The context makes that abundantly plain and clear. Ephesians 4 : 22 is concerned about conduct, behaviour; Romans 6 : 6 is concerned about the old man himself, not his conduct or behaviour.

The teaching of verse 6, then, is that my 'old man' was crucified in order that the remaining use of my body by sin might be disannulled, might be rendered ineffective. A good way of translating 'body of sin' is to call it 'the old nature'. The difference between the 'old man' and the 'body of sin' is the difference between my 'old self' and my 'old nature'. Now that is the very translation adopted by Arthur S. Way, a very good translator of Paul's Epistles. He translates 'old man' by 'former self', and 'body of sin' by 'old nature'. That is an excellent translation. What the Apostle asserts is that the whole object of my 'old man' being crucified with Christ is that I might be delivered entirely and completely from the slavery of sin, 'that henceforth we should not be slaves of sin'.

We have not yet reached the stage of application, but as most of us are anxious to go on to the stage of application and to say, 'Well, how does all this help me?' – this is the answer. If you do not realize that you yourself are more important than your nature, then obviously you cannot follow the Apostle's argument. The greatest truth we can ever be told is that our old self has gone. I can deal with my old nature only as I realize that my old self has gone and that I have a new self. This is a most striking and amazing truth. The problem of my old nature becomes much easier once I realise that my old self has gone. My old self, that self that was in Adam, was an utter slave to sin. That self has gone; I have a new self, I am a new man. The moment I realise that I am a new man I am in a better position to deal with this old nature that remains in my body, in what Paul calls my 'mortal flesh'. We shall find the Apostle saying in chapter 7, 'It is no more I that do it but sin that dwelleth in me' (verse 20). Is not that a marvellous thing to be able to say? I am not doing this or that, it is this sin that remains in my members that does so. Sin is no longer in me, it is in my members only. That is the most liberating thing you have ever heard! That is the Apostle's assertion. This, he says, is the way of salvation. Cannot you realize, he says, that your self, your old self, has gone? Never think of yourself in those terms again.

It is wrong to go on to the practical before we have finished with the theoretical, but lest someone is really unhappy about all this, let me say this for your encouragement and comfort as we go along. This is how it works out. I find that many Christian people are unhappy because every time they fall into sin they raise again the whole question as to whether they are Christians at all. They fall into sin and immediately begin to say to themselves, 'Is it possible that I am a Christian at all? If I really were a Christian how could I possibly sin like this?' That is the error the Apostle nails here. He says: You must not do that, you must not raise again the whole question of your salvation every time you sin. You yourself, as a being and as a person in the sight of God, are in Christ. You are joined to Christ indissolubly – 'planted together in the likeness of His death and of His resurrection', and (as he will add in the grand climax at the end of chapter 8) there is nothing, 'neither death, nor life, nor angels, nor principalities, nor powers, nor things present, nor things to come, nor height, nor depth, nor any other creature which shall be able to separate us from the love of God which is in Christ Jesus our Lord'.

The difference such teaching makes is this, that if I grasp it truly when I fall into sin, I shall not again ask 'Am I a Christian or not?'. I shall say 'Of course I am a Christian, my old man has been crucified, I am justified, I am a new man in Christ, I am accepted of God, I am a Christan'. What then about that sin? Thank God it is something that cannot separate me from Him. This is not something that affects my salvation, I do not need to be converted all over again; I am a new man. Why then do I sin? Because sin is in my members, because this 'body of sin' remains. But I am sharing in a salvation that will even rid me of that. I realize that I am behaving in an inconsistent manner – inconsistent because I am a Christian, not because it is doubtful whether I am a Christian. That is why Paul is so anxious that we should realize that 'our old man', our old self, was crucified, that he has gone. I must never bring him back again in thought by wondering whether I am a Christian. That is simply to bring back 'the old man' that has been crucified, that died, that was even buried, and has gone for ever.

That is the practical aspect, but it is when we come to verse
11 that we shall be really dealing with it.

This having been said, we can now proceed to the seventh
verse: 'For he that is dead is freed from sin.' Here again there is
much disagreement about, and varying expositions of, this verse.
What does the Apostle mean by this? He is winding up his
argument concerning the negative first half of verse 5. He has
made the main statement in verse 6, but he now puts it again in
what amounts to a summing up of the whole position. The
difficulty arises in connection with the translation. In the Revised
Version you will find that it reads, 'He that hath died is justified
from sin'. And on the basis of that translation a particular exposition is put forward. It is very interesting to notice that while the
Revised Version translates it as 'justified from sin', the Revised
Standard Version has the same expression as the Authorized
Version, and reads 'freed from sin'.

What difference does it make to translate this as 'justified'
instead of 'freed?' The difference is this. The argument of certain
expositors is that this word which is translated here as 'freed',
and which should be translated as 'justified', is everywhere else in
this Epistle, and in other places, always translated as 'justified'
and not as 'freed'. It should not therefore have been translated as
'freed' here. They argue that the statement which the Apostle is
making is this, that all of us who have died – then they have to
put in, 'with Christ' – have been justified from the guilt of sin.
Certain well-known commentators interpret the Apostle's words
in this way, and say that he means that we are 'justified from the
guilt of sin'. They say, 'The word here is "justified", so what the
Apostle is saying is that all of us who have died with Christ have
been justified from the guilt of sin'. Immediately they are in
difficulties, because they can see that that is not the subject with
which the Apostle is dealing here. So they have to ask, 'Why does
he say that?' They answer that he says it for this reason: Because
we have been justified from the guilt of sin we are once more in a
living relationship with God, and therefore we can now be blessed
by God, we can therefore receive power from God. In other
words they say that our justification inevitably leads to our
sanctification, because it puts us into touch with God, and that
means that we can get from God the power we need to fight the
battle against sin. That is their argument.

There is a further argument which I must mention in order to be fair to this position. They point out that the word 'freed' is used in the Authorized Version again in verses 18, 20 and 22. Verse 18: 'Being then made free from sin, ye became the servants of righteousness'. Verse 20: 'For when ye were the servants of sin, ye were free from righteousness'. Verse 22: 'But now being made free from sin, and become servants of God, ye have your fruit unto holiness, and the end everlasting life.' There, they say, the word 'free' or 'freed' is used three times, but there the Apostle did not use the same word in the Greek as the word he uses here in verse 7. In verse 7 he used the word that is generally translated as 'justified'; the word he uses in verses 18, 20, and 22 is not the word that is generally translated as 'justified' or 'justification'. If he meant 'freed' they argue, he would have used the same word as he uses in verses 18, 20, and 22, but he deliberately used the word that is normally translated as 'justified'.

The question is, Do we accept this exposition? Do we agree that what the Apostle is saying here is that all of us who are joined to Christ, and who have therefore died with Him, have been justified from the guilt of sin? Let me say at once that I do not accept it. Let me try to defend the Authorized Version translation as being undoubtedly the correct representation of the meaning of what the Apostle was saying. Here are my arguments.

First, as all these statements which the Apostle makes in this whole section emphasize that what happened to the Lord Jesus Christ has also happened to us, this exposition which holds on to the word 'justified' implies, of necessity, that the Lord Jesus Christ was justified from sin. But that is something that is never said of Him in the Scripture. It is never said that the Lord Jesus Christ had any need to be justified, or was ever justified from sin. Even when He bore our sin He had no need to be justified. It is we who are justified; we are never told that He was justified. But if you translate it as 'We who have died with Him have been justified from sin', well then, because what is true of Him is true of us, He therefore must have been justified from sin.

Secondly, that exposition also carries the suggestion that we are justified because we have died to sin. It must mean that if the translation and explanation are true. 'He that has died is justified from sin'; therefore the cause of our justification is our having died with Christ to sin. It is because our old man has died that

[86]

we are justified. But we have seen at great length in chapter 4, and elsewhere, that the Apostle's argument is that God justifies the 'ungodly'. We are justified before we are joined to Christ; it is a forensic, declarative, statement by God. He does not justify the godly, and any man whose old man has died with Christ can no longer be described as 'ungodly'; he is 'in Christ' and joined to Christ. So it seems to me that that exposition is a serious denial of the doctrine of justification by faith only, and that God justifies the ungodly. It is to reverse the true order of justification and our union with Christ. Justification comes before our union and not after it. So I reject that exposition on those grounds also.

Then in addition to that I would urge this, that in this whole chapter the Apostle is not dealing at all with the question of justification itself. He has dealt with that already, and has finished with it. It is because he has finished with it that he is able to go on in this way. The Epistle is no longer dealing with justification, and therefore to re-introduce the idea of justification of the sinner from the guilt of sin at this point is to introduce an irrelevancy, is to introduce something that is entirely extraneous to the point and the issue that the Apostle has in hand.

Why then do expositors land themselves in such trouble? It is because they have been so fascinated by this one word which is normally translated 'justified' that they can see nothing else. While an expert knowledge of Greek is good, it can also be dangerous. So the scholars tend to take this one word 'justified' and allow that to determine their whole outlook. It makes them ignore the context.

Have you noticed that here in this seventh verse the Apostle makes a sudden change? From the beginning of the chapter he has been talking about 'us' – 'we'. For example, 'Know ye not that so many of us as were baptized into Jesus Christ were baptized into his death? Therefore we are buried with him by baptism into death; that like as Christ was raised up from the dead by the glory of the Father, even so we also should walk in newness of life. For if we have been planted together in the likeness of his death, we shall be also in the likeness of his resurrection: Knowing this, that our old man was crucified with him, that the body of sin might be destroyed, that henceforth we should not serve sin.' But suddenly the Apostle says here, 'For he – he that is dead'. Why does he not say 'we that are dead?' If he is talking about us, and that we are united to Christ and have therefore died with Him, why does he suddenly talk about 'he'? All along he has been writing 'we' and he goes on in verse 8 to do so again – 'Now if we be dead with Christ we believe that we shall also live with him', and so on back again to the 'we'. It is 'we' everywhere except in verse 7 where he suddenly says 'he'.

What is the significance of this? The Apostle here, I suggest, is not referring to us as such; he is making a general statement. He is not referring here to those of us who have died with Christ, because what he says is, 'he that has died'. He does not add 'with Christ'. But those who accept the other exposition have to say 'with Christ' – 'died with Christ'. But the Apostle did not say that here. 'He that has died', are his words; and he means what he says. If he had meant those who have died with Christ he would have continued saying 'we' or 'all of us' or 'so many of us' as have died with Christ; but here he deliberately says' 'He who hath died is freed from sin'.

What then does he mean? My explanation is that here he is making a general, universal, axiomatic statement about any man who has died. It is an axiomatic statement of universal validity. He is saying that when a man dies, by his dying he is acquitted from sin, and remains absolutely free as far as sin is concerned. When a man dies he can no longer sin; when a man dies he goes out of the realm of sin; when a man dies he cannot be tempted because he is dead. Sin cannot do anything to him, neither can the law which works with sin. Once a man dies he is outside the jurisdiction of sin and law. You cannot bring a charge against a dead man in a court of law; he is outside the realm of man's jurisdiction. The very fact that he has died puts him quite clear of it. He is no longer in the realm where sin and law operate.

The Apostle is simply making a general statement. He says, 'You know surely. . . . For', he says. This is something axiomatic, something which we can all see at a glance, that the moment a man dies he is outside the realm of sin altogether. A modern scholar has translated it very well like this. He says, 'Once a man has died he is quit of the claims of sin upon him'. I believe that is the correct translation. Once a man dies you can no longer charge him with the guilt of sin. You cannot bring a charge against a dead man. A man who has died is a man who has changed his realm, he is outside the realm and the reign and the rule of everything that is connected with sin, it has no power over him. The moment a man dies, automatically the power of sin over that man has come to an end. Hence the Apostle was saying what the Authorized Version represents him as saying. The Authorized Version is right; a man who dies is 'free' – freed altogether from sin, and all its realm and its territory, in every single respect; it has no power whatsoever with respect to him. So that we can now put verses 6 and 7 together like this, 'Our old man was crucified with Christ in order that we might be delivered in every respect from the slavery of sin; because every man who has died is entirely free from the power and the reign and the slavery and the tyranny of sin'. In other words, because we are united with Christ we have died with Him, and, therefore, as is true of any man who dies, we are entirely outside the realm of sin.

Thus we are back again to the statement that Paul made in verse 2: 'How shall we that died to sin, live any longer therein?', where our interpretation was that 'died to sin' means 'died to the realm and the rule and the power and the reign of sin'. The Apostle is simply going on with what he was saying in chapter 5 verse 21: 'That as sin hath reigned unto death, even so might grace reign through righteousness unto eternal life by Jesus Christ our Lord.' He has come back to it once more. He is winding up an argument, and saying in effect, 'I have now demonstrated what I set out to demonstrate. I told you at the beginning that it is impossible that we should continue in sin as we did before we became Christians, for we have died to the realm and the rule and the tyranny and the reign of sin.' He has been showing how that has happened; it is that the old man has died. Sin still dwells in the mortal body, but not in my true self; it is in my members, in my body, in my flesh. I am like a man who has died, I have nothing more to do with it, I am entirely outside its territory, its realm and its rule and its jurisdiction. 'Sin hath reigned unto death.' It cannot go any further than that; but it does go as far as that. That is why the Apostle goes on to emphasize that we have also risen with Christ.

But if my explanation is correct I still have to answer this question. What do I make of verses 18, 20 and 22, where, as I have reminded you, this word 'free' and 'freed' is used? Why did the Apostle not use the same term, – that is, in the Greek – in all these instances? My answer is that he was not concerned to say

[89]

the same thing. In the section we are looking at now he is dealing with sin as a great legal power; in the section from verse 15 onwards he is dealing with sin as a kind of slave-master, a slave-owner, which is a very different conception. So he is thinking in different pictures, in different terms. He is thinking here of sin as a legal system, as a government, as an authority, as a realm, as a kingdom; so he very naturally uses a legal term. But in verses 18, 20 and 22 he is thinking in entirely different terms. He is thinking there of slavery, and slave-owners, and a slave market, and so on. It is an entirely different realm, a different world; a much more practical one. So there he uses a term which is appropriate to the whole context of slaves and slavery and of freedom being given to a slave. Verse 18 could well be translated, 'Being then emancipated from sin's ownership'. It is emancipation from the ownership of sin. There you have a different shade of meaning.

What the Apostle wants to establish from verse 1 to the end of verse 14 is that we as persons have entirely finished with the rule, the reign, the dominion of sin; and he says that, as far as all that is concerned, we have nothing to do with it. It is possible to say that we are justified from it, but I prefer to say with the Authorized Version that we are freed from it. We have entirely finished with it, not only its guilt, but its power, its everything. We are no longer in that realm, our old man has died with Christ, and as Christ is no longer in the realm of sin, as He was when on earth, (and as we shall find Paul explaining in the next verses), neither are we. We have died to that once and for ever. That is what Paul is concerned to prove, and surely he proves it completely.

To round off my argument, let me show that there is a very powerful supporting argument to be found in the First Epistle of Peter, chapter 4, verses 1 and 2: 'Forasmuch then as Christ hath suffered for us in the flesh, arm yourselves likewise with the same mind: for he that hath suffered in the flesh' – and this means to die – 'hath ceased from sin; that he should no longer live the rest of his time in the flesh to the lusts of men, but to the will of God.' These two verses are an exact parallel to this section we are considering in the sixth chapter of Romans. Peter in his way is saying exactly the same thing as the Apostle Paul. Our Lord, he says, has suffered for us once in the flesh. He came to do that. But, he adds, you must realize that he that hath suffered in the flesh has finished with sin. He puts it, 'hath ceased from sin'. He has no more to do with it, he has quit it, he does not belong to it any longer, he is entirely outside it. The famous Grimm-Thayer lexicon at this point puts it like this. It says that it means 'hath got release from' – 'he that hath suffered in the flesh hath got release from sin'. To have release from sin is just another way of saying 'is freed from sin', 'set at liberty from sin', 'no longer under its dominion or its rule or its reign'. It is finally put perfectly in the glorious statement in verse 14: 'Sin shall not have dominion over you, for ye are not under the law, but under grace.'

Both Paul and Peter are saying the same thing, namely, that the man who has died with Christ has once and for ever as a being, as an entity, as a soul, finished with sin. He should never again raise the question of his justification or of his forgiveness or of his final arrival in glory. 'Whom he justified, them he also glorified.' 'Being justified by faith, we have peace with God' – yes, 'and we rejoice in hope of the glory of God'. Though we are still here in the body, and though we know that sin is in the body, and though we fall into sin, because I have died with Christ I am saved. I am as surely saved now as I shall be when I am in the glory. Augustus Toplady has seen it –

> *The terrors of law and of God*
>   *With me can have nothing to do;*
> *My Saviour's obedience and blood*
>   *Hide all my transgressions from view.*

Then he goes on to say –

> *My name from the palms of His hands*
>   *Eternity will not erase;*
> *Impressed on His heart it remains,*
>   *In marks of indelible grace.*
> *Yes, I to the end shall endure,*
>   *As sure as the earnest is given;*
> *More happy, but not more secure,*
>   *The glorified spirits in heaven.*

They are more happy. Why are they more happy? Because they no longer have sin in the body. They know no failure now; they no longer need repentance. 'More happy, but not more secure.'

That is what the Apostle tells us here. The way to overcome

depression, and the way to overcome failure, is to realize that you are safe, and that you are going there. 'Every man that hath this hope in him purifieth himself, even as he is pure' [1 *John* 3 : 3]. But if you are not certain about this, every time you fall into sin you will say, 'I wonder whether I am a Christian after all. Have I ever really been converted, born again?' And immediately you are down in the depths of depression, and the moment you are depressed the devil has a very easy target. He gets you down again and again, and you remain on the ground, grovelling in the dust. What is the cure for that? The cure for that is to realize that, whether you have sinned or not, you are in Christ; that sin does not affect you yourself as a person, and that it cannot bring you again into its realm and reign; that sin only remains in your mortal body, and that – even that – because you are in Christ, is going to be entirely set free. The Apostle goes on to say: 'Now if we be dead with Christ we believe also that we shall live with him', and much else. But so far he is only dealing with the negative half of verse 5 – 'that we have been planted together in the likeness of his death'. That is almost enough in itself. It tells me this – that I, as a man, as a being, as a personality, as an entity, have already by my death with Christ finished with the realm and the rule and the reign and the dominion of sin. Any man who has died is automatically, axiomatically, inevitably, free – 'freed from sin'.

That is the negative aspect. We shall go on to look at the positive aspect, and having done that, we shall listen to the tremendous exhortation which he makes on the basis of it all.

Eight

*

*Now if we be dead with Christ, we believe that we shall also live
with him:*

*Knowing that Christ being raised from the dead dieth no more;
death hath no more dominion over him.*

*For in that he died, he died unto sin once: but in that he liveth,
he liveth unto God.*   Romans 6 : 8–10

In these verses we begin to look at the exposition of the second
half of verse 5. We have noticed that the Apostle's method in this
chapter is to make a general statement and then to proceed to an
explication of it. The key verse in many ways is verse 5 which
says, 'For if we have been planted together in the likeness of his
death, we shall be also in the likeness of his resurrection'. We have
seen that verses 6 and 7 are an exposition of the first half of that
statement. Now in verses 8, 9, and 10 the Apostle takes up the
second half of verse 5 which says, 'We shall be also in the likeness
of his resurrection'. As the first half of verse 5 is negative, so
verses 6 and 7 are negative; but now we come to the positive side
corresponding to the second half of verse 5 which is positive.
Death is negative, resurrection is positive. So these three verses
expound and explain this positive aspect. It is a great thing to
know that we are dead to sin, as a man who dies is outside the
territory of sin. Sin cannot do anything to him, cannot tempt
him, cannot bring a charge against him; he is freed from sin.
But that is not all that is true of us. We are not left in a void. We
have come out of that territory, but we have also been promoted,
or translated into another territory. This is positive; and this,
of course, is much more striking and more reassuring and comforting to our faith.

The Apostle states the matter as a general proposition in verse
8; 'Now if we be dead with Christ, we believe that we shall also

live with him.' That is but a repetition of what he said in the second half of verse 5, 'We shall be also in the likeness of his resurrection'. He says that this is something that follows quite inevitably. We must not be tripped by the expression 'We believe that we shall also live with him'. There are some who assert that the Apostle is merely saying, 'We just hold on to a belief in the resurrection by faith'. But that is not what he is saying. This 'believe' really stands here for 'We are well aware of the fact', 'we are sure'. He says that if we be dead with Christ it follows of necessity that we shall rise with Him. If we really are joined to Him, and everything that happens to Him of necessity happens to us, it follows that if we have died with Him we must also rise with Him. There are many affirmations in Paul's Epistles which are put in the form of 'We believe'. Take for instance the end of chapter 8 where he says, 'I am persuaded that neither death nor life' – That really means, 'I am absolutely certain', 'I am confident', 'I am assured'. What the Apostle is saying, is that because of this doctrine of our union with Christ it follows beyond any question that if we have died with Him we must of necessity rise with Him.

But, again, a slight difficulty arises in people's minds because of Paul's use of the future tense at this point: 'If we have been planted together in the likeness of his death, we *shall be* also in the likeness of his resurrection.' The tense used leads some to argue that the Apostle is referring here to nothing but the future resurrection of the bodies of believers in the Lord Jesus Christ. As usual, the authorities differ greatly concerning the matter. There are those who say quite plainly that the Apostle's use of the future tense makes it certain that he refers to our future bodily resurrection, and to nothing else. I regard that way of viewing this matter as completely wrong. I tried to show that in my comments on verse 5, and I must do so again. I have no doubt that this statement includes our future resurrection, but I am anxious to stress that that is the least important aspect of what the Apostle has in mind at this particular point. At the moment he is not concerned to deal with something that is yet to be true of us; he is concerned, rather, to show what is true of us now. The whole object of the passage is to refute the charge that we may now in the present continue in sin that grace may superabound. The entire discussion is about what is true of us in the present. It is true of us in the present that we died with Christ, that we are no longer in the realm and territory of sin. In the same way it is true of us now in the present that we 'live with him'. This is the main thrust of the Apostle's words. He is not concerned to speak only of what will happen to us in the resurrection which is to come. I can prove that. I have already given one proof. To throw it right forward into the future would mean that it would be more or less valueless from the practical standpoint in this particular context.

But here is a further argument. In verse 4 the Apostle says, 'Therefore we are buried with him by baptism into death, that like as Christ was raised up from the dead by the glory of the Father, even so we also should walk in newness of life'. When? Is that after the resurrection? Is it in the eternal state? Of course not! 'We should also walk in newness of life' here and now in this world. Paul says this because it is the best way to refute the suggestion that this doctrine of justification by faith, and by grace, means that it does not matter how we live in the present. That is a false deduction, he says, because we have been raised, as Christ was raised by the glory of the Father, in order that we should walk in newness of life here and now. That, in and of itself, would be sufficient to clinch this argument that it is not merely a reference to the resurrection.

But I have yet another proof which is surely conclusive and final. Take the exhortation in verse 11. There Paul draws a deduction from all this argument, in the following words: 'Likewise reckon ye also yourselves to be dead indeed unto sin, but alive unto God through Jesus Christ our Lord.' When? Is all that to be reserved to the future resurrection? Of course not! We are to 'reckon ourselves to be dead indeed unto sin, but alive unto God in Jesus Christ' now. This is the whole point. But if you throw 'shall also live with him' into the future, and postpone it to the resurrection, then you cannot show how verse 11 is a legitimate deduction from all this argument.

I am taking this trouble because, regretfully once more, I find myself in complete disagreement with Robert Haldane who says that this statement in verse 8 has no reference except to the life after the resurrection. There are others who agree with him. Take, for instance, a quotation from the well-known Commentary on this Epistle by Sanday and Headlam, regarded by most scholars as the best commentary on it. Here is what they say about this matter. 'The different senses of "life" and "death" always lie near together with St. Paul, and his thought glides backwards and forwards from one to another almost imperceptibly; now he lays a little more stress on the physical sense, now on the ethical; at one moment on the present state, and at another on the future.'

What they are saying is that the Apostle in his use of the terms 'life' and 'death' sometimes uses the terms in a physical sense, sometimes in an ethical sense; that sometimes he is thinking of the present, sometimes of the future. So they go on to say: 'Here (in verse 8) and in verse 9 the future eternal life is most prominent; but verse 10 is transitional, and in verse 11 we are back again at the standpoint of the present.'

That is, surely, really amusing. They have to postulate that the Apostle's meaning is constantly gliding – now this, now that – that it is always on the move, in order to say that. How comes it that great scholars like Sanday and Headlam should be capable of writing what I must describe as such rubbish? The answer is clear. Verse 11 makes it plain to them, as to everyone else, that the Apostle is dealing with the present – there is no question about that. So they have to say that in verse 11 'We are back again at the standpoint of the present'. Now if they had realized that that should have governed their exposition in verses 8, 9 and 10 also, they would have avoided having to write about what they term Paul's shifting, changing position. They do not tell us how we are to decide which it is in any one case, whereas if they had adopted the exposition that I am putting forward there would be no need to write about shifting meanings and changing positions. Indeed the difficulty entirely disappears. So by paying too much attention to this 'shall be' they put themselves in that ludicrous position.

But someone may ask, 'Why then does Paul say "shall be"?' For this reason: He is looking at the position from the standpoint of our being joined with Christ in His death; then he looks beyond that death to something that follows. So he says in effect, 'We are here now; and if we are here now with Him, we shall also be there with Him'. It is simply future from the standpoint of the place at which he left off at the end of verse 7, which leaves us with the death. Resurrection is always future to death; that is all. So it means that, if we be dead with Him, we know that of necessity we also rise with Him, or have risen with Him. That is precisely what it means, and nothing more. That other view confuses the exposition of the entire paragraph. This becomes yet clearer if you read Haldane on the last phrase of verse 10 – 'But in that He liveth, He liveth unto God'. I confess that I cannot follow his argument or discover what he really is saying.

Consider now certain parallel statements elsewhere, as supporting arguments. Take the parallel which we have in Ephesians 2, where the Apostle says precisely the same thing. 'You hath he quickened who were dead in trespasses and sins' (verse 1). But go on especially to verse 4 – 'But God, who is rich in mercy, for his great love wherewith he loved us, even when we were dead in sins, hath quickened us together with Christ, (by grace ye are saved); and hath raised us up together . . .' Paul does not say that God is going to do this; He has done it already, 'and made us sit together in heavenly places in Christ Jesus'. There, quite plainly, the Apostle is not talking about something that is going to happen to us. It will yet happen in a physical sense, thank God for that, but his object here in Romans chapter 6 as in Ephesians chapter 2, is to show what is true of us now. He does that in order to show how it affects our conduct and behaviour here and now, not our conduct and behaviour when we shall be glorified and entirely free from sin.

Another parallel is found in Galatians 2 verses 19 and 20: 'For I through the law am dead to the law, that I might live unto God'. Not after I am resurrected, but now! 'I am crucified (was crucified) with Christ, nevertheless I live' – not 'I am going to live', I live now – 'yet not I, but Christ liveth in me: and the life which I now live in the flesh I live by the faith of the Son of God, who loved me, and gave himself for me.' That is exactly the same as what we have here. It does not refer to what will be true of me after the resurrection; it is what is true of me in the here and now. If we but realized the object of this entire argument, which is to deal with our living in the present, we should be saved from all those vagaries of interpretation.

Let me sum it up like this. Here, then, is the general proposition, that we have died with Christ to sin, and have risen with Him also to an entirely new life, in an entirely new realm, which has nothing to do with sin. We have finished with the realm of sin, he says, not only by dying but also by rising again. The dying really does make it complete, but if you further realize your rising again into another different realm, then it becomes quite clear. We have not only died, we have risen again into a new and resurrection life with the Lord Jesus Christ. That is the proposition of verse 8.

The Apostle is obviously anxious that we should be clear about this, and that we should grasp the full meaning of this wonderful statement. How can we be sure of it? How are we to grasp it? The way to be established in this doctrine, and to understand the great assertion in verse 8, is to be quite clear in our minds as to what has happened to the Lord Jesus Christ Himself in this question of relationship to sin; because, on account of our union with Him, what is true of Him is true of us. So this is what the Apostle expounds in verses 9 and 10: 'Knowing this', he says. Here it is once more; we gave attention to this 'knowing' before in verses 3 and 6. There are certain things the Apostle says which we ought to know very well. Indeed that is what 'knowing' means here – 'You know very well'. He means, It is clear to you. But the question arises, Is it clear to us? You will find that many, in interpreting these verses 9 and 10, write about 'us and our experience', and therefore obviously do not know what the Apostle says we all ought to know.

The way to understand it is this. We must for the moment forget all about ourselves and our experiences and consider only what is true about the Lord Jesus Christ, and what happened to Him in this matter of relationship to sin. That is the way to understand this truth. Our *present* position is the concern of the Apostle at this point. So far he has not come to the realm of experience; that will start in verse 11 and then go on. So if you push in experience, our own personal experience, into these verses you are mistaking what the Apostle is saying. What is that? He is showing us clearly what happened to the Lord Jesus Christ. Until we are clear about that, we shall never be clear about our own position, and consequently shall never get victory in our lives. This is a most important principle; this is how the New Testament deals with us and our problems and our difficulties. It never starts with them directly. What the New Testament tells you to do always, in the first instance, is to forget yourself altogether – to forget all your problems, your temptations, your difficulties, everything else; to forget yourself and look at the Lord Jesus Christ. Consider first what has happened to Him, consider first

His relationship to sin. Then when you have got that clear, the next step is to say, 'I am joined to Him, and what is true of Him is true of me, therefore I deduce this about myself.' That is exactly what the Apostle does here; and he does not come to the 'Therefore' until verse 11.

First, then, we must forget all about ourselves and our experiences and our subjective moods and states and conditions. You say, 'Ah, but there is a statement here about dying to sin'. My answer is, that Paul is not writing about you at all at this point; he is writing about the Lord Jesus Christ in verses 9 and 10. That is the key to the whole question. What does he say about Him? This is what he says we ought to know, 'That Christ being raised from the dead dieth no more; death hath no more dominion over him'. What does this mean? Why is this true? Why is this true of necessity with respect to Him? How can we know this, and understand it, and be sure of it? You notice his statement: 'We know', he says, we are certain of this, 'that Christ having been raised from the dead dieth no more; death hath no more dominion over him.'

Let us look at these words. Here is the first thing – 'Christ having been raised from the dead'. That statement prompts us to ask this question: If Christ has been raised from the dead, as we know to be true, by whom has He been raised from the dead? The Apostle has already given us the answer in verse 4, 'Christ was raised from the dead by the glory of the Father', which we saw meant 'by the glorious power of the Father'. So it was the Father who raised Him from the dead by His glorious power. The statement tells me this: The very fact that God raised Him from the dead is proof positive that God was fully satisfied with the work which His Son had done upon the cross. The resurrection is God's announcement and proclamation to the whole universe that Christ has completed the work which He sent Him into the world to do. You remember how Paul has stated the same truth in the last verse of chapter 4: 'Who was delivered for our offences, and was raised again for our justification'. The resurrection of Jesus Christ is an announcement, a proclamation to the whole universe by God that His Son has completed the work of atonement and of redemption and of salvation. That is the Apostle's argument here. He says, 'We know this, that Christ being (having been) raised from the dead dieth no more'. Why? Because there is no need for Him to die any more. He does not go on dying, He has done that once and for ever. The resurrection proves that; it proves that He has finished the work and that the end in view has been accomplished.

But the Apostle puts that still more strongly in the next verse: 'Death', he says, 'hath no more dominion over him.' This is a tremendous statement, 'Death hath no longer any dominion, or power, over him'. It means that there was a point, there was a time, when death did have power over Him. That was why He died. But how did death ever come to have power over Him? That is the vital question. The Apostle tells us in the First Epistle to the Corinthians that 'the sting of death is sin' [1 *Corinthians* 15 : 56]. What enables death to come upon us is sin; sin is the agent that produces death. So as we look at the Son of God dying we see that He has come under the power of death and its sting. How can this have happened, for He was without sin in His nature, and He never sinned at all? But it is the glorious message of the Gospel that He has taken upon Himself our sins. What we have to explain is how death at any time had any power over the Lord Jesus Christ; and this is the only explanation. He took our sins upon Himself, and thereby, He put Himself under the penalty of the Law. We must always remember that it is the Law that gives to sin the power to reign unto death. Paul expresses it strikingly in 1 Corinthians 15: 'The sting of death is sin, and the strength of sin is the law.' Note the sequence. How does sin lead to my death? It does so because sin is a breaking of the Law, and the Law pronounces death as the punishment for the sin. 'The sting of death is sin; the strength of sin is the law'.

Here, then, is our Lord who was sinless, and death could not touch Him; but He takes our sins upon Him. By identifying Himself with us, and by taking our sins upon Him, He puts Himself under the Law and its dominion, so death now has power over him. What the Law therefore pronounces as punishment for sin comes upon Him, and so, because He bore our sins, death had power over Him. For that reason, and that reason only, He died; death hath no more dominion over Him now, but it did have at that point, and it killed Him. From the moment that 'He was made of a woman, made under the law' [*Galatians* 4 : 4], He was under the power of death.

But how can I know that death no longer has that power over Him? The answer is, as I have been showing, the resurrection. The resurrection is a proof of the fact that the Law has been satisfied. The resurrection is a declaration of that fact. That is why Christ was 'raised again for our justification'. His resurrection means that the Law is not only satisfied, but that He is no longer under this Law, He has gone back to the glory. He was 'made of a woman, made under the law'; but He is no longer in that condition, He has finished with the Law. And because He has finished with the Law death cannot touch Him any longer. Death could only touch Him as long as He was under the Law; apart from the Law it could not. His resurrection shows that He has finished with the Law and that in, consequence, death cannot in any way touch Him. As Paul puts it in 1 Corinthians 15, Christ by His resurrection has conquered the last enemy. He puts it like that: 'The last enemy that shall be destroyed is death.' Here is One who has actually defeated and conquered the last enemy. He has risen again. So He has finished altogether and entirely with death, He has defeated death completely.

Let me remind you of the glorious statement at the end of 1 Corinthians 15, beginning at verse 54: 'So when this corruptible shall have put on incorruption, and this mortal shall have put on immortality, then shall be brought to pass the saying that is written, Death is swallowed up in victory. O death, where is thy sting? O grave, where is thy victory? The sting of death is sin, and the strength of sin is the law. But thanks be to God, which giveth us the victory through our Lord Jesus Christ.' That in the main, of course, deals with the resurrection in a physical sense, but it is true in a spiritual sense also. So the argument is that our Lord Himself has already accomplished the work. He has already conquered the last enemy; and He has conquered it for us. That is why we need not fear death; that is why we can be certain of our resurrection. But at the moment we are looking only at Christ, and what the Apostle is asserting in this ninth verse in Romans 6 is that He really has achieved this conquest, that 'death hath no more dominion over him', and never shall have. In every way He has finished with death. By dying He has conquered death, He has rendered it inoperative in every sense of that word.

Further, let me remind you how the Epistle to the Hebrews states the truth. We read in its second chapter: 'that through death he might destroy him that had the power of death, that is the devil' [verse 14]. That is just another way of saying the same thing, looking at it from a slightly different angle. All these state-

[101]

ments are really asserting that the Lord Jesus Christ in His resurrection has once and for ever finished with death; and because this is so, He has altogether finished with the realm and the rule and the reign of sin. That is what the Apostle was setting out to prove, 'That as sin hath reigned unto death, even so might grace reign through righteousness unto eternal life by Jesus Christ our Lord' [*Romans* 5 : 21]. That, then, is the meaning of the statement in verse 9.

So far we are not thinking about ourselves at all. All we can see is this, that the Lord Jesus Christ was once under the power of death, under the dominion of death; but that is no more the case. That has gone, that is finished with once and for ever. His rising from the dead is a proclamation that death is conquered and vanquished by Him, and that He will never die again. He came here to deal with the problem of sin. He has done it, and He is back in the glory. He is no longer related to the whole realm of sin and of death in that way. That is the statement.

In verse 10 he puts that yet more clearly. 'For', he says, – and the word 'For' tells us that he is going to give an explanation – 'For in that he died, he died unto sin once; but in that he liveth, he liveth unto God'. What does he mean by 'in that he died, he died unto sin?' You will find that some interpret it as if the statement was that 'He died to sin'. Then they go on to say, 'That is what I want to do – to die to sin'. They bring in their own experience, and so get into an impossible muddle from the standpoint of exposition. I say again, forget yourself for the moment. The Apostle is talking about the Lord Jesus Christ, and he says that 'He died unto sin'. Now he says elsewhere that 'He died for sin', and some of the commentaries say that that is all the Apostle is saying here. It is quite true, of course, that He died for sin; but it is not what the Apostle is saying here. That statement is true as regards justification; but here Paul is not dealing with justification.

How can I prove that Paul does not say here that our Lord died 'for sin' in this manner? I answer that the parallel makes it impossible. The parallel is, that what is true of Him is true of me. Therefore if the Apostle is saying here that Christ died 'for sin once', then it must also be true that I have died for sin once. But that is not true. It is He alone who died 'for sins'. We do not and cannot die for our sins. He alone could do that. So it does not mean that He died 'for sins'. The Apostle says that He died 'unto sin'.

Neither does the Apostle mean – and this is most important – that He died to the 'power' of sin as we know it in our lives. It does not mean that He died to 'indwelling sin'. It does not mean that He died to the 'liability to sin'. It does not mean that He died to the 'force of sin' as the evil power in our lives that drags us down. It does not mean any one of these things, and for this reason, that such things were never true of Him. There was never any power of sin in His life. There was never any liability to sin in His case. There was no such thing as 'indwelling sin' in Christ. He was not a sinner, and there was no sin in Him. He was 'harmless' and 'undefiled', and 'separate from sinners'. So it does not mean that.

We must realize that the term is that He died 'unto sin'. I suggest that it means exactly what it means in verse 2, in verse 6, and in verse 7, as we have already seen. Paul is just stating it once more so that we shall be clear about it. 'How shall we that died to sin . . . ' [verse 2]; and we interpreted that as meaning 'died to the realm and to the rule and to the reign of sin'. Not 'to sin' as 'indicating the justification of believers' from its guilt as Haldane puts it. But it means that we have died not only to the condemnation of sin, but to the whole realm and rule and reign of sin. It means exactly the same in verse 6: 'Knowing this, that our old man was crucified with him.' We saw the same in verse 7: 'He that is dead is freed from sin' – not 'justified from sin' but freed from the whole realm and rule and reign of sin. So here Paul says it again: 'For in that He died, He died unto sin once.' He died to that whole relationship to sin into which He once put Himself voluntarily for our salvation. He has died unto it as a power, as something that reigns, as we have seen in chapter 5 – something that has a realm and a rule and an authority.

Further, he says 'In that he died, he died unto sin once.' Let us be clear about this word 'once'. The Authorized Version translation is not good. The meaning is 'once, and and once only'; 'once, and once and for all'; 'once, and once for ever'. 'Once', standing alone, does not tell us enough. We sometimes use the expression, 'once and again'. But it does not mean that. The word used by the Apostle means 'once, and once only', 'once, and once for ever, never to be repeated'.

This point can be illustrated best by reference to the Epistle to the Hebrews where the word is constantly and powerfully emphasized. My first reference is in chapter 7, verse 26. The author is contrasting our Lord as High Priest with the priests under the Old Testament dispensation, and he says, 'For such an high priest became us, who is holy, harmless, undefiled, separate from sinners, and made higher than the heavens; who needeth not daily, as those high priests, to offer up sacrifice, first for his own sins, and then for the people's; for this he did once (once and for ever) when he offered up himself'. The contrast is between the repetition of the sacrifice and the 'once, and once for ever'. The next example is to be found in chapter 9 in several verses. Take Hebrews 9 : 12: 'Neither by the blood of goats and calves, but by his own blood he entered in once (once and for ever) into the holy place, having obtained eternal redemption for us.' Next we turn to verses 25 and 26, where the same comparison and contrast is again made: 'Nor yet that he should offer himself often, as the high priest entereth into the holy place every year with blood of others; for 'then must he often have suffered since the foundation of the world; but now once in the end of the world hath he appeared to put away sin by the sacrifice of himself' – once and for ever! And then again in verse 28: 'So Christ was once offered to bear the sins of many; and unto them that look for him shall he appear the second time without sin unto salvation'.

In chapter 10 you will find the word used three times. Verse 10: 'By the which will we are sanctified through the offering of the body of Jesus Christ once and for all.' (The context emphasizes the contrast, 'And every priest standeth daily ministering and offering oftentimes the same sacrifices, which can never take away sins'). Again, verse 12, 'But this man, after he had offered one sacrifice for sins for ever, sat down on the right hand of God'. In verse 14 we have the third example, 'For by one offering he hath perfected for ever them that are sanctified'. Christ has done it by 'one offering', never to be repeated, once and for ever. He has 'perfected them that are sanctified'.

Observe, then, what the Apostle is doing in this sixth chapter. He has made the great pronouncement in verse 8; he demonstrates it in verse 9, and then he gives the full explanation of it in verse 10. The point we have reached is this, that he is showing the finality of what Christ has done. How can I be sure that Christ, being raised from the dead, dieth no more, that death hath no more dominion over Him? This, he says, is the answer. When He died unto sin, He did it once and for ever; and the work is so complete that there is never any need for Him to come back to do it again. The priests under the Old Testament had to keep on doing the same thing day after day; and the high priest year after year. Not so here! Because He is the Son of God, because He is who and what He is, and because of the way in which He accomplished His work, He by one act has done it once and for ever. It needs no repetition; and there will be no repetition. So I know that 'Christ being raised from the dead dieth no more, sin hath no more dominion over him'.

We shall go on to complete Paul's argument, and then to draw the grand deduction about ourselves, yes, even in an experimental sense.

Nine

For in that he died, he died unto sin once: but in that he liveth, he liveth unto God. Likewise reckon ye also yourselves to be dead indeed unto sin, but alive unto God through Jesus Christ our Lord.

Romans 6 : 10, 11

What we have found so far in verse 10 is summed up very clearly in the Epistle to the Hebrews in verse 28 of chapter 9 which reads, 'So Christ was once (once and for all) offered to bear the sins of the many; and unto them that look for him shall he appear the second time without sin (apart from sin) unto salvation'. He came the first time, when He came as the Babe of Bethlehem into the realm of sin, in connection with sin, into this world of sin, and under the Law. He was 'made of a woman, made under the law'. But says the word in Hebrews, 'unto them that look for him shall he appear the second time without sin'. 'Without sin' does not mean that He Himself will be without sin, for He was without sin when He came the first time. It is a statement with regard to His nature or His character or His being. What it means is, that in His first advent He came in connection with sin, in relation to sin, but when He comes the second time He will come with no such relationship to sin, 'without sin'. He will come 'without sin unto salvation' for the final working out of His great salvation. We can sum it up by saying that His relationship to sin was only temporary; it was just for that short period of time. But that will never happen again, because He did once and for ever everything that was necessary to deliver His people from their relationship to sin and death. He is the last Adam; there will never be another. He is not the second Adam, He is the last Adam, there is no need of another. He has done all; it is finished. He said on the cross, 'It is finished'; and it was finished.

He died once for all; and He has finished with sin and death once and for ever.

We can now take up the second half of this tenth verse, where the Apostle turns to the other side and says, 'but in that he liveth, he liveth unto God'. He died once. That is one action finished. But He goes on living: 'in that he liveth, he liveth unto God'. This is our Lord's condition now. The words form one of our key statements in the interpretation of the whole of this section from verse 1 to verse 14.

What does 'He liveth unto God' mean? It obviously cannot refer to His obedience to God because He was always obedient to God. It cannot refer to the type of life He lives, for His life even when He was here on earth was a life that was lived entirely to God. It has no reference at all to His obedience, or His behaviour or conduct, because that has always been a constant. What makes the interpretation of this phrase so vitally important is that we are told that what is true of Him is true of us. We shall be told in verse 11: 'Likewise reckon yourselves also to be dead indeed unto sin but alive unto God.'

What then is the right interpretation? Surely this, that Christ is now living exclusively in the realm of God. In other words, this tenth verse presents us with a contrast. There was once a time when Christ was in the realm of sin and death; but He is no longer there, because 'in that he liveth, he liveth unto God'. He is no longer living in the realm of, and under the reign of sin and death. He was there for a while, but He is no longer there. He is now living in this other realm, in the realm of the power and the glory of God – and in that alone. Clearly the purpose of the second half of the verse is to present us with a contrast to the statement made about Him in the first half of the verse. So we can put it like this. Our Lord for a short period of time came out of the realm of glory into the realm of 'sin and death'. It was temporary only. He is no longer there. He has been 'received up into glory' [1 *Timothy* 3 : 16].

Let us look at this more closely. Christ came out of the realm of glory into the realm of sin and death. What was true about Him in that condition? This is what the Bible says – 'He was a man of sorrows, and acquainted with grief'. Though He was the eternal Son of God, though He was the second Person of the blessed holy Trinity, He became 'a man of sorrows, and acquainted with grief', because He had come into the realm of sin and death. He came voluntarily, He humbled Himself. He chose to do it, and so He came. And while He was in that condition, as we are reminded in the fourth chapter of the Epistle to the Hebrews, 'He was tempted in all points like as we are, yet without sin' [Chap. 4 : 15]. While He was in the realm of glory before the Incarnation He was not only not tempted, He could not be tempted. We are told that 'God cannot be tempted with evil, neither tempteth he any man' [*James* 1 : 13]. But Christ came into this world, into this other realm of sin and shame; and because He had humbled Himself and was 'made of a woman, made under the law', He had come into a realm where He could be tempted. And He was 'tempted in all points like as we are, yet without sin'.

But more: Look at Him standing in that cemetery, outside the grave in which His friend Lazarus had been buried. We read that 'He groaned in the spirit' [*John* 11 : 38]. He has come into the realm of sin and death, and He 'groans in the spirit'. But go further and look at the shortest verse in the Bible, 'Jesus wept' [*John* 11 : 35]. He was the eternal Son of God, but He wept. That was because He had put Himself voluntarily into this realm of sin and of death. Then take that statement about Him in the fifth chapter of the Epistle to the Hebrews, verses 7 and 8, 'Who in the days of his flesh, when he had offered up prayers and supplications with strong crying and tears unto him that was able to save him from death, and was heard in that he feared; though he were a Son, yet learned he obedience by the things which he suffered'. That is all a part of it. He is no longer in the realm of glory exclusively; having become man, having become 'Jesus', He has entered into this other realm of sin.

But we must go yet further in order to bring out the meaning of this verse. Look at Him there in the Garden of Gethsemane. Observe again the agony and the groaning, but much more intense; so intense now that He begins to sweat great drops of blood. He did not do that at the grave of Lazarus. His agony of soul and of spirit was so great that He began to sweat those drops of blood. But there was something even worse than that. He had been from all eternity in the bosom of His Father – Father, Son, Holy Spirit, co-equal, co-eternal, without any mixture or any change or any variation. That was His eternal state. But He has come out of that, and here is the climax of what He has entered into. Look at Him upon the Cross and listen to Him crying out, 'My God, my God, why hast thou forsaken me?' For that brief moment – we do not know how long it lasted – He was in a condition in which He was actually separated from God the Father. The eternal communion which had subsisted eternally between Him and His Father is broken, and for that terrible moment He is outside the realm of God's love. He says, 'My God, my God, why hast thou forsaken me?' That was because He had come voluntarily into the realm of sin and of death. It meant that for that brief passing moment He was entirely cut off from the realm of God and from communion with His Father.

But now says the Apostle in the second half of this tenth verse, He is no longer in that condition – 'In that he died, he died unto sin once'. That one fleeting moment produced that work. But, he says on the other side, 'in that he liveth, he liveth unto God'. The Apostle means that Christ is now restored to the position where He was before He came into this world. The prayer that He offered, His great High-Priestly prayer that is recorded in the seventeenth chapter of John's Gospel, and especially verse 5, has been answered. What was His petition? 'And now, O Father, glorify thou me with thine own self with the glory which I had with thee before the world was.' From eternity He had shared this glory with the Father; but, in order to redeem us, He had put on one side some of the signs and the insignia of that eternal glory. He humbled Himself, He made Himself of no reputation. He came in the likeness of man, in the form and likeness of sinful flesh, and His glory was veiled and was hidden. But now He realizes that He is about to die, and to finish the work, so He offers up the petition. He says, 'I have completed, I have finished the work which thou gavest me to do'; and because He had done so, He goes on to say: 'glorify thou me with thine own self with the glory that I had with thee before the world was.' That prayer has been answered. He has returned fully to His eternal glory, He has re-entered into the realm and the sphere out of which He had come. 'In that he liveth, he liveth unto God.'

There is a similar statement of this truth in the first chapter of the Book of Revelation, verse 18, where, appearing to John, He says, 'I am he that liveth, and was dead; but behold, I am alive for evermore, Amen; and have the keys of hell and of death'. Another statement to the same effect is found in the Epistle to the Ephesians, chapter 1, verses 19 to 23. The Apostle prays in verse 19 that these Ephesians might know 'what is the exceeding greatness of his power to us-ward who believe, according to the working of his mighty power, which he wrought in Christ when he raised him from the dead, and set him at his own right hand in the heavenly places, far above all principality, and power, and might, and dominion, and every name that is named, not only in this world, but also in that which is to come; and hath put all things under his feet, and hath given him to be the Head over all things to the church'. There is the same truth once more.

In other words, Christ is no longer 'in the realm of sin and death'. He is in the realm of God, and of glory, and of majesty. He is again enjoying the glory which He had with His Father, and which for the time being He had set aside to do this work of redemption. He is enjoying it again in an unbroken manner; and it will never be broken again. 'In that he died, he died unto sin once.' Repetition is unnecessary and impossible. He is back in the glory. 'In that he liveth, he liveth unto God.' There will never be another break, there will never be need for another break. He has done all that was necessary once and for ever; there is no need for any further action. So when He comes again He will come in glory, riding on the clouds of heaven, surrounded by His holy angels. As the everlasting King He will come to judge the world, destroy all evil, set up His Kingdom, and reign in glory for ever and for ever. That is what the Apostle is saying here. That is the teaching of this tenth verse.

Let me sum it up. What is the teaching concerning our Lord? These three verses 8, 9, and 10 look entirely and exclusively at the Lord Jesus Christ. I have been emphasizing that, but must do so again, because it is so essential to our interpretation of what is to follow. Our Lord has finished with sin and death once and for ever. He will never die again. Death hath no more dominion over Him. He has conquered and vanquished death; He has taken the sting out of death. His resurrection is the defeat of death. He is now altogether and entirely without limit in the realm of God and His glory. And He will remain there for ever. His relationship to sin and death was only temporary and for our sakes, for your sake and mine. This is the good news of salvation, that this eternal Son of God came out from the glory once. That is the story, 'That once the King of glory came down on earth to dwell'. There was no reason for it but His own grace and mercy and everlasting love. He did it all. He humbled Himself, He came into a world like this, He put Himself into the realm of this power of sin and death, in order that you and I might be redeemed and reconciled to God. It was a temporary relationship altogether for our sakes. But having accomplished His work He has gone back into the glory. 'In that he liveth, he liveth unto (now entirely in the realm of) God.' He is no longer in the realm of sin and death. That is the truth concerning the Lord Jesus Christ.

We can now look at verse 11: 'Likewise reckon ye yourselves also to be dead indeed unto sin, but alive unto God through Jesus Christ our Lord.' We come to a real turning-point in this verse. At last we come to the realm of application, to what impatient Christians try to do so much earlier in this chapter. But you cannot come to the realm of application until you are clear as to what has to be applied. That is why the Apostle has taken these three verses 8–10 in particular, and in a sense the eleventh verse, to tell us the truth about the Lord, because he is going to show that what is true of Him is true of us. Had you realized that this is literally the first word of exhortation in the Epistle to the Romans? Until we reach this eleventh verse of chapter 6 it has been nothing but sheer doctrine. The entire first five chapters and nearly half the sixth consist of exposition and doctrine. You cannot come to application and to practice, to conduct and behaviour and experience, until you are clear about the doctrine. That is the great lesson we should learn at this point. So far we have simply been told the truth about ourselves. Now, he calls upon us to realize the truth he has been teaching us up to this point.

Let me make this clear. So far we have simply been told the truth about ourselves. Now the Apostle wants us to lay hold of it, to realize it, and to begin to apply it. He calls upon us to realize, and to reckon, these things. Why is he doing so? Why does he want us to 'reckon ourselves also to be dead indeed unto sin'? It is because he is still answering the objection which he reports and takes up in verse 1. He is still dealing with the people who said, 'I can see what your teaching is, your teaching of the free grace of God and so on. It just means this, Let us continue in sin that grace may abound. The more we sin the more grace will be given; therefore, let us plunge even more deeply into sin.' 'Impossible'! says Paul. If you realized the truth of this doctrine, far from saying that, you would say the exact opposite; you would see that everything that is taught in this doctrine is designed to bring you out of sin, and to conquer sin, and to make sin unthinkable to you. That is what the Apostle is doing.

How does he do it? The first thing that is absolutely essential to our being delivered from sin and to our realizing that we are not to continue in sin, is that we should realize the truth about ourselves as it is expounded in this eleventh verse. Nothing, therefore, can be more important for us at this point than to understand exactly what this eleventh verse says, and what it does not say. Let us look at it again. 'Likewise reckon ye yourselves also to be dead indeed unto sin, but alive unto God through Jesus Christ our Lord.'

What does it mean? There are three principles which we must bear in mind before we come to the details of the statement. The first principle the Apostle asserts is that what is true of the Lord Jesus Christ is also in this respect true of us, because we are joined to Him. We have seen how he has been proving that at length. He says, 'Know ye not that so many of us as were baptized into Jesus Christ were baptized into his death?' We have been crucified with Him, we have died with Him, therefore we are buried with Him by baptism into death, 'that like as Christ was raised up from the dead by the glory of the Father, even so we also . . .' We are united to Christ. And because we are united to Christ, what is true of Him is true of us. I remind you of the old comparison. We used to be united to Adam; that is why we are what we are by nature. Adam fell, we fell. Adam sinned, we sinned with Adam. That is the argument of chapter 5 verse 12 to the end. Now we are joined to Christ, and therefore what is true of Him is true of us. The two words 'likewise' and 'also' prove that. 'Likewise' – in the like manner, in the same way – 'reckon ye yourselves also'. Not only true of Him, but also of you! 'Likewise' – 'also'. That is what he is saying, that what is true of Christ is true of us.

The second principle is that the statement in the eleventh verse is entirely non-experimental; it has nothing to do with our experience. The very word 'reckon' which he uses proves that clearly. You cannot tell a man to reckon an experience; that would be ridiculous. If he has had the experience there is nothing to reckon. The very word 'reckon' settles the matter, as does also the parallel which Paul is drawing between the Lord and ourselves. The experimental aspect of this matter only comes in with the next verse. The main trouble about Christian living is that people will rush to the experimental before they have understood the truth. The experimental is the outcome of an understanding of the doctrine, of the truth. Now this verse is entirely non-experimental. The practical, experimental aspect comes in verse 12 and following.

The third principle is that this verse does not deal directly with the question of our holy living and sanctification; but it does introduce us to a truth that will lead on to that, and which promotes that, in a most wonderful manner. Verse 11 has nothing to do directly with sanctification, but indirectly it is a most important verse with regard to the whole question.

Those are the three principles which we must hold in our minds. They are of crucial importance, and I repeat, non-experimental. What Paul asserts is that what is true of Christ is true of us. His experience does not come in at all. He was always holy, He never had any sin at all. So we must get rid of the whole notion of experience here. It is the comparison that matters, the 'likewise – also'. What happened to Him has happened to us.

Now we come to the detailed exposition. Let us start with the word 'reckon'. It really means 'to regard oneself as something', or alternatively, it means 'to consider'. The Apostle is saying, 'Reckon ye also yourselves', 'Consider yourselves to be what you are'. That would be quite a good translation. Or a better one perhaps would be this, 'Consider, and keep before you' – that idea is in it. You have to go on 'reckoning'. 'Consider, and keep constantly before you, this truth about yourself.' Another very good translation is 'conclude', 'draw the deduction'. It is interesting to note that the word 'reckon' here in this eleventh verse of this chapter is exactly the word the Apostle used in chapter 4 in a whole series of verses. It occurs in verse 3 of that chapter: 'For what saith the Scripture? Abraham believed God, and it was *counted* unto him . . . ' You will find the same word also in verses 6, 8, 9, 10, 11, 22, 23 and 24. Sometimes it is translated 'counted', sometimes 'imputed', and sometimes 'reckoned'.

The same word is also found in chapter 3 verse 28 of this Epistle; and this is an important use of it. The Apostle has been arguing out the matter of justification by faith, how it is not by 'the deeds of the law' and so on. Then, summing up his argument, he says, 'Therefore we conclude that a man is justified by faith without the deeds of the law'. 'We conclude' – it is exactly the same word. If could well have been translated, 'Therefore we reckon'. This, he says, is the 'conclusion' at which we have arrived'.

That then is the connotation of this word 'reckon'. I am emphasizing the matter for this reason, that there are people who have regarded, and still regard this eleventh verse as something which can be used in the practice of Couéism, in which people endeavour to persuade themselves that something is true of them which is not actually true of them. When ill they are taught to say, 'Every day and in every way I am getting better and better'. According to Couéism if you keep on saying that to yourself you will begin to feel 'better and better'. Many have interpreted Romans 6 : 11 in that way; but it is a complete travesty of it. This is not something of which you persuade yourself psychologically; it is a conclusion, it is a deduction, it is a bit of logic. It is the inevitable result of the truth the Apostle has been laying down. It is indeed the opposite of Couéism, so we must get rid of that false notion.

What it means is that you accept God's Word and draw the inevitable conclusion from it. Do what Abraham did when God came to him at the age of ninety-nine, Sarah being ninety, and said to him, Sarah is going to conceive and bare a son. It sounded monstrous, it sounded impossible, but 'Abraham believed God'. Because God said it Abraham believed it, in spite of everything to the contrary. In other words Abraham reckoned that what God said was true. Abraham came to the conclusion that what God had promised God could also surely perform. He drew the right conclusion, he came to the solemn conclusion. It is not a bit of Couéism, but it is logic that is based upon the veracity of the Word of God. That is the context of this term – acceptance of God's Word and drawing the inevitable deduction from it.

Then we come to the expression, 'ye yourselves'. 'Likewise reckon ye yourselves also to be dead indeed unto sin'. Who is this 'self', 'yourself'? I have already been explaining this. Let me remind you of it. It means your essential personality. We shall have to deal with this in greater detail when we come to chapter 7, but he means 'you yourself', this distinct personality that God has given to you, and to me, that makes us all separate and different people, the individuals that we are. I was once a man in Adam. *I* was once in Adam. *I* am no longer in Adam but I am in Christ. I can talk about the 'old man' and the 'new man', but I myself can look on at the two men, as it were. It is my being, my entity that he means here. 'You' -- this being that you are, that came from God, and will go back and stand before God -- you, your own individuality and identity, yourself, your personality. 'Reckon that you yourself are dead indeed unto sin, but alive unto God through Jesus Christ our Lord.'

That brings us to the third expression -- 'through Jesus Christ our Lord'. That is how it is found in the Authorized or King James version. It is a pity that it was so translated, for the Authorized version is not only unfortunate here but indeed wrong. What Paul wrote was, 'Likewise reckon ye also yourselves to be dead indeed unto sin, but alive unto God in Jesus Christ our Lord. Not 'through' Him, not 'by' Him, but 'in' Him. What a world of difference there is there! We found precisely the same thing in verse 10 of chapter 5, and we made a big point of it there. In the Authorized Version it reads, 'If, when we were enemies, we were reconciled to God by the death of his Son, much more, being reconciled, we shall be saved by his life'. I was at great pains to show that it is not 'by' His life, but 'in' His life. There the Apostle started to expound the great doctrine of our being in Christ -- joined to Him -- that he has followed through the remainder of chapter 5 and in all these first ten verses of chapter 6 -- 'In Christ Jesus'. 'How much more shall we be saved in his life!' We have seen at length in working through this sixth chapter that his basic argument all along is that we who are Christians are not merely forgiven because of what Christ has done for us, we have been united to Christ, we are joined to Christ, we are indeed 'in Christ' -- 'in Christ Jesus'. He is the Vine, we are the branches; we are in Him, a part of Him. That is the basis of his whole argument; and here, therefore, he says, 'Likewise reckon ye also yourselves to be dead indeed unto sin, but alive unto God'. Why? Because you are 'in Christ Jesus'. That is why you are dead to sin and alive unto God – because you are 'in Christ Jesus'.

That brings us to the fourth matter, which is the practical one. What are we, then, to realise as being true of us in the Lord Jesus Christ? What is this that I have to conclude and to reckon and to hold always before me? The first thing is this, that we are 'dead indeed unto sin'. We have seen that Christ is dead indeed unto sin. He died unto sin once, He is no longer in that realm, He is living unto God. As He is dead indeed unto sin, so are you, says Paul, if you are in Him. You must be, if you are in Him, because what is true of Him is true of you. So you are 'dead indeed unto sin'! Notice that I am emphasizing 'unto'. You remember that we saw in His case that it was 'In that he died', He died not *to* sin, but 'He died *unto* sin'. We must not say that Christ died to sin; He never had any need to die to sin. He died unto sin, He died to His relationship to sin. The same word is used of us. He does not say 'Reckon ye yourselves also to be dead indeed to sin' but 'Reckon ye also yourselves likewise to be dead indeed unto sin'. As it was 'unto' in His case, it is 'unto' in our case. That, of course, helps to determine the interpretation.

What does it mean then? What am I to do when I am told that I must reckon myself to be dead indeed unto sin? Let us consider first what it does not mean. No verse, perhaps, has been so abused, and so misinterpreted, as this one. Here are some of the things it does not mean.

It does not mean that it is my duty, in view of my profession of faith, and in view of my vows as a Christian, to die unto sin. Some have interpreted this verse in that way, as if the Apostle is saying, 'You say that you believe that Christ died for your sins, and that you are forgiven by God because He died for your sins, that you are justified by faith. Therefore cannot you see that it is your duty to be dead indeed unto sin?' Surely the answer to that is that the whole context makes it impossible. The very fact that what is true of me is what is primarily true of Him makes that a sheer impossibility. The interpretation here must conform to what we have seen to be true about Him.

Secondly, this is not a command to me to die to sin, or to become dead to sin. Many have interpreted it as just an injunction commanding Christian people to die to sin because of what Christ has done for them. It does not mean that either.

Thirdly, it does not mean that I am to reckon that sin as a force in me is dead, and that I, because I am a Christian, have altogether finished with sin. Why does it not mean that? Because sin was never a force like that in the life and experience of the Lord Jesus Christ; and what I am told here is that something is 'likewise' true of me as it was of Him. What was never true of Him cannot become true of me. Furthermore, if I said that, I would be uttering a lie. If I am told to say to myself that sin as a power is dead in me, that it does not exist, and that as I go on repeating the words I shall not sin and fall, I am trying to cure myself by telling myself a lie. I am saying to myself that something is not there in me which I know very well in experience is there. Indeed if it were not there, there would be no problem.

Neither does the Apostle's statement mean that sin is dead, or that sin has been eradicated out of me. The simple answer to that proposition is that sin is not dead; it is very much alive. Sin has not been eradicated, rooted right out of our constitution, because we know well that it is still here in our flesh and in our bodies. So this verse does not teach eradication.

Neither is the Apostle saying that we are dead unto sin as long as, or while, we are gaining a victory over sin. That is a popular and common interpretation of it. Some say, 'Reckon yourself to be dead indeed unto sin'; as long as you go on doing that you will be having your victory, and as long as you have your victory, sin is really dead as far as you are concerned. It does not mean that, because again the whole analogy with our Lord makes it an utter impossibility; it cannot be true. In any case, to argue thus means that you have already become experimental; and as I have been pointing out, it cannot be experimental because of the parallel with our Lord. But this verse is commonly interpreted and taken in an experimental sense. We are told, 'The way to get victory is just to go on repeating this verse to yourself. You say to yourself: Sin is not there as far as I am concerned since I have become a Christian, sin is really non-existent for me. You go on saying that, and by doing so you will get your victory.' That is not what this verse means. It does not deal directly with my experience or with my daily life.

Finally, it is not saying that it is my 'reckoning' of this fact that makes me dead unto sin. Many have interpreted it in this way. They say, 'If you engage in this reckoning you will indeed be dead unto sin'. The Apostle is actually saying the exact opposite.

What precisely is he saying? Positively, this is his exhortation: We are to reckon as true about ourselves not something that we want to be true, but something that is actually true of us. 'Reckon ye yourselves', he says, (because of your union with Christ) 'to be dead indeed unto sin.' Realize, he says, conclude that you are already dead unto sin because Christ is dead unto sin. The Apostle has taken all this trouble to tell us in detail what is true of the Lord Himself, because he is going to tell us that what is true of Him is true of us. I am to 'reckon' therefore, not something that I want to be true, but something that is true. It is not my reckoning that does this for me. No, this has already been done for me by Another. I am to reckon something that is already a fact; and the fact is that because I am united to Christ, and from the moment I became united to Him, I am already dead to sin, to the law, to death itself. So I am to reckon on something that has already happened. And this something that has already happened is not something that I do, it is not my reckoning that brings it into being. This – my death to sin and being alive unto God – is something that has been accomplished for me by the Lord Jesus Christ, who died unto sin once. I have come into this position because of the work of the Holy Spirit who baptizes me into Christ, and as He baptizes me into Christ I am 'in Christ', and I reap all these consequences of what happened to Him. So this verse is not telling me to accomplish anything; it just tells me to realize what has been done for me once and for ever by the Lord Jesus Christ. He died unto sin once, therefore I with Him died unto sin once and for ever. That is what I have to keep on holding before myself. So you see that this is not experimental, it does not tell me anything about my experience.

What does it tell me? It tells me about my position, my standing, my whole status. It tells me about the realm in which I now am as a Christian. Christ was once in the realm of sin and death, He is no longer there. I was once in the realm of sin and death; everybody who is not a Christian is still in the realm of sin and death, is under the dominion of sin, and of Satan, and of death, belongs to the darkness, belongs to the kingdom of Satan. What the Apostle tells me here is that as Christ once entered into that realm for a while but no longer does so, in exactly the same way I no longer belong to it either; I have been taken out of it with Him because I am in Him.

That is the great principle which we shall now have to work out in detail. You and I have to 'reckon' on this; this fact, this truth about ourselves. It is not experience; but the Word of God comes to us and tells us that if we are Christians at all, then by the action of the Holy Spirit we are in Christ. And because we are in Christ what is true about Him in His relationship to sin and death is equally true about us in our relationship to sin and death. Therefore I am to realize, to believe, to reckon, to hold it constantly before me, that as He died unto sin once and for ever and for all, I also have done so. I am no longer in the realm of sin and death, I belong to this other realm – 'alive unto God'. This is not my experience but my standing, my position, my status. It is the realm in which I myself now live.

Ten

*

Likewise reckon ye also yourselves to be dead indeed unto sin, but alive unto God through Jesus Christ our Lord. Romans 6 : 11

In referring to this most important and vital verse last time I indicated that it is the first exhortation, actually, in this Epistle. We must therefore pay great attention to it, and make certain that we are indeed doing what the Apostle asks us to do. As we do so I must remind you that there are certain general principles which must govern our interpretation. These we derive from what he has been saying in the previous ten verses. The first guiding principle is that we are to reckon as being true of ourselves what the Apostle has previously been telling us is true of the Lord Jesus Christ. The very words 'likewise' and 'also' make this abundantly clear.

The second principle is that this is not an experimental statement, not a question of experience. This is so because, as I have just been saying, we are to 'reckon' something as being true of ourselves which is already true of Christ. Therefore we must not begin to think in terms of a consciousness of sin within us, and how we are going to get rid of it, for there never was any sin in Christ at all, and He never had any consciousness of sin. So it is a non-experimental statement. We are told to realize, and to hold before ourselves and in our consciousness constantly, something that is already true of our position or status. It is not an exhortation to us to do anything with regard to sin, but to realize what has already been done for us with respect to our relationship to sin. It is an exhortation to us to remember what is already true of us; it urges us to realize what has already happened to us as Christians, those of us who are joined to the Lord Jesus Christ.

And what is true of us is that we are already in an entirely new position and standing with respect to sin.

This is something which we have to believe solely because the Word of God teaches it. You do not 'experience' your position, you are told about it and you believe it. That is what justification by faith alone means. We have this Word of God which tells us that this is God's way of salvation; and we have nothing but the Word of God. As we have seen, we have all got to do what Abraham did, as the Apostle has already reminded us in chapter 4. We must just take the bare Word of God, believe it, submit to it, and act upon it. That is what we have to do with this statement. Should someone come to me and say, 'But how can I say that I am indeed dead unto sin when I am conscious of sin within me, and I feel that I am a terrible sinner?' my answer is, that you have got to believe it in spite of those feelings, exactly as Abraham had to believe God's word that Sarah was going to bear a son though he knew that as he had reached the age of ninety-nine and Sarah ninety, the thing was a sheer impossibility on the natural level. Naturally, Abraham knew that it could not happen. In spite of this he believed God; and you and I must do the same. Now that is what this statement exhorts us to do. It is not experimental, not a matter of experience, but we just have to take this word, that if we are in Christ, if we are joined to Christ – and that is true of every believer in Him – then we are already 'dead to sin', even as He is dead to sin.

Let us work this out. What does it mean? We are to realize constantly that it means, first and foremost, that we have died once and for ever to the realm and the rule and the reign of sin and death. I have said that many times before, but I must go on repeating it. The Apostle himself has said it many times, and he goes on repeating it. He does so for this good reason, that we all know that it is precisely what the devil would hinder us from believing. We must believe that, because we are in Christ and joined to Him, as it is true to say of Him that He died unto sin once and for ever, so we also have finished with the realm and the rule and the reign of sin.

Secondly, we have to believe and to realize that we have done that once and for ever. You notice that we read about our Lord that 'in that he died, he died unto sin once', which we saw meant 'once and for ever'. Then Paul goes further and says, 'Knowing that Christ being raised from the dead dieth no more'. He died once, once and for ever; He will never die again. He has finished that work, He has done it once and for ever. Now we have to believe that the same is true of us, that our finishing with the rule and the realm of sin and death is final. As a believer in Jesus Christ I can never again go back into the bondage and the captivity of the realm and the rule and the reign of sin – never! That is true of Him; and as I am in Him, joined to Him, it is true of me; it must be true of me. That is the point the Apostle sets out to prove; because he is still dealing with the man who says, 'Ah, this teaching of yours means, Let us continue in sin that grace may abound'. Not at all, says the Apostle, you have been taken out of that realm, and you can never go back into it, you can never again return to that bondage.

But we must go even further, in the third place, and say, that as it is true to say of the Lord Jesus Christ that 'death hath no more dominion over him', it is true to say that of ourselves also. What we are exhorted, therefore, to say to ourselves as Christians is, 'Death has no more dominion over me because I am a Christian and because I am in Christ Jesus'. 'But surely', says someone, 'that must be wrong, because we all have to die. Christian people, though they are Christians, and though they are in Christ, still have to die. How can you say, therefore, that death has no more dominion over the Christian, over the believer?' The fact is that this is such a wonderful statement that it is not surprising that even Christian people constantly tend to misunderstand and forget it. Let us look at the assertion again. 'Likewise reckon ye also yourselves to be dead indeed unto sin'. In other words what is true of Him is true of me. What is true of Him? Here it is: 'Knowing that Christ being raised from the dead, dieth no more; death hath no more dominion over him'. I am arguing therefore that as I am delivered from the dominion and the territory and the realm of sin, so I am also delivered from the dominion of death. 'How do you establish that?' asks someone. I do so in this way. The Apostle himself goes on to do this very thing. Take what he says in chapter 8 verses 10 and 11, for instance, where we read, 'And if Christ be in you, the body is dead because of sin; but the Spirit is life because of righteousness. But if the Spirit of him that raised up Jesus from the dead dwell in you, he that raised up Christ from the dead shall also quicken your mortal bodies by his Spirit that dwelleth in you.' That is part of the answer.

But further answers are found in the Apostle's statements elsewhere. Take for instance 2 Corinthians 4: 16: '. . . though our outward man perish, yet the inward man is renewed day by day'. Then consider 2 Corinthians 5: 1 : 'For we know that if our earthly house of this tabernacle were dissolved, we have a building of God, an house not made with hands, eternal in the heavens' and so on. Then add to those statements a statement made by our Lord in the fifth chapter of the Gospel according to John and in verses 24 to 26, 'Verily, verily, I say unto you, he that heareth my word and believeth on him that sent me, hath everlasting life, and shall not come into condemnation; but is (has) passed from death unto life. Verily, verily, I say unto you, the hour is coming, and now is, when the dead shall hear the voice of the Son of God: and they that hear shall live'. But the most striking statement of all is in the eleventh chapter of the Gospel according to John verses 25 and 26: 'Jesus said unto her (that is, Martha), I am the resurrection, and the life: he that believeth in me, though he were dead, yet shall he live: And whosoever liveth and believeth in me shall never die. Believest thou this?' Let each one at this moment ask the question that our Lord asked Martha, Do you believe this? Listen to it again in verse 26: 'Whosoever liveth and believeth in me shall never die'. How do you explain such statements? Here is a statement that whosoever believeth on the Lord Jesus Christ shall never die. 'But', you say, 'we have to die. There have been thousands, not to say millions of Christians since our Lord uttered those words who have believed on Him and on His Name, but they have died and have been buried; and yet He says, "Whosoever liveth and believeth in me shall never die" '. I am suggesting that all these verses are the explanation of Paul's statement here that 'death hath no more dominion over a Christian'. It has no more dominion over our Lord, it has no more dominion over us.

How do we interpret the statement in John 11: 26? Clearly it means this, that whosoever lives and believes in the Lord Jesus Christ shall never taste everlasting death, shall never know what it is to be separated in soul and body from God. This is surely one of the most glorious and comforting truths that, as Christian people, we will ever hear or can hear. Have you noticed that in the New Testament we are not told that Christians 'die'? Christians 'fall on sleep'. Have you noticed the statement in the fifteenth chapter of the First Epistle to the Corinthians verse 51? Paul says, 'We shall not all sleep, but we shall all be changed'. What does he mean by saying 'We shall not all sleep?' You and I would put it like this, 'We shall not all die'; but he says, 'We shall not all sleep'. Christian 'fall on sleep'. There are many statements to this effect. For instance, in the First Epistle to the Thessalonians in chapter 4 verse 14: 'For if we believe that Jesus died and rose again, even so them also which sleep in Jesus will God bring with him.'

This is a very important doctrine; and what it tells us is that because we are in Christ, though we may pass through death, death has no more dominion over us. Death no more has prescriptive rights over us; it has no legal claim upon us. In being delivered from sin we are delivered also from the dominion of death. And we have been seeing the reason for that as we have been working our way through this chapter. The Lord Jesus Christ was 'made of a woman, made under the law', and it was because He was made 'under the law', and took our sins upon Him, that death ever did have power over Him. That was why He died. But He has conquered death, and He has not only conquered it for Himself, He has conquered it for all His people. That is why you get that extraordinarily interesting statement in the second chapter of the Epistle to the Hebrews, where we read in verse 14, 'Forasmuch then as the children are partakers of flesh and blood, he also himself likewise took part of the same; that through death he might destroy him that had the power of death, that is, the devil; and deliver them who through fear of death were all their lifetime subject to bondage'. This means that if you and I 'reckon ourselves to be dead indeed unto sin' we shall never be any longer in bondage to the fear of death. He died to deliver us from that bondage, and He does so by telling us here quite plainly that 'death has no more dominion over us'. It has dominion over all others; they are under 'the law of sin and death', and 'the sting of death is sin, and the strength of sin is the law'. But we who are Christians have been delivered from all that.

Let me now put the matter in the form of plain and clear doctrine. Because of what the Lord Jesus Christ has done, and because of what has happened to Him, and because of our union with Him, it is true to say of us that our whole relationship to sin and all it can do has been fundamentally changed. We are no longer in the position in which we were when we were born as the children of Adam. We were under the dominion, under the reign and the rule of sin. That is no longer the position, we have been 'translated' out of that 'into the Kingdom of God's dear Son' [Colossians 1 : 13].

We can go further and say in the second place that sin no longer has any dominion over us, though we may still have contact with it in our bodies. That is a vital distinction: it has no more dominion over us though we still have contact with it in our bodies.

Thirdly, we are no longer 'under the law'. Our Lord has finished with the Law, and so have we, in that sense. We are no longer 'under law', we are under grace, as we shall see in verse 14. Our relationship to the Law has finished, in that sense. The point is that we are no longer under the dominion of the Law. Paul say that in the first verse of chapter 8 : 'There is therefore now no condemnation to them that are in Christ Jesus.' But I go still further. There never can be, there never will be condemnation to believers in Christ. We cannot state this too strongly; because this is an essential part of the Apostle's teaching. Our Lord's relationship to the Law, which was temporary, has finished for ever. He is no longer under the Law, He is alive unto God. So are we. I am not only not under the dominion of the Law at this moment, I never shall be. My whole relationship to the Law as something that is against me, that condemns me, has finished once and for ever. There is no such thing as 'falling from grace'. If I am in Christ, I am in Christ. 'He dieth no more' – neither shall I die. The sting of death has been taken out as far as believers are concerned. That is why Paul at the end of that great fifteenth chapter of I Corinthians asks us to rejoice and be triumphant, and exhorts us to look at death and the grave and challenge them, saying, 'O death, where is thy sting? O grave, where is thy victory? The sting of death is sin, and the strength of sin is the law. But thanks be unto God who giveth us the victory'. I have finished with those things once and for ever.

The next deduction is that even the dominion of death over us no longer remains. In the wisdom of God it may be that we shall have to pass through death. There will some time be a generation of Christians that will not even have to pass through it. The

Apostle says that those who are living on the earth at the Second Coming of our Lord will not die at all, they will not pass through death. That is because death has no legal right any longer: death has lost all its power. They will be 'changed' without passing through death. But it may be that those of us who are now alive will have to pass through death; but it will have no claims upon us, there will be no bitterness in it, there will be no suffering in it, we shall 'sleep in Jesus', we shall 'fall on to His bosom', as it were. Its perils have gone, the terror of death is taken away once and for ever. Indeed, as the Apostle himself puts it so plainly and clearly at the end of the eighth chapter, in that tremendous challenge of his, 'I am persuaded that neither death (he puts it first), nor life, nor angels, nor principalities, nor powers, nor things present, nor things to come, nor height, nor depth, nor any other creature shall be able to separate us from the love of God which is in Christ Jesus our Lord'.

Let me be very practical. There are far too many Christian people who say, 'I am afraid to die, I am afraid that in the physical act of death my mind may become clouded; I may lose my faith, or I may say things that I do not really believe; how can I be responsible then?' They are afraid of the dissolution of the body, indeed many are afraid of becoming old, and afraid of the failure of their faculties and powers. But you have no right to be afraid of that. There is nothing that can ever separate us from the love of God which is in Christ Jesus our Lord. You may develop thickened arteries and failure of your brain; you may die in a state that appears like insanity, in which you may almost blaspheme and deny all you have ever believed; but it will not matter, it will not make the slightest difference. The decay of your body does not affect your relationship to the Lord Jesus Christ. You are 'in Him' and the failure and the decay of the body does not matter at all, and what you may do or say as a consequence of that decay will make no difference.

I am emphasizing this because I have known Christian people to be very troubled about it. I was once called to see a saintly old man who was on his deathbed. I was called in by his doctor as well as by the members of his family. They were in great distress because that dear old saint was using the most foul language that I think I have ever heard. One wondered where he had even heard such words. But there he was, swearing and cursing.

It was a puzzle and a problem to his family and to everybody else. How could this saint of God be behaving in such a manner? Had he ever truly been a Christian? Was it conceivable that he ever could have been a Christian in view of the fact that he was behaving in this manner? To me it was no problem at all, and for one reason only – the sheer failure of his circulatory system. He was not responsible for what he was saying, he was not himself. He was no longer the man he had been; his poor body was near to dissolution, the mechanism was breaking down, he did not know what he was doing. The man's name happened to be Thomas Davies. What I explained to them was that it was not Thomas Davies who was speaking those things, the trouble was that the poor 'tent' in which he had been living was dissolving, was breaking up, disintegrating, and therefore physically and in a 'machine' sense he was not functioning as he should have been. But it made no difference whatsoever to his soul and his relationship to God.

We must believe the words of Scripture when they tell us, 'I am persuaded' – I am certain – 'that neither death, nor life, nor angels, nor principalities, nor powers, nor things present, nor things to come, nor height, nor depth, nor any other creature shall be able to separate us from the love of God which is in Christ Jesus our Lord'. No! death no longer has any dominion over us. You need not be afraid of death; death cannot separate you from Him and from His love. It is incapable of doing so. Its sting has been taken out, it has been shorn of its powers. We may still have to pass through death, but we do not really die, for 'he that believeth in me shall never die'. Had you realized that you are never going to die? There may be dissolution of your bodily functions and powers, but you are never going to die. But the unbeliever is going to die, he is going to experience the horror of death, he is going to 'taste death'; but a Christian will never taste death.

Let us not be misled, therefore, by that which is purely physical; let us 'reckon ourselves to be dead indeed unto sin'. Indeed I must go on to say this – and this is a further deduction from it – that we must learn to say with the Apostle Paul, that not only has death no more dominion over us, but that death indeed to us is a 'gain'. He is in 'a strait betwixt two', he tells the Philippians, in the first chapter of his letter to them. He knows it is good for them that he should stay with them; but not as far as he himself is concerned. As far as he is concerned the 'good' is to be 'with Christ', 'which is far better', he says. 'For me to live is Christ, and to die is gain.' If to die is gain, death cannot have any dominion over him. A thing that tyrannizes over a man, and has dominion over him is not gain. But it is no longer that, Paul says. He can smile in the face of death; death has no power over him, has no legal rights over him. It is the will of God, perhaps, that he should be required to pass through it; but it is gain. He has a complete victory over it because it leads him immediately into Christ's presence. 'To be with Christ, which is far better.'

These are the things which we are to reckon, these are the things we are to remind ourselves of constantly. We look into the future; we do not know what is going to happen to us. Many things may happen to the body, but that does not matter. If we are 'in Christ' we have finished for ever with the dominion and the rule and the reign of sin and of death. We have nothing to look forward to except complete and perfect glory. Death, as far as we are concerned, is such a defeated enemy that to pass through it really becomes the greatest gain imaginable. And that is why it is really sinful for those of us who are Christians to be afraid of death in any shape or form. It is sheer ignorance of what it means to be with Christ, it is sheer ignorance of the glory to which we are going, the 'mansions' which Christ has 'prepared' for us, and for our reception. That is part of the meaning of this statement, 'Reckon ye yourselves also to be dead indeed unto sin'.

But we must draw one other deduction, which is, that we must learn to look at ourselves in our relationship to sin and death in the way indicated, so that we may learn one further practical lesson. Sin can never make me its slave or its captive again. Look at the way in which the Apostle John states that truth in his First Epistle, chapter 3, verse 9: 'Whosoever is born of God doth not commit sin', by which he means 'does not practise sin', does not go on living in sin and committing it and practising it – 'for his seed remaineth in him: and he cannot sin because he is born of God'. He does not say that he is incapable of committing an act of sin; what he does say is that he cannot go on in slavery and the dominion of sin. That is impossible. So the position of the Christian now is this: when a Christian sins he does not sin as a slave, but he sins as a free man who is choosing to do that which is wrong.

Do we get the significance of that distinction? A man who is not a Christian sins as a slave, he is in 'bondage', he is in 'captivity' he is one of the people, part of the goods, whom 'the strong man armed keepeth in peace'. He has no choice, he cannot get out. He cannot stop sinning, he cannot live the Christian life. It is impossible for him to do so because he is under the dominion of sin and of Satan. Such men try to break out of their captivity frequently, but they never succeed, because they are slaves, and they sin as such. But the Christian, when he sins, does not sin as a slave, for he has been brought out of slavery. He belongs to a new territory, he has been 'delivered from the power of darkness and translated into the kingdom of God's dear Son' [*Colossians* 1 : 13]. That is where he is, and when he falls he falls there, not where he once was.

This is of tremendous significance, and yet I find in my pastoral experience that more people trip up over this than perhaps over anything else. Cannot you see that it is your status and your position that chiefly matters? I sometimes use this illustration. Imagine yourself at the foot of a mountain and that you are walking along the level, and you fall. Very well, you have fallen. But now imagine that you have been climbing up that mountain, and that you have got two-thirds of the way to the summit. Suddenly you fall. Is your falling there identical with your falling down at the bottom? Of course it isn't. But there are many Christian people who seem to think that it is. They come to me and they say, 'I have fallen into sin; I do not think that I have ever been a Christian'. They are simply putting themselves back at the foot of the mountain again; they do not realize that while it is true to say that they have fallen, they have not fallen back to the ground level at the foot of the mountain. They have simply fallen two-thirds of the way up. Does not that make a difference? They do not have to climb all that two-thirds of the mountain once more; they have simply to get up from where they are and go on. The point at which you fall is of tremendous importance. You do not go all the way back to the foot of the mountain because you fall, you can fall just short of the summit. You have fallen into sin, but you are nevertheless near the summit of the mountain.

Now that is the position of the Christian. He is no longer where he was, he is in an entirely different position, he is in a different realm. He can certainly fall there, but he never falls again into the slavery, he never goes back under the dominion and into the territory of sin. He has fallen at a different point. He does not sin as a slave, he sins as a free man.

Or we could use again the familiar illustration about the slaves that were set at liberty after the American Civil War. There were many thousands of people then who had been born as slaves and brought up as slaves and who had lived as slaves. They had got into the habit of thinking as slaves. But the American Civil War settled the question of slavery, and slavery was abolished. However, many years afterwards many of those former slaves, and especially the old ones, kept on forgetting that they were at liberty. They had to learn to reckon themselves to be no longer slaves. And it took some time because all men tend to act according to habits and customs and practices which have been long ingrained. The way to get rid of all this evil is to tell yourself what is true about yourself; that you are no longer a slave, but that you are a free man. That is what I mean when I say that the Christian no longer sins as a slave but as a free man; and that is why I say he is always a fool when he sins. The compulsion has gone; it is he who now yields voluntarily; his whole position, his whole condition is changed.

But I must go on and add even to that; and it is an essential part of this teaching. Nothing and no one, not even the devil himself, can ever make a Christian a slave again to sin and its consequences. We are dead indeed unto sin, to its realm, its rule, its reign, its power. I may be conscious of its activity in my body but I am not under its dominion. And surely this is something which is even true in experience. It certainly becomes increasingly true in experience as you realize it. As soon as you begin to apply it and to examine yourself you will find that it is actually true. Look back to the days when you were a non-Christian and living the life of sin. Do you remember your attitude towards sin then? Is that your attitude towards it now? Of course it is not. Your whole attitude to sin has changed.

All this is most important if we are to realize the truth concerning the person termed a backslider. What is a backslider? A backslider is a child of God, a Christian who falls into sin. Why do we call him a backslider? Why not say of him that he was never a Christian at all? That is what many people do say about a man who falls into grievous sin. Why do I draw the distinction? I do so for this reason. The way to test whether a man is a backslider or one who has never been a Christian at all is this. If he is a Christian who is backsliding he is miserable as he goes on sinning. If, on the other hand, the truth about him is that he has never been converted at all, and never been a Christian, but has merely come under some passing psychological or moral or emotional influence and as a result has given up a particular sin, but has now returned to it, he will not be miserable as he returns to it again. He will enjoy it, and may well feel that he was a bit of a fool when he gave it up. But if he is a child of God, if he is regenerated and in Christ, though he is actually committing acts of sin he is miserable, he is under a sense of condemnation, he is unhappy. He is in a terrible condition, he hates himself, he hates the whole thing, and yet he goes on doing it. And I will add one further thing about him; he will for certain be restored; that is one of the final proofs that a man is a backslider. A backslider, because he is a child of God, will not be allowed to continue like that; it will be stopped; he will be brought back because he is 'in Christ'.

I trust that that makes it plain and clear that we must 'Reckon ourselves' to be dead indeed unto the whole realm and rule and reign and dominion of sin, and of the law, and death. We have finished with that once and for ever. And of course the moment you realize that, you will begin to see the inevitable consequences in the realm of conduct and behaviour. But before we come to draw these deductions we shall have to go on to the positive half of this verse, where we are told that we are to 'Reckon' not only that we are 'dead indeed unto sin' but also that we are 'alive unto God through Jesus Christ our Lord'. I do trust that we are clear about our relationship to sin and to death. I hope we can all say that death no longer has terrors for us. I hope we can all say, 'Thanks be unto God who giveth us the victory through our Lord Jesus Christ'. I hope that we can stand and challenge death and the grave, and defy them, because we know that Christ has conquered them and that we are in Him, and that they no longer have any dominion over us. We may pass through them, and we may be troubled and harassed very much by Satan while we are still here, but sin and death and Satan no more have dominion over us, no more have power, no more have authority, no more have rights. We have finished with them, we are free from sin and death, we are free in Jesus Christ.

[131]

Eleven

*

Likewise reckon ye also yourselves to be dead indeed unto sin, but alive unto God through Jesus Christ our Lord.   Romans 6 : 11

We have dealt with the first half of this momentous and all-important statement, so we can now look at the second half which, you notice, is no longer negative but gloriously positive. The first half, as we have seen in detail, is of tremendous importance; but it is vital that we should realize that the truth does not stop at that point.

You will find that certain commentators for some extraordinary reason seem to end at the negative and fail to go on to the positive. That is because they had originally gone wrong in their exposition of verse 2; and so, in order to be consistent with what they said there, they had to emphasize the negative in verse 11 at the expense of the positive. However, we must emphasize that this is most positive, and for the reason that we are still dealing with the false charge that is brought against the preaching of justification by faith and which is mentioned in verse 1 – 'Shall we continue in sin that grace may abound?' The first half of the answer to that is that it is an impossible suggestion, because we are 'dead indeed unto sin'. But that is not all; there is something that clinches the argument and makes it doubly certain, and shows, therefore, what a monstrous suggestion it is. It is this – that we are 'alive unto God'. We are not only to hold before ourselves the fact that we are 'dead indeed unto sin', we are equally to hold before ourselves this positive truth, that we are 'alive unto God'.

Once more we bear in mind that the Apostle is telling us that this is true of us as it is true of our Lord and Saviour Jesus Christ Himself. 'Likewise also.' He has just been telling us that 'Christ being raised from the dead dieth no more'. He has already told us that, 'if we be dead with Christ, we believe that we shall also live with him'. Indeed he had already told us in verse 4, 'Therefore we are buried with him by baptism into death: that like as Christ was raised up from the dead by the glory of the Father, even so we also should walk in newness of life'. All he tells us about ourselves in this context is that that which is essentially true of the Lord Jesus Christ Himself is true of us. I have therefore once more to repeat my second point also, which is, that this is not primarily an experimental statement, it is not a description of any experience we have. It leads to experience, but in itself it is not experience. As it was true to say of being 'dead unto sin' that it was not primarily experimental or experiential, so it is true to say the same of this. They both lead to experience, but in and of themselves they do not belong to the realm of experience; but they do very definitely belong to the realm of that which we believe by faith because we find it clearly stated in the Word of God.

That then being the setting, the context, what does it tell us? As we expounded it in the case of our Lord we saw that it meant this – that He is no longer in the realm of sin and death, He is no longer 'under the law,' He is no longer under the rule and reign of sin and of death. He was for a while. He put Himself there deliberately. But He is no longer there: 'Knowing this, that Christ being raised from the dead dieth no more, death hath no more dominion over him. For in that he died, he died unto sin once; but in that he liveth, he liveth unto God'. It is a change of sphere. He is no longer in that sphere, He is now in the sphere and the realm of God, sharing again with God 'the glory that He had with Him before the foundation of the world', and which He, in part, as regards its external manifestation, laid aside when He became incarnate and was born of the Virgin's womb. That is what it means in His case.

Now we, on our part, are to reckon ourselves 'likewise . . . alive unto God', and in the realm and the sphere of God and His operations. Otherwise stated, we are in the realm of the operation of the reign of grace. That was the statement in verse 21 of chapter 5, 'That as sin hath reigned unto death, even so might grace reign through righteousness unto eternal life by Jesus Christ our Lord'. In the second chapter of the Epistle to the Ephesians, Paul himself expresses it by saying 'We have been raised with Christ'. We were dead in trespasses and sins, we were buried, we were in a grave, but we have been quickened, we have been enlivened, we have been raised, we have been raised 'together with Him' into an entirely new realm and a new sphere – 'made to sit together in heavenly places in Christ Jesus' [*Ephesians* 2 : 6]. That is a statement that balances the first half of this eleventh verse. It is not merely and not only that we are dead to the condemnation of sin. Unfortunately Robert Haldane stops at that and goes no further. But we have finished with the realm, the power, the whole reign of sin, and we are in this other realm and under this other power, which is the power of grace. You find this stated clearly in that portion of the Epistle to the Ephesians which begins in verse 15 of chapter 1 and goes on to verse 10 of chapter 2. The Apostle emphasizes there that it is precisely the same power that God used to bring His own Son out of the grave that is working in us. So in the third petition of his prayer for those Ephesians, having prayed that they might know 'what is the hope of his calling,' and then 'what the riches of the glory of his inheritance in the saints', he goes on, 'and what is the exceeding greatness of his power to us-ward that believe according to (by means of) the working of his mighty power which he wrought in Christ when he raised him from the dead and set him at his own right hand in the heavenly places.'

Now it is important that we should realize that and bear it in mind. He has already said it, as I have reminded you, in verse 4 in this very chapter. 'Therefore we are buried with him by baptism into death; that like as Christ was raised up from the dead by the glory of the Father' – which means, you remember, 'the glorious power of the Father' – 'even so we also should walk in newness of life'. How can we walk in newness of life? Only because we have been raised up by the selfsame glorious power from the grave of sin. The same thing is stated very explicitly in Ephesians 2, verses 4 to 10.

That is what, the Apostle tells us, we must be holding constantly before our minds, that we are now 'alive unto God'. What does he mean by these words? They include a variety of blessings. We are to remind ourselves that in and through our Lord Jesus Christ, and because of our union with Him – which is the basic thought – it is true to say of us that we are in an entirely new relationship to God. That is the most staggering thing of all. We are no longer under the wrath of God. That is where we were. We were all by nature 'children of wrath, even as others' – every one of us, not only born in sin, but because of that, under the wrath of God. And, of course, that is why the world is as it is, for it is under the wrath of God. That is why the life of every unbeliever is what it is; it is a life lived under the wrath of God.

But now we have been delivered from all that through our Lord Jesus Christ. What does that deliverance signify? That we are reconciled to God! We are now in a position in which we are in God's favour instead of being under His wrath. 'God heareth not sinners' [*John* 9 : 31]. A sinner is not in the favour of God; but we are, for we are 'alive unto God'. That means we are alive in His presence, we have access to His presence; He is open to us. We are reconciled to God, and not only so, but we have become His children and objects of His love and His very special concern. There is one verse which states this perfectly. It is John 17, verse 23. 'I in them, and thou in me, that they may be made perfect in one; and that the world may know that thou hast sent me, and hast loved them as thou hast loved me'. That is one of the most staggering statements in the whole of the Bible. Our Lord's prayer there is that the world may know that God has loved us who are Christians as He has loved His only begotten Son. There is nothing beyond that. That is one of the results of realizing that we are 'alive unto God'. God loves the Christian as He loved His only begotten Son.

That, in turn, leads to this – that we are now open to all the blessings of God. It follows inevitably. And this is what the Bible teaches everywhere; we are open to all the blessings of God. The Apostle has already said this in verse 2 of chapter 5 of this Epistle. He says, 'By whom also we have access by faith into this grace wherein we stand'. It is all there. This is an exposition of it; and there is nothing that is more wonderful than to be open to all the blessings of God. The most terrible thing about a man who is in sin, and who is not a Christian, is that he is cut off from the blessings of God. That is much worse than the misery and all the suffering to which sin leads, and all the subjective elements in which people are so interested today.

It is true that there are certain general blessings which God gives to all and sundry. He 'sendeth rain on the just and the unjust', 'He maketh his sun to rise on the evil and on the good'. They are just parts of the blessings of 'common grace', so called; but they are not the choicest blessings of God. I am not detracting from their value. Health and strength, and life and power, are all very wonderful gifts, but they pale into insignificance when you put them by the side of spiritual blessings such as Peter talks of when he says, 'All things that pertain unto life and godliness' and 'the exceeding great and precious promises'. Those are the blessings of which the sinner knows nothing. He gets the benefit of the sun and the rain and other boons and benefits; but he knows nothing about God's choicest gifts and God's most precious blessings. But as Christians we are open to them because we are 'alive unto God'. We are no longer buried in a grave of sin, we are standing on our feet, we are looking into the face of God and are therefore open to all that pertains to His children. That is what the Apostle means by 'Reckon ye also yourselves to be alive unto God'. Hold it before yourself constantly, whatever may be happening to you. God made man originally for communion with Himself, but as the result of sin and the Fall man has got out of that relationship, is estranged from God, and left to himself. That is why he is as he is. He is not obeying the law of his being, he is not in the right relationship with his Maker, the Author of his being. But in Christ all that is cancelled, and we are back in the relationship, and even beyond the relationship, that Adam knew at the beginning. I quote again those lines out of that verse in the great hymn of Isaac Watts which is unfortunately left out of so many hymn-books:

> *In Him the tribes of Adam boast*
> *More blessings than their father lost.*

'Alive unto God' and enjoying that freedom of communion and of access that Adam enjoyed; and even more!

But not only are we open to all the blessings of God; more particularly we are the special objects of God's concern and attention and purpose. This is what I want to emphasize. To be 'alive unto God' means that we are in God's purpose, in God's plan. We shall find later that the Apostle emphasizes this concept. You get it perfectly, for instance, in chapter 8, verse 28: 'We know that all things work together for good to them that love God, to them who are the called according to his purpose'. That is it – God's purpose! Being alive unto God means that you are in God's purpose, in His great and eternal plan which dates from before the foundation of the world.

What is this plan? What is the purpose of God with respect to us? At this point we come to the very nerve and centre of the argument that the Apostle is conducting here. The charge brought against him and his preaching is that it really leads to but one conclusion – the antinomianism that says, 'Let us continue in sin, that grace may abound'! 'Impossible!' says Paul, because being alive unto God means that we are in the eternal purpose of God. What is the eternal purpose of God with respect to His children? The best answer to that question is found again in the Epistle to the Ephesians, chapter 1 verse 4: 'According as he hath chosen us in him before the foundation of the world'. What for? Here is the answer, 'that we should be holy and without blame before him in love'. Now that is God's purpose for His people; that is the thing He had in His mind when He planned our salvation before the foundation of the world. The whole end of salvation, the whole end of the scheme and the plan and the purpose of salvation in Christ Jesus, is that we are to be holy and without blame before Him in love. That is the force of the Apostle's argument. If that is God's plan and purpose for us who are in Christ, how, then, can anybody say, 'Let us continue in sin that grace may abound'? To live in sin is to go contrary to the whole purpose of God. This plan of salvation, far from allowing and encouraging people to sin, does the exact opposite. The whole end and purpose and object of the plan is that we might 'be holy and without blame before him in love'. So to be 'alive unto God' means that I am alive to this purpose of God, which is, that I should be holy and without blame before Him.

That leads to our fourth point. To be 'alive unto God' means not only that we are in God's plan and purpose, but still more vital, this purpose is being worked out in us. How does this happen? The Apostle has already been partly answering the question. By nature we are 'born in sin and shapen in iniquity', under the wrath of God, the power of sin and the power of Satan. But Christ has come to set us free from all that, and to make us holy.

How, then, is this purpose of God to make us holy and without blame being worked out in us? The first thing – that which in a sense includes everything – is that we have been united to Christ. In exactly the same way as we were united to Adam, and in

[137]

him, we are united to Christ; we are in Him in a most mysterious manner which we cannot understand. We belong to Him. 'Ye are the body of Christ, and members in particular.' That, I say, is the staggering fact. This teaching is found frequently in the New Testament. Our Lord Himself announced it first. He said, 'I am the vine, you are the branches'. It is all there in that relationship. Our attachment to Him is not a mechanical one; it is living, it is vital, it is organic. We receive life from Him, we are in Him, we are engrafted into Him, receiving life and power from Him. As Paul has put it here in verses 5 and 6 in this sixth chapter of Romans, we have been 'planted together', grafted together, united together, in the most intimate manner conceivable.

The Apostle states this same thing in many places. We read at the end of the first chapter of the Epistle to the Ephesians, 'And hath put all things under his feet, and given him to be the head over all things to the church, which is his body, the fulness of him that filleth all in all'. Then there is a particularly clear statement of it in Ephesians 4 : 16: 'From whom (Christ) the whole body, fitly joined together and compacted by that which every joint supplieth, according to the effectual working in the measure of every part, maketh increase of the body unto the edifying of itself in love.' We cannot expound that fully now, but it means that our relationship to Christ is comparable to the relationship that is maintained and sustained by various parts of the body to the living head. Every part of my body receives energy from my brain through joints of supply; the blood carries it and the nerves carry it in a marvellous way. There is some sort of electricity in the body, and all this gives sustenance even to my little finger. It is joined to the head, it is joined to the heart, and through the joints of supply the energy, the life, the power is flowing through the entire body and every part.

Now because we are joined to Christ, and are members of His body, parts of this whole of which Christ is the Head, one result as stated by the Apostle, is that 'I can do all things through Christ which strengtheneth me' [*Philippians* 4: 13]. What can be impossible? 'I can do all things through Christ who is infusing His power into me.' That is another way of saying that I am joined to Him, that I am in Him. Again, take that mystical statement of the matter which was made by the Lord Himself. It is found in the sixth chapter of John's Gospel verse 57: 'As the living Father hath sent me, and I live by the Father; so he that eateth me, even he shall live by me.' Do not stumble at the expression 'eateth me'. It has nothing to do with the Communion Service. It means living on Him. It is another way of describing this union, and what Christ is saying is, that a man who is in Him and joined to Him and lives on Him – as He had lived by His Father – 'shall live by me', by My life, My power, by My sustenance, and all that I am and have.

It is in the light of all these glorious statements that our Lord could say such things as the following. You remember His statement to the woman of Samaria? Standing there by the side of the well, and pointing at it, He said, 'Whosoever drinketh of this water shall thirst again, but whosoever drinketh of the water that I shall give him shall never thirst'. Never thirst! 'But the water that I shall give him shall be in him a well of water springing up into everlasting life' [*John* 4 : 13, 14]. That is the consequence of being united to the Lord Jesus Christ. He says it again in chapter 6, verse 35, 'I am the bread of life: he that cometh unto me shall never hunger; and he that believeth on me shall never thirst'. Notice particularly the word 'never'. It was that word 'never' that proved to be the most liberating word in the life of Hudson Taylor, the founder of the China Inland Mission. The biggest thing that ever happened to him was to realize the force of that word 'never'. 'He that cometh unto me shall never hunger' – and he had been hungering a good deal. 'And he that believeth on me shall never thirst' – and he had known the thirst. Never again! That is the result of being 'alive unto God'. You are 'in Christ', and if you are in Christ you shall never hunger. Have you realized this? Hold it before yourself – never hunger, never thirst! That is the first thing.

My being put into Christ means that God is working out His plan for me and in me. He looked at me and determined that I was to be made holy and without blame before Him in love. How does He do that? He puts me into Christ, joins me to Him, engrafts me into Him. As I go on receiving from Him this process continues. But it does not stop at that. Another way of looking at it is to know that the Holy Spirit dwells within us. As the Holy Spirit dwelt in the Lord Himself when He was here in the days of His flesh, so He dwells in us. The same Spirit that came upon Him comes upon us. 'God giveth not the Spirit by measure unto him.' He gave Him more of the Spirit, but it is the same Spirit – by measure unto us, without measure unto Him. So the Apostle can say to the Corinthians, 'Know ye not that your bodies are the temple of the Holy Ghost that dwelleth in you?' To be a Christian, to be 'alive unto God', means that God puts the Holy Spirit within you. And yet people say, 'This preaching of yours leads to this, "Let us continue in sin that grace may abound"'. How can it do so when God puts His Spirit within us? The Spirit that was in Him is in us. 'As He is, so are we in this world,' says John [1 *John* 4 : 17]. The Holy Spirit dwells within us; our very bodies are the temples in which He dwells.

The Holy Spirit's indwelling also means that the Holy Spirit works in us. In order to effect His purpose of making us 'holy and without blame before Him in love' God puts the Spirit in us, and then the Spirit works within us. What does He do? Take, for instance, what Paul says in Philippians 2: 12 and 13: he says, 'My beloved, not only as in my presence only, but now much more in my absence, work out your own salvation with fear and trembling. For it is God that worketh in you both to will and to do.' That is the work of the Holy Spirit; He is working in us to will and to do. How does that happen in experience? You may be sitting down, you may be reading a book, and suddenly you feel an impulse, a desire to read the Word of God; and you do so and derive great benefit to your soul. Where did the impulse come from? 'It is God that worketh in you, both to will . . .' He governs the will, He stimulates us, brings things into our mind, moves our hearts 'to will and to do'.

God does all this by the Holy Spirit, and it is a part of the plan and the purpose of making us holy and without blame before Him in love. It is constantly going on; there is a working of the Spirit constantly in the life of every believer. Such is the teaching of Scripture. It is not just a question of being converted, and then remaining like that for years, and then going to a convention and getting a second blessing. Not at all! From the moment you become a Christian this 'working' begins, and it goes on and on, leading, prompting you 'to will and to do'. Indeed, as I have already reminded you, the Apostle Paul in a sense was more concerned that those Ephesians should understand this than anything else. He says he wants them to know it, to have the eyes of their understanding enlightened that they might know, 'what is the hope of his calling'. Glorious! Wonderful! That is something that is going to come. 'And what the riches of the glory of his inheritance in the saints.' What a marvellous thing it will be to look at the host of the redeemed when the great day of glory arrives! You can even see something of it now. Paul wants them to have a glimpse of it. But, further, 'that you may know the exceeding greatness of his power to us-ward who believe' – this power that is working in us now, even here and now, though we do not realize it as we should. Paul says that he was praying that the eyes of their understanding might be enlightened though they had been converted for some time. They had assurance of salvation, many things had happened to them, they had been sealed by the Spirit, but they did not know, as they should know it, 'the exceeding greatness of his power to us-ward who believe'. It is the same power that God exercised when He raised Christ from the dead; that is 'the power to us-ward who believe'.

The Apostle gives a further definition of this blessing in the third chapter of the Epistle to the Ephesians verses 20 and 21: 'Now unto him that is able to do exceeding abundantly above all that we ask or think, according to the power that worketh in us, unto him be glory in the church by Christ Jesus throughout all ages.' Notice the emphasis upon the fact that 'the power that worketh in us' is beyond our highest thoughts, beyond the highest flights of our imagination. This power is working in us. 'That ye may be filled', he has just been saying, 'with all the fulness of God'. So what I am saying is that the moment you are 'alive unto God' you are alive to this power; and it is a power that is designed to produce holiness and to make us 'blameless and faultless' before the Lord.

I go on to one further step, the fifth – the certainty, the absolute certainty, of the completion of the purpose. The purpose is 'that we might be holy and blameless before him in love'. We have glanced at the way in which the purpose is being carried out: but in addition, the perfect carrying out of this purpose is something that is absolutely certain; nothing can stop it. 'He that hath begun a good work in you will perform it until the day of Jesus Christ' [*Philippians* 1:6]. It is as certain as God's promise. 'He that hath begun' – Who is that? It is God; and because it is God, it will never be left half completed. Men are guilty of that fault. They get excited and have their enthusiasms; they take up an idea and they are absorbed by it; but they may forget it in a few months and abandon it. God never behaves in that way. 'He that hath begun a good work in you will perform it until the day of Jesus Christ.' Or, take the same truth as it is found in Ephesians 5, verses 25-27: 'Christ loved the church and gave himself for it.' Why did He do so? 'That (in order that) He might sanctify and cleanse it with the washing of water by the word, that he might present it to himself a glorious church, not having spot, or wrinkle, or any such thing; but that it should be holy and without blemish.' Such was God's purpose before the foundation of the world. Such was the purpose that animated the Lord Jesus Christ and filled His mind and heart when He laid aside the insignia of the eternal glory and humbled Himself unto the Virgin's womb. Why did He do it? Why did He go to the Cross? Why did He die? Why was He buried? Why? This is the purpose, 'that he might present the church to himself a glorious church, not having spot, or wrinkle, or any such thing, but that it should be holy and without blemish'. That is the purpose of Father, Son and Holy Spirit. And that is why it cannot fail. It is going on, and it will go on until it is finally completed.

We are 'dead indeed unto sin, and alive unto God'; and because we are 'alive unto God', God's purpose is being carried out in us whether we realize it or not. He is going to make every one of the children whom He has put into Christ, perfect, blameless, completely without spot, or wrinkle, or any such thing. It is going to happen; He will bring it to pass; it is His power that does it. He has already put His purpose into operation in all believers, and He will continue the execution of it until every one of us is saved and entire and complete and perfect in His holy presence. That is why the Apostle says here, 'Reckon ye also yourselves to be dead indeed unto sin, and alive unto God through Jesus Christ'. That is your position, that is your status, that is your standing, that is now your relationship. You are no longer under the reign of sin, you are under the reign of grace, He will bring it to pass; nothing can stop it. Paul will eventually sum up all this in that mighty asseveration at the end of chapter 8: 'I am persuaded, that neither death, nor life, nor angels, nor principalities, nor powers, nor things present, nor things to come, nor height, nor depth, nor any other creature, shall be able to separate us from the love of God, which is in Christ Jesus our Lord.' And yet some foolish people say, 'Such preaching leads people to say "Let us continue in sin that grace may abound".' The answer is, You are no longer in sin, and you shall not continue in sin. It is clear in verse 14 of our chapter, 'Sin shall not have dominion over you: for you are not under the law, but (you are now) under grace'. 'Sin shall not . . .' God's character – if I may so put it – would be exposed to the laughter of the devil, and all hell, if any one of the chosen and the called and the redeemed did not arrive in heaven absolutely perfect and spotless. So that can never happen; the result is guaranteed because it is based upon the character and the power of God Himself. That is what is meant by 'reckoning ourselves to be dead indeed unto sin, but alive unto God'.

'How does all this help me?' asks someone. 'You expound this verse, saying that it is not experimental. How then does it help me to fight sin? That is what I want to know. I want something practical, but you have taken so much time on the doctrine. How does it work out?' Here is the beginning of the answer. If you reckon yourself, as you should, to be 'dead indeed unto sin', and 'alive unto God', the first effect will be that next time you fall into sin you will not raise the question as to whether you have ever been a Christian or not. Doubtless we have all done that many times. We fall into sin, and the devil comes and says, 'You thought you were a Christian, but this proves that you have never been a Christian'. And we listen to him and believe him, and then go back to God and plead for pardon and forgiveness as if the relationship had been broken, as if we had 'fallen from grace' and are again 'under sin' and under condemnation. If you really understand the meaning of this eleventh verse of chapter 6 of this Epistle you will never do that again. 'Knowing this, that Christ being raised from the dead dieth no more; death hath no more dominion over him. In that he died, he died unto sin once, but in that he liveth, he liveth unto God. Likewise reckon ye also yourselves.'

You cannot go in and out of grace; you cannot be saved one day and not be saved the next, and go back and forth. You are either under the dominion of sin and Satan, or else you are under the dominion of grace and of God. If you are a child of God you remain a child of God, and when you sin you do not cease to be a child of God. When your own child deliberately does the opposite of what you have told him to do, he does not cease to be your child. He is sinning as a child, he does not become a stranger because he has sinned. The same is true of us as Christians when we sin against God. So if we realize this, we shall never again allow sin to take us right back, as it were, to the beginning, and cause us to wonder whether we are saved or not. We must realize, rather, that every time we sin, we sin deliberately and as a child of God. We are no longer merely breaking or offending against the Law, we are now wounding love. That is much more grievous, but it is not a legal offence.

Secondly, if we understand this verse and the argument implicit in it, it gives us a right view of ourselves and our standing, both in relationship to sin, and in our relationship to God. Irrespective of what you may feel if you are a Christian, you must say to yourself, 'I have finished with the realm of sin, I am exclusively in the realm of God'. You must say that to yourself, hold it before yourself, remind yourself of it. That is your position in Christ. Whatever your feelings, say that to yourselves, believe it, hold to it, act upon it.

Thirdly, to realize this, therefore, takes away from us that old sense of hopelessness which we have all known and felt because of the terrible power of sin. You have said, 'I am never going to do that again. I am going to read my Bible regularly, I am going to pray constantly, I am going to do this and that'. Then you go back and commit the same sin again and you say, 'Who can stand up against such a power? "O wretched man that I am! Who shall deliver me?" Sin is too strong for me, it gets me down, it is in my very members, what can I do?' The only way I know of to get rid of that sense of hopelessness is the teaching of this chapter and especially this verse. Thank God, I do know it, because this sixth chapter has been to me, since I came to understand it, the most liberating chapter in my whole Christian experience.

How does it work? It works in this way. I lose my sense of hopelessness because I can say to myself that not only am I no longer under the dominion of sin, but I am under the dominion of another power that nothing can frustrate. However weak I may be, it is the power of God that is working in me; and it is God's purpose to deliver me from every vestige and trace and remnant of sin, until I become faultless and blameless. I know that that is true. There is a power working in me which is against sin and sin's power. I have been taken out of the realm of sin and I am being purged and purified, God is working in me. However great the power of the devil may be, I know that this power is greater: 'Greater is he that is in you, than he that is in the world' (1 *John* 4: 4).

When I say that, and believe it, I can smile at the devil, I can defy, I can resist him and see him fleeing from me. I can resist him, 'steadfast in the faith'. I used to be terrified of him, but no longer! Oh yes, if I were still alone I should be terrified; but Christ is with me, I am in Him. Therefore I need fear nothing that the devil can do to me. I can defy him, though he is 'a roaring lion roaming about seeking whom he may devour'. In Christ I can resist him. 'They overcame him by the blood of the Lamb and by the word of their testimony' [*Revelation* 12 : 11].

To realize all this, furthermore, leads to a sense of joy and of hope. When you realize these things you begin to smile; you stand up, you shake yourself. You say, 'What a fool I have been for being so depressed for so many years! Why did I ever allow the devil to tyrannize over me? Why have I listened so much to 'the accuser of the brethren?' You stand up on your feet, and you begin to rejoice. You may indeed indulge in a holy laughter as you realize your position, and what is happening to you. 'The joy of the Lord' comes in, and as Nehemiah reminded his hopeless people, 'The joy of the Lord is your strength' [*Nehemiah* 8 : 10]. When we are miserable and unhappy and defeated and pessimistic and morbid and introspective we are in no condition to fight and conquer the world, the flesh, and the devil. You cannot do your daily secular work properly if you wake up in such a condition. If you wake up feeling dull and lethargic and unhappy, and sorry for yourself, nothing seems to go right. You cannot write letters, you cannot add up columns in your ledgers, you cannot use a typewriter properly; but if you are feeling well and happy, everything comes so easily and you go through your work like a knife through butter. 'The joy of the Lord is your strength.' Well, this is the way to that joy. It is to realize that this is true of me, that I am 'dead indeed unto sin, but alive unto God', and that because I am in Christ this power is coming down through the ligaments of supply to me. I am no longer left to myself, I am receiving power from the Head, the life of God is in my soul, and I am filled with a joy which turns into further strength.

Lastly, and as we have seen in the exposition, I know that whatever may be true of me and of this world at this present time, the purpose of God is sure and certain; nothing can stop it – nothing whatsoever! That is the great message of this Epistle to the Romans, as indeed it is of the whole Bible. God has set this plan of salvation in process, and neither devils nor hell nor the whole universe can stop it. 'We rejoice in hope of the glory of God' because we are 'dead indeed unto sin, and alive unto God'. We are going to glory, and nobody can stop us, nothing can frustrate God's plan. The devil has done his utmost, but he has been defeated, and his doom is certain. Once you are in the scheme, the plan, the purpose of God, nothing can stop your ultimate glorification. I must quote Toplady again –

My name from the palms of His hands
Eternity will not erase;
Impressed on His heart it remains,
In marks of indelible grace.

Yes, I to the end shall endure,
As sure as the earnest is given;
More happy, but not more secure,
The glorified spirits in heaven.

Nothing is so important as to realize that, though you may be ignorant and weak and frail and fallible, and though the world, the flesh and the devil are mighty and strong, God is still working in you, and His object is to make you 'holy and without blame before Him in love'. Christ died. What for? For the church, his bride. He will look at her, present her to Himself as it were, and then present her to God 'without spot, or wrinkle, or any such thing'.

What fools we are to listen to the devil! How wrong-headed we are when we say, 'Doesn't this mean that we can continue in sin that grace may abound?' The answer is that you cannot continue in sin. Child of God, I warn you to be careful. If you try to live a life of sin, then be prepared for the application of the words, 'Whom the Lord loveth he chasteneth'. He will not allow you to continue in sin, He will pull you up. He may strike you with illness, He may rob you of a loved one, He may smash your business, He may ruin some bright hopes and prospects you may have. He may level you to the dust, He will not let you go. He has set His mark upon you; you belong to Him, and He is going to perfect you; and nothing is going to stop Him.

You are 'dead indeed unto sin, and you are alive unto God'. If you but realize that, if you but keep on holding it before yourself, and never forget it, it will make you such that you will not fall as you have been falling, you will see everything in a new light, and you will say with the Apostle John, looking forward to the future, 'Every man that hath this hope in him, purifieth himself even as he is pure'. And He will give you the power to purify yourself. He is working within you, and He will show you how to do it. He will lead you on and on, and you will 'grow in grace and in the knowledge of the Lord'; you will increasingly be 'conformed unto the image of his Son'. 'Reckon ye also yourselves likewise to be dead indeed unto sin, but alive unto God, through Jesus Christ our Lord.'

> *O for a thousand tongues to sing*
> *My great Redeemer's praise,*
> *The glories of my God and King,*
> *The triumphs of His grace.*

Twelve

*

*Let not sin therefore reign in your mortal body, that ye should obey
it in the lusts thereof. Neither yield ye your members as instruments
of unrighteousness unto sin: but yield yourselves unto God, as those
that are alive from the dead, and your members as instruments of
righteousness unto God. For sin shall not have dominion over you:
for ye are not under the law, but under grace.*

Romans 6 : 12–14

With this twelfth verse we come, in a sense, to a new section,
at any rate to a new sub-section of the argument which the Apostle
unfolds in this sixth chapter. It brings us to the application in a
practical manner of the argument the Apostle has been working
out in the first eleven verses. Let us, therefore, not lose sight of
the fact that he is still dealing with the false charge that is brought
against his teaching, and which he has mentioned in the first
verse – 'Shall we continue in sin, that grace may abound?' He is
still refuting that charge, and showing how, actually, the effect
of his teaching, when properly understood, is the exact opposite
of what his critics alleged. So far he has been showing it in a purely doctrinal manner, but now he proceeds to work it out along a
more practical line. In verse 12 he states this practical teaching
in general, in verse 13 he puts it in a little more detail; and then
in verse 14 he again reminds us of the one great source of encouragement and of stimulus to us in our effort to put into daily
practice the great principles he has outlined.

When we began our study of the chapter we analysed its con-
tents and showed that it was divided into two sections, the first
section running from verse 1 to verse 14, and the second from
verse 15 to the end of the chapter. We also suggested that we could
sub-divide the first section into verses 1–11, and then verses 12–

14. Here, then, we have now reached this practical section in which the Apostle applies his teaching. It is not surprising therefore that he introduces it with the word 'therefore'. 'Let not sin therefore reign in your mortal body.' There is, in a sense, no more important word in the writings of this Apostle than the word 'therefore'. If we have not learned to watch him when he uses the word 'therefore', we are indeed very ignorant of his method.

He had an essentially logical mind and always builds up a case. He does not make statements at random, but always proceeds from one thing to another; and the connecting link is generally this all-important word 'therefore' – 'Let not sin therefore reign in your mortal body'. Let us look then at some of the important matters he introduces in this particular instance by the use of the word 'therefore'.

First: Doctrine is always to be applied; it is never to be considered as an end in and of itself. That is a statement we could elaborate at great length. Speaking very generally, Christian people today can be divided into two main groups. The larger group is not interested in doctrine at all, but devotes all its attention to practical matters. The second group, a much smaller one, is concerned with doctrine only, and tends not to be interested at all in practical matters. Both, of course, are wrong – again speaking generally. But what is emphasized by this word 'therefore' is that, however much we may have been interested in the argument and doctrine we have met in verses 1–11, they will be of no value to us unless we put them into practice. It is as dangerous to take a purely detached, intellectual, theological, academic interest in doctrine, and to stop at that, as it is not to be interested in doctrine at all.

We are warned constantly in the Scriptures against both these extremes, and also constantly reminded that if we do have a knowledge of doctrine our responsibility is correspondingly greater. 'If', said our blessed Lord Himself – 'If ye know these things, happy are ye if ye do them [*John* 13. 17]. It will avail us nothing in the day of judgment to say that we understood 'all doctrine', or had 'all knowledge' – as the Apostle puts it in the thirteenth chapter of 1 Corinthians – if that has not had a vital effect upon our whole life and conduct and behaviour. 'Let not sin therefore reign in your mortal body.' That is the application of the knowledge. I have been giving you all this doctrine, says

Paul in effect, but beware of the danger of being content with the knowledge alone. Content of that kind is a terrible possibility, a dangerous possibility. What can be more fascinating to some people than Christian doctrine? It can become an intellectual hobby, something that delights the mind without touching the practice and the conduct. That is, according to the Apostle, the most direct way of bringing his teaching into disrepute, because it plays into the hands of this very enemy whom he is refuting, the man who says that it does not matter very much how we live if we are Christians and under grace. That is our first deduction.

The second: As this practical section is the outcome of, and a deduction from, the doctrine that has gone before, what is stated in this practical section, therefore, becomes a very valuable check on our interpretation of the previous section. That, surely, follows of necessity. This section is the logical sequence of verses 1 to 11. So what we find here must correspond to what we said there. It may happen that a consideration of the practical section will tend to contradict or clash with our exposition of the doctrinal section. If that proves to be the case it means that we were wrong in our interpretation of the doctrinal section. The two must go together, they must correspond; they must work in the same direction. I trust that it will become clear, as we proceed, that our previous interpretation was correct when we rejected totally any exposition of the first eleven verses which would teach sinless perfection, or say that a Christian can ever in this life be in a position in which he has nothing whatsoever to do with sin. We have seen enough already, by the mere exhortation in this verse, to convince us that sinless perfection has not been taught in verses 1 to 11.

The third principle can be put in the form of a question. What does this section tell us about ourselves as Christians in our relationship to sin? That is an important matter. We have already been looking at it, of course, in verses 1 to 11, but here again it is put in a very explicit and plain manner. This will help us to see whether or not our interpretation has been correct. You notice that the Apostle seems to draw a distinction here between ourselves and our mortal bodies. He says, 'Let not sin therefore reign in your mortal body' – you, and your mortal body. There is a distinction, clearly, between the two. I must emphasize that he does not say, 'Let not sin reign in you'; what he says is, 'Let not sin reign in your mortal body'. That reminds us of something we noted when we were considering verse 6, 'Knowing this, that our old man is crucified with him, that the body of sin might be destroyed, that henceforth we should not serve sin'. You remember that we interpreted 'the body of sin' as meaning 'sin as it remains in our bodies', and distinct from ourselves as personalities. Here it is once more, 'Let not sin therefore reign in your mortal body'. We must look again at the terms. 'Body' really means what it says; it means literally our physical body. It does not mean our sinful nature.

Even the great John Calvin went astray at that point. He interprets it as 'sinful nature'; but it does not mean that. The Apostle is talking about the body, not about our souls, because he says *mortal* body. That in itself is sufficient to prove that he really does mean the physical body. He does not mean our total personality, for that is not mortal; he means this body of ours, flesh and bones and blood – what we normally mean when we use the term 'body'. And what he says is that you must not let sin reign in your body. But then he adds this adjective, 'mortal'. Why does he call it, significantly, 'your mortal body'? One thing he means is that it is a dying body. He says that to encourage us. The position we are in as Christians is only a temporary one. We ourselves have been saved, but we are still in this life and in this world, and sin is still left in the body. But it is not going to be so for ever, Paul says; it is only temporary because the body is mortal. You have not got to face this for all eternity. It is only something transient; it is going to be our condition only as long as we are in these 'mortal bodies'. No longer! That is a very comforting thought in and of itself.

But there is also a second meaning here. The Apostle is contrasting the mortal body with the body of our glorification that is to come. Take the perfect expression of this which you find in the Epistle to the Philippians, chapter 3 and verse 20. He says, 'Our conversation (citizenship) is in heaven; from whence also we look for (expect) the Saviour, the Lord Jesus Christ: who shall change our vile body, that it may be fashioned like unto his glorious body, according to the working whereby he is able even to subdue all things unto himself'. Here we see the contrast between 'our vile body', or 'the body of our humiliation', 'our mortal body', and what He will yet fashion, namely, a body 'like unto his glorious body,' 'the body of his glorification'. That, I believe, is the very contrast we have here – the 'mortal body' is to be contrasted with the 'glorified body'. This clearly carries the implication that as long as we are in this 'mortal body' we shall be bothered by sin. But there is a day coming when we shall not be bothered by sin in any respect at all. We ourselves are already delivered out of its territory and its realm; but it still remains in the body. But there is a day coming when the body will be glorified, and sin will be altogether finished with and left behind once and for ever.

You notice that in all the teaching concerning the body in Scripture, mortality and corruption are always linked together. Take, for instance, 1 Corinthians 15 verses 50–54, where the Apostle argues saying, 'flesh and blood cannot inherit the kingdom of God; neither doth corruption inherit incorruption'. That is why he says that believers who will be alive on the earth, when the Lord returns, shall be changed. They must be changed, they cannot inherit incorruption while they are in a corruptible body. 'This corruptible', he says, 'must put on incorruption, and this mortal must put on immortality.' In other words, mortality and corruption always go together. So what the Apostle is teaching here, quite clearly, is that while we are in this mortal body, sin will remain in the body. His whole appeal, therefore, is that we are not to allow it to reign and rule in our mortal body.

You notice that the Apostle does not say that sin must not reign in *us*. He cannot say that because he has already told us that our 'old man' has indeed been crucified with Christ, that he is already dead to sin. It is impossible that sin should reign in us who are Christians, but what is possible is that sin should reign in our mortal body. And his exhortation to us is that sin must not be allowed to reign in our mortal body. When he uses a phrase like this, he does so very deliberately. After all he has been arguing in verses 1 to 11, he cannot turn to us suddenly and say, 'therefore, in the light of all this, let not sin reign in you'. He could not possibly say that; he says, 'Let not sin therefore reign in your mortal body'. You yourself have already finished with it – 'dead indeed unto sin'. Christ died unto sin once. 'Reckon ye also yourselves to be dead indeed unto sin, but alive unto God through Jesus Christ our Lord'. Do not go back on that. And clearly the

Apostle himself does not go back on it, so he says, 'Let not sin therefore reign in your mortal body'.

Thus we have seen certain obvious implications of the Apostle's teaching. Let me now present them to you as principles, and emphasize them, so that we may have them clearly in our minds. The first is, as I have already been saying, that sin still remains and is left in our bodies; not in us, but in our bodies. As persons, as souls, we have already finished with it, but not so the body. This body of sin – this body which sin inhabits and tries to use – still remains.

Secondly, sin not only remains in our bodies; but if it is not checked, if it is not kept under, it will even reign in our bodies, and it will dominate our bodies. We must be clear about this teaching – sin is not in me, but in my body. The Apostle tells us that sin, while we are left in this mortal body, will be always seeking to dominate our body, and to dominate us through the body. The way in which it does so, he says, appears in the words, 'Let not sin therefore reign in your mortal body, that ye should obey it in the lusts thereof'. That is exactly what sin does; it turns the natural instincts of the body into lusts. The instincts are good in and of themselves; there is nothing sinful in the natural instincts. But sin tries to turn the natural instincts into 'inordinate affections', into lusts. So what the Apostle asserts here is that, while we are left in this mortal body, sin will go on trying to bring that about. It will try to trip us, it will try to dominate over the body. And we must not allow it to do so. All along, it will be trying to do so, but we must restrain it, we must resist it, we must fight it.

There is no exposition of verse 11 which is quite so wrong as that which regards it as saying (as it has so often been put) that we are to reckon that sin is dead to us, for that is the exact opposite of what the Apostle is saying. He never says that sin is dead; what he does say is that we are dead to sin. He says that sin is not only not dead, but that it is still in our mortal body; and if we do not realize that, and deal with it, it will soon reign in our mortal body. His very appeal insists upon the interpretation, that sin is not only not dead, but that it is very much alive. Sin is not eradicated out of us, and it never will be as long as we are in this mortal body. We must hold on to this word 'mortal' because it is virtually synonymous with 'corruptible'. Sin is in our bodies, and it is always striving for mastery and for control in the Christian. It can never dominate over him again, but it is always striving to dominate his body. It may indeed dominate his body for a time, and when it does so, it is what we call 'backsliding'. It is only the believer, the true Christian, who is capable of backsliding. That, then, is another implication of this extraordinary statement, 'Let not sin therefore reign in your mortal body'. Sin is there; it will always be trying to control and master and reign in your body. You have always to remember that, and not allow it to do so.

It is because of this truth that we have so many statements in the Scripture about this body of ours, and the relationship of sin to it. For instance, we shall see in verse 19 of this chapter that the Apostle puts it in this way, 'I speak after the manner of men because of the infirmity of your flesh: for as ye have yielded your members' – 'members' meaning 'parts of the body' – 'servants to uncleanness, and to iniquity unto iniquity; even so now yield your members servants to righteousness unto holiness'. And when we get to chapter 7 the same teaching will be yet more plain. Take verse 18, 'For I know that in me (that is, in my flesh), dwelleth no good thing'. Or take it in verse 20, 'Now if I do that I would not, it is no more I that do it, but sin that dwelleth in me'. Or again in verse 23, 'But I see another law in my members, warring against the law of my mind, and bringing me into captivity to the law of sin which is in my members' – always, you see, in the body. And so verse 24, 'O wretched man that I am! who shall deliver me from the body of this death?' All those statements are in line with this statement in this twelfth verse which we are studying.

Again, you have the same thing in chapter 8 in verse 23, 'And not only they, but ourselves also, which have the firstfruits of the Spirit, even we ourselves groan within ourselves, waiting for the adoption, to wit, the redemption of our body'. That means the literal physical body, and that he was waiting for the glorification of the physical body. You find precisely the same teaching in chapter 12 in the first verse, 'I beseech you therefore, brethren, by the mercies of God, that ye present your bodies a living sacrifice, holy, acceptable unto God, which is your reasonable service'. The same thing exactly is seen in 1 Corinthians 6: 13, and in 1 Corinthians 9: 27 where he says, 'I keep under my body' – and he means his body physically – 'lest having preached to others, I myself should be a castaway'. He says, I buffet my body, I hit my body, I bruise my body, I pummel my body, I keep under my body, because that is the place in which sin is still resident. He does not pummel himself, but his body.

This is in many ways the key to the understanding of this entire teaching, as it is the key to the understanding of the whole doctrine of sanctification. It is because many expositions lack a clear understanding at this point that there is so much confusion over the question of sanctification, and especially in this sixth chapter of the Epistle to the Romans. Is it clear to us then? I myself as a new man in Christ am dead indeed unto sin, I have nothing more to do with it, and it has nothing more to do with me. I have finished with it as such – I myself. But it is here still in my mortal body, and it will continue to worry me, and I shall have to deal with it as long as I am in the mortal body. Thank God, I know that it can never get me back under its dominion; never again can it master me, never again can it ruin my soul. Impossible! All it can do is to worry me in the body. It cannot affect my salvation, it cannot affect my final destiny – 'sin shall not have dominion over you'. 'Reckon ye yourselves therefore to be dead indeed unto sin, but alive unto God.' Yes! but in the meantime it will go on worrying you. But do not let it master, do not let it reign over your mortal body.

My third deduction therefore is this, that it need not do so; the Apostle's very exhortation to us not to allow it to do so, means that it need not happen of necessity.

There, then, we finish with our third main principle, which was that this verse tells us all about ourselves as Christians in our relationship to sin.

We come now to the fourth main principle. The word 'therefore' introduces us to the New Testament doctrine of holiness and of sanctification. This is obviously a crucial matter. What does it tell us? Let me again emphasize the principles as taught here. What is the first principle in the New Testament doctrine of sanctification? It is, obviously, that this doctrine is something that you and I have to put into practice. An exhortation is addressed to us: Do not allow sin to 'reign in your mortal body'. I deduce from this that sanctification is not a gift to be received. There are many who err at this point. They say, 'You have al-

The New Man

ready received your justification by faith, now you must receive your sanctification by faith'. But sanctification is clearly not a gift to be received, for here, we are face to face with an exhortation.

Secondly, sanctification is not a sudden experience of deliverance once and for ever. It cannot be, because sin is going to remain in the body as long as it is mortal, and as long as sin remains in my body I shall never have an experience of a sudden deliverance once and for ever from sin. I have known numbers of Christian people who have been miserable most of their lives because they have been seeking such a deliverance. They believe that it is possible, they have been taught that it is possible, that in one act they can be entirely rid of sin finally and completely. They have sought it, have longed for it, have tried to get it, but have never succeeded, and so they feel discouraged. Some of them even wonder whether they are Christians at all. It is entirely because they have not understood this chapter. Sin remains in the mortal body, and will remain in the body as long as it is mortal. Therefore we shall never be free from it in that sense. So we must get rid of the thought that there is such a thing as a sudden experience of complete deliverance from sin once and for ever.

It is clear also that the New Testament method of teaching sanctification and holiness is not a constant appeal to us to surrender. That is a very familiar teaching. We are always being taught, and appealed to, to 'surrender' and to 'be willing to be made willing', and so on. We are asked, 'Are you willing to be delivered from sin and to be kept in a sanctified holy state?' If you are uncertain or in trouble the next question is, 'Are you willing to be made willing?' But that is not the teaching here. We are exhorted, rather, to act.

Again, take another negative. The New Testament teaching about sanctification is not just an appeal to us to 'look to the Lord', or as it is sometimes put, 'Allow Him to live His life in you'. We are told, 'Your trouble is due to the fact that you are struggling and fighting against sin; and, of course, you are defeated. That is where you go wrong. You have nothing to do but to surrender yourself, and to look to the Lord and to allow Him to live His life in you. He will give you victory, and He will keep you victorious, and you will have no more trouble.' Has not that been the teaching, the prevailing teaching, common in

evangelical circles for a hundred years or so? All I ask is this –
How do you reconcile that teaching with this, 'Let not sin therefore reign in your mortal body'? That is an exhortation addressed
to us, an admonition, a call to a positive activity of the will.

Is it not clear that the other teaching is unscriptural in that it
by-passes the Scriptures. Indeed it ignores much scriptural
teaching. It makes the second half of most of the New Testament Epistles entirely unnecessary, because it tells us that we
have nothing to do but simply to realize that we must stop struggling, and just allow the Lord to live His victorious life in us,
and all will be well. But here we are given these practical exhortations; and we shall find the Apostle putting them in actual detail,
as he does in other Epistles. He tells the Ephesians not to steal
any more, and not to use foolish talking and jesting, not to lie to
one another. He is urging them not to do such things. Yet this
other teaching dismisses all that, and says that we have nothing
to do but to be 'willing to be made willing', and to allow the Lord
to live His life in us, and all will be well. But the exhortation in
this verse is addressed to us, and obviously must be because of
the doctrine which Paul has been elaborating in the first eleven
verses.

'But', asks someone, 'how do you reconcile all this with what
you have been telling us in the previous verses? You have assured us that because we are under grace, and not under the Law,
and not under the power of sin, that our sanctification is absolutely guaranteed, that God is going to do it. You have been
emphasizing that, how do you reconcile that with what you are
saying now?' It seems to me that the reconciliation is quite
simple. God accomplishes this great work through us; that is
His way of doing it. Turn to Philippians Chapter 2 verses 12 and
13: 'Work out your own salvation with fear and trembling, for
(because) it is God that worketh in you both to will and to do.'
Of course it is God's work, but this is God's way of doing it.
He does not accomplish it by telling us to do nothing and just
to 'look to the Lord' or to 'let go and let God'. God tells us to do
it in the way taught in this twelfth verse. This is the New Testament method of sanctification. What exactly is it?

Sanctification proceeds as we are led by the Holy Spirit to draw
deductions from the doctrine we have already considered. 'Let
not sin therefore reign in your mortal body.' We have to imple-

ment this 'therefore', we have to draw certain deductions, we have to see that certain things are inevitable as the result of the doctrine that has already been laid down.

That brings us to the actual practical details. Do you long to be holy? Do you long to have victory over sin in your mortal body? How can you do so? First, understand the doctrine. You cannot work out the 'therefore' unless you are clear about the doctrine. Have you understood verses 1 to 11? Have you understood what the Apostle means by saying that you cannot 'continue in sin that grace may abound' because you are already dead to sin? Have you understood that you have really died to sin, that your old man has been crucified with Christ? Do you know what it means to 'Reckon yourself to be dead indeed unto sin' as Christ is dead unto sin? Understanding the doctrine – that is the place to start. You must not say, 'I am not interested in doctrine; all I do is to look to Christ and allow Him to live His life in me'. The 'therefore' insists that you must understand the doctrine. Then, having understood it, you must remind yourself of it constantly. 'Reckon' – go on reckoning, keep on reckoning, realize it, apply it to yourself, and then draw the inevitable deductions from it.

What are the deductions? Here are some of them. If I really believe and understand the doctrine, and realize its implications, I am bound to ask this question: What sort of a person ought I to be in the light of this doctrine? You cannot consider the doctrine truly without drawing that deduction. Here is the truth about me; I have died with Christ! Why have I died with Christ? You are bound to ask the question. If you really understand the doctrine, you say, 'What is my position now? What sort of a man or a woman ought I to be in the light of all that has happened to me?' And, immediately, you are promoting your sanctification; you are beginning to turn against sin as it resides in your mortal body.

In the same way the doctrine provides us with the true motives for holiness. What are the true motives for holiness? They are not just a reaction against the evil nature of sin, they are not just the desire to be happy. These are a part of it, but not the chief motive. Still less should we seek to be holy in order to make ourselves Christians; and still less merely because we are afraid of hell and the punishment of hell. Our motives must be entirely positive. Why must I not allow sin to reign in my mortal body? Because I am a man who claims to know what God's purpose is for me. And what is God's purpose for me? It is that all the works of the devil shall be undone in me. God made me in His own image, He made me perfect; and His whole purpose in salvation is to bring me back to that state. I believe that, I know that, I realize that; therefore I cannot allow sin to reign in my mortal body. That is my motive. I know what God's purpose for me is, and all He has planned, and all He has brought to pass. That is my grand motive, but there are others.

I know what the Lord Jesus Christ has done for me. Knowing this doctrine, I believe that the second Person in the blessed holy Trinity left the courts of heaven and came into this world, and not only lived as a man but humbled Himself so as to come in the likeness of sinful flesh. I believe that He went to Calvary and bore my sins in His own body on the tree, and suffered the agony and the indignity of it all for me. Why did He do all that? That we might continue in sin? No! but 'that He might redeem us from all iniquity and purify unto Himself a peculiar people zealous of good works' [*Titus* 2: 14]. So how can we go on with sin?

These are the motives, this is the way in which I become sanctified. It is because I know these things that I will not allow sin to reign in my mortal body. I therefore go on to draw this deduction, that the very honour of God, and of the Lord Jesus Christ, is involved in this matter of my behaviour. I claim to be a child of God, I claim to be one who has been adopted into the family of God, I am of the household of God. I believe this, the doctrine has taught me this, therefore I say to myself: 'If I allow sin to reign in my mortal body I am disgracing my Father, my Saviour, and the family of heaven to which I belong. I cannot do that.' This is how the New Testament teaches sanctification: 'Sanctify them through thy truth; thy word is truth' [*John* 17: 17]. It is the truth that sanctifies: 'Ye shall know the truth and the truth shall make you free', said our Lord to the people [*John* 8: 32]. The truth that makes us free is that which tells us who we are, what we are, what has been done for us, and how the whole honour of the family is, as it were, in our hands. It does not just say to me, 'let go and let God', or 'do nothing but allow Him to live His life in you'. Reason it out, it says, work it out. 'Let not sin therefore reign in your mortal body.'

The truth reminds me constantly of the wonderful position in which I am. I can say that sin and death shall never again have dominion over me. They had dominion over me in Adam, but never again. I have been separated from that dominion, I have been crucified with Christ. My old man is dead. I am already seated with Christ in the heavenly places. And it is as I realize these things that I say, 'sin shall not reign in my mortal body'. Or, if you like, you can argue in this way. If I allow sin to reign in my mortal body, then I am in an utterly contradictory position. I say I believe the Gospel, I believe in Christ in order that I may be delivered, and that as the result of my belief I am in this new position; and yet I go on living as if I were not in a new position. I am utterly contradictory, I am in an utterly foolish and untenable position.

Not only that! If I allow sin to reign in my mortal body, it is a complete denial of everything that I claim to be looking forward to. As a Christian who understands this doctrine, I say that I know that a day is coming when Christ shall have conquered every enemy and shall reign over all. My mortal body shall then be glorified, I shall be with Him and like Him. I say that on the one hand; and on the other hand, I am living the old life as if I had never heard all these things at all and as if I had not believed them. It is utterly contradictory. These are the doctrines which we are told to apply; these are the deductions which we are meant to draw.

But I have yet another reflection. If I allow sin to reign in my mortal body I am then setting myself against the purpose of God in me and in my salvation, and there is nothing more dangerous that a believer can ever do than that. 'This is the will of God, even your sanctification' [1 *Thessalonians* 4 : 3], and He is working out that purpose. We are under the reign of grace, and nothing can overthrow it. I have been emphasizing that repeatedly in all the eleven verses. If, therefore, I allow sin to reign in my mortal body, what am I doing? I am for the time being standing against the purpose of God in me. And what will happen? I do not know what may happen to me. What the Apostle says to the members of the church at Corinth is this, 'For this cause many are weak and sickly among you, and many sleep' [1 *Corinthians* 11 : 30]. There were Christian people in Corinth who were allowing sin to reign in their mortal bodies. The result was, says Paul, that some of them were ill, and some had actually died. In the same way the Epistle to the Hebrews teaches that 'Whom the Lord loveth he chasteneth' [12 : 6ff]; and if you do not endure chastisement in some shape or form at some time or another, you are not a son, you are a bastard. God's purpose is to make us holy, and He is working in us to that end, so if we stand against His purpose by allowing sin to reign in our mortal body, we must not be surprised if we are chastised and chastened. It may be by an illness, or by an accident, or by death, or by sorrow. If you belong to Him He will bring you to the desired goal of holiness; therefore a man who allows sin to reign in his mortal body is exposing himself to the chastisement of the love of God. Is there anything more foolish, more insane, than that?

The final deduction is this: the very exhortation, in the light of the doctrine that has preceded it, reminds us of what is possible to us and for us. 'Let not sin therefore reign in your mortal body.' 'But wait a minute', says someone, 'are you not putting me back in the position I was in before I was a Christian?' That is certainly not the case, because what Paul says is 'Let not sin *therefore* reign in your mortal body'. I know that there is nothing more futile than to turn to a natural man and to say, 'Conquer sin, do not let it reign in your mortal body'. He cannot act thus, he is the slave of sin, he is under the dominion and power of sin. It is useless to tell him not to let it reign; it will reign in him and his body, and it does reign. But I am not talking to him. I say 'Let not sin *therefore* reign in your mortal body'. Who are you? Oh, you are the man who has died with Christ, who has been crucified with Christ; you are the man who is 'alive unto God'; you are the man in whom the Spirit of God is working; you are the man in whom God's great purpose has been set moving. You have got the power in you, and therefore I can exhort you. 'Therefore' – the doctrine has already told you that 'Greater is he that is in you than he that is in the world', so you are left without any excuse at all. You are not left to battle with sin alone and by your own power. Because you are a child of God the Spirit of God is in you, the mind of Christ is in you, the purpose of God is working itself out in you. And it is because of this that we are not told just to 'let go and let God', or to be passive and to allow Christ to live His life in us; but, instead, 'Let not sin therefore (do not let sin therefore) reign in your mortal body'.

You are in a position to stop it. 'Resist the devil and he will flee from you.' 'Your adversary the devil, as a roaring lion, walketh about seeking whom he may devour; whom resist steadfast in the faith' [1 *Peter* 5 : 8, 9]. If you do that, you will conquer him, you will defeat him. For us as Christians, there is no need for sin to reign in our mortal bodies, because God is working in us both to will and to do of His good pleasure, and has given us the power to resist.

There, then, we have the introduction, as it were, to the New Testament doctrine of sanctification, introduced by this important and vital word 'Therefore'. In the light of the glorious doctrine of verses 1 to 11, 'Let not sin therefore reign in your mortal body, that ye should obey it in the lusts thereof'.

Thirteen

*

*Neither yield ye your members as instruments of unrighteousness
unto sin; but yield yourselves unto God, as those that are alive from
the dead, and your members as instruments of righteousness unto
God.* Romans 6 : 13

The theme of this verse is clearly a continuation of what we have
already considered in verse 12. Indeed verses 12, 13 and 14 should
be taken together because they are a part of one statement. It is
the practical application of the doctrine laid down in verses 1 to
11. We must bear in mind also that the Apostle's object in doing
this, in giving the doctrine and the practical application, is to
refute and to dismiss once and for ever the suggestion that had
been made that this doctrine of justification by faith only, and the
assurance which follows from it, is a teaching which encourages
people to say 'Shall we continue in sin that grace may abound?'
The Apostle's object is to show that that is a monstrous suggestion, that both the doctrine, and the inevitable practical deductions from it, indeed lead to the opposite result, namely, that we
are delivered from sin and the practice of sin.

'Therefore', says the Apostle in verse 12 – and this 'therefore'
as we saw is most important – 'let not sin reign in your mortal
body'. The 'therefore' still continues in this 13th verse. We have
seen the light that this teaching throws on the New Testament
doctrine and teaching with regard to sanctification and holiness.

But the Apostle does not leave the matter at this point. He says
that not only must we not allow sin to reign in our mortal bodies,
we must not even afford it any opportunity of doing so. Still
less must we make any provision for it to do so, or in any way
encourage it to do so. This is a theme that the Apostle often deve-
lops. We shall find at the end of chapter 13 where he says, 'Put

[163]

ye on the Lord Jesus Christ, and make not provision for the flesh'; and he is really anticipating that exhortation in the verse we are now studying. Obviously, therefore, this is something which we must consider in detail; the Apostle compels us to do so by the very terms which he uses in pressing the matter. At the same time let us remember that we are considering the New Testament teaching concerning holiness and sanctification. This is essential, indeed almost classical New Testament teaching on this subject which to so many seems to be so confusing and 'hard to be understood'.

We resume our study of it, therefore, by calling attention to the fact that once more we are confronted by a command, by an exhortation: 'Neither yield ye your members.' These words are addressed to our wills; this is something that we are told to do, something, therefore, that we can do. I emphasize this once more for this reason, that any teaching concerning sanctification or holiness which tells us that we really have nothing to do, and that the main call to us is to stop trying to do anything in the matter of our sanctification, is obviously a contradiction of this. There is, as I have already indicated, a teaching that does that quite definitely. It says that sanctification is quite simple, that the mistake you have been making all your life is that you have been trying to fight the sin that is in you, that that is where you have gone astray. What you have to do is to give up struggling, to give up fighting; you have just to hand yourself and your whole problem to the Lord Jesus Christ, and He will do it for you and in you. The greatest mistake of all, they say, is to attempt to fight sin; our business is rather to stop trying to do so. I am suggesting that that teaching cannot be reconciled with the verse we are considering, any more than it can be reconciled with the previous verse. 'You must not allow sin to reign in your mortal body,' says the Apostle, 'neither must you yield your members as instruments of unrighteousness unto sin.' So a teaching which tells us that sanctification and holiness are really quite simple is clearly not in accord with this. Yet we are told that it is as simple as is the case of a man in a dark room with glorious sunshine outside. All he needs to do is to lift up the blind or draw back the curtains, and the moment he does so the sunshine comes streaming in, the darkness is dispelled and the problem is solved!

How can such teaching be reconciled with the Apostle's teaching here, with these verses that call upon us not to do one thing, and to do another? In both instances these verses call upon us to do something. They do not tell us that we can do nothing, and that we merely have to allow the Lord to do it for us. They are both exhortations, and nowhere is the impression given that it is as simple as allowing the sunshine to come in to a darkened room and then just abiding in that position.

These matters are of urgent and vital importance because there is great confusion concerning them. There are people, as I say, who seem to spend the whole of their lives in trying to surrender themselves; whereas the first thing that is needed is that we should realize that this is an appeal addressed to us as Christians to exercise our wills, to do certain things and not to do other things.

Let us then follow the Apostle as he works this out in detail. His command divides itself into two sections, a negative and a positive. Let us start with the negative: 'Neither yield ye your members as instruments of unrighteousness unto sin.' We must sub-divide this negative again into two sections. In the first we have what the Apostle does say to us, in the second, what he does not say to us. They are both very important.

First let us take what he does say to us, and observe the terms he uses. He says that we must not yield our members unto sin. That is the best way to read it, 'Neither yield ye your members unto sin as instruments of unrighteousness'. Notice that once more, as he has already done in chapter 5, and elsewhere, the Apostle personalizes sin. He regards sin, as it were, as a great power, a great enemy which is confronting us. He does this, of course, in order to make the matter real and vivid to us, and to bring it to us with force. Sin is a great enemy who is always looking for his opportunity; and we must always bear that in mind. Here, then, is the exhortation – you must not yield your members to sin, to this enemy.

What does he mean by 'members'? The context surely determines the answer. The members are the parts of that mortal body to which he has already been referring; they are the various parts of the body in which the powers, the faculties, the propensities which we all have as natural men and women reside. The various activities of our bodies, our physical bodies as such, come into this category of 'members'. It does not stop at that. The term also includes the mental powers, the power of thought, the power of reason, the power of imagination. It seems to me that in this teaching it is quite clear that the Apostle puts all such things under this general heading of 'the mortal body'. The natural man has brains, he has understanding, he has mental powers which he can use, he has imagination. All these belong in a sense to the physical man and are parts, therefore, or members of this mortal body. But the term also includes the emotions. In other words the term 'members' is a way of describing the functioning of man. A man is a being who is endowed with these powers and faculties and propensities. And so the Apostle, having talked about the mortal body as a whole in verse 12, now divides it up into its component parts. He lays emphasis upon the fact that not only are we not to allow sin to reign in the body as a whole, but we are not to present any single part or portion of the manifestation of the activity of this bodily life to sin, to this power that is against us.

That brings us to consider the word 'yield'. Here is a word which the translators handle in differing ways. But surely it means, 'present', 'put at the disposal of', 'allow to use', or 'allow to be of service to'. Here is this power, the power of sin personalized, as over against God, and what the Apostle tells us here is that we must not present these members of the body – these powers and faculties and propensities – we must not put them at the disposal of sin, the tremendous power that is always anxious to get hold of them, and to use them.

Then we come to the word 'instruments'. 'Neither yield ye your members unto sin as instruments of unrighteousness'. Here again is a very interesting word. Some would argue that this word should be translated as 'weapons', as if the Apostle is saying 'Do not present your members, the parts of your body and the faculties of your body, to sin, that he may use them as weapons in the warfare that he is waging against God and the forces of light'. I believe that there is good reason for regarding it partly in that way. But whether it is as definite and as positive as that, I am not quite sure. But it certainly means what is indicated by the word 'instruments' which appears in the Authorized Version. Sin personalized has his programme. We have already read in chapter 5, verse 21 about 'sin reigning unto death'. He is a mighty power, and he has reigned unto death. He uses certain means in order to extend his kingdom, and to manifest his reign, and to introduce the death and the chaos that he is anxious to produce. 'Do not allow anything that is in you,' says the Apostle, 'to be used by him as an instrument'. That is what it really means. The word 'instrument' means anything which enables him to bring his purposes to pass, and to extend his rule.

Paul's reason for saying all this, of course, is that the ultimate end and object of sin, and of the devil, and all that belongs to that realm of darkness and of evil, is to lead to unrighteousness. What is unrighteousness? It is everything that is opposed to God who is eternal and everlasting righteousness. God is a righteous God; He declares Himself to be such. So unrighteousness is everything that is opposed to His rule, to His reign, to His way of life. It is that, therefore, which is not straight; it is not upright, it is not true, it is not beautiful. It is twisted, perverted, foul, and ugly. It is evil in and of itself, and it leads to consequences which are always evil and ugly and foul. So the Apostle makes this statement; he presents us with this command. We can sum up his message in this way. We all have these powers and faculties, says the Apostle, but you must never allow a single one of them in any way, or in any shape or form, to become an instrument of sin; because that will only lead to unrighteousness.

It is important that we should not only grasp this as a principle, but that we should really work it out in detail. The Apostle does this for us in the Epistle to the Colossians. In doing so he says among other things, 'But now ye also put off all these; anger, wrath, malice, blasphemy, filthy communication out of your mouth. Lie not one to another . . .' [*Colossians* 3 : 5–9]. He goes on later to put the matter in its positive form. That is what we must learn to do in detail. We must not allow any one of the faculties of the body to be used in the service of sin. I must not allow my strength, I must not allow my energy, my appetites, my speech, my mind, my thinking, I must not allow my imagination or my emotions – all these things which are part of me and the expression of my personality – I must now allow any one of them ever to be used by sin, and in the service of sin.

Such is the picture that Paul draws of our fight against sin. We have to be aware of this enemy all the time: that is why you find so frequently in the New Testament exhortations to watch, to be on guard. That is why we are told to 'put on the whole

armour of God'. It is because there is always this threat from the
devil and sin trying to get at us in one form or another. If the
devil cannot get at you in your physical frame he will get at you
in your mind; if he cannot do it through the mind he will do it
through the imagination; and if he cannot succeed there, he will
attempt it in a subtle way through your emotions. He does not
care how he does it as long as he can get some part of you, or some
expression of your personality, and use it for his own nefarious
ends. So the Apostle tells us that we must never allow this to
happen.

One has only to speak thus, to realize immediately how frequently we are guilty of this, how frequently we allow our imagination, for instance, to be taken hold of, and to be used, by sin
and the devil. There are certain things which we would not dream
of doing actually with our bodies, but we have often enjoyed
doing them in imagination. But that means presenting one of
our members to sin, that sin may use it as an instrument of unrighteousness. It is not sufficient that we regard ourselves as a
whole; we must also regard ourselves in parts and portions.
Many of us, perhaps, peculiarly need this particular exhortation
and command. We are responsible for every one of our members.
Whatever or whichever it may be does not matter; we must always be keeping our eye upon them all. It is not enough that I
do not sin with my literal physical body. Do Is in in my mind,
in my imagination? Do I sin in thought, in my emotions? To do
so in any one of these ways is to be guilty of handing over, of
presenting to sin – the great enemy of man and of God – these
vital powers that have been given to us by the great and glorious
Creator.

In other words we can sum it up in this way; these powers
and faculties and propensities which we all have are in themselves
good and harmless. But they can always be used in one way or
the other, good or bad; and the devil and sin are always trying to
get hold of them. That does not mean that, when the devil and
sin are using them, they themselves are bad; it is, rather, that they
are being used by the wrong power. In verse 17 of this same chapter the Apostle puts it quite clearly, and, indeed, in verse 19
particularly it is still more clear. 'God be thanked', he says, 'that
ye were the servants of sin, but ye have obeyed from the heart
that form of doctrine which was delivered you' [verse 17], and

'Being then made free from sin, ye became the servants of righte-ousness' [verse 18]. Then verse 19, 'I speak after the manner of men because of the infirmity of your flesh; for as ye have yielded your members servants to uncleanness and to iniquity unto ini-quity, even so now yield your members' – the same members exactly – 'servants to righteousness unto holiness'. The 'servants' are still the same. A man who in the past used his mind, his brain, his ingenuity, his imagination, his gift of speech or of eloquence, or whatever it was, the man who used all those in the past as servants of sin, is now to use exactly the same powers as instru-ments and servants unto righteousness and unto God. We do not receive new 'members', new faculties when we are converted. They are the same as they were before; the difference is that they are no longer being used on the side of sin but now on the side of God. The exhortation, therefore, is, Do not be content with not allowing sin to reign in your mortal body; never in any shape or form even allow sin to make use of any faculty or power that you may happen to have. That is the negative aspect of the exhortation.

But now let me point out what he does not say under the negative. This is of extreme importance. Had you noticed that there is a kind of lack of balance in this verse? 'Neither yield ye your members as instruments of unrighteousness unto sin, but yield yourselves unto God as those that are alive from the dead, and your members as instruments of righteousness unto God'. Do you notice the difference? There is something lacking on the negative side which the Apostle puts in on the positive. It is the word 'yourselves'. He tells us positively to 'yield ourselves unto God'; but he does not tell us not to yield ourselves unto sin. Is there any importance in that, or is it just accidental? Did he just forget to say that on the negative side, and then suddenly remember it when he came to the positive side? No, we believe that the Apostle was divinely inspired, and that there are no accidents in what he wrote, and no omissions. This is something deliberate; and it must be so in view of the doctrine of verses 1 to 11. He does not tell us not to yield ourselves unto sin, for this reason, that we cannot do so if we wanted to. Is that going too far? No, for the reason that I am simply repeating what the Apostle has been saying from verses 1 to 11. He has already asked in verse 2, 'How shall we that have died unto sin' – you remember I emphasized that it was the aorist, that it belongs to the past, indeed, that it means 'once and for all' – 'live any longer therein?'

But look at the verses where he says it quite explicitly, namely, verses 8 to 10: 'Now if we be dead with Christ, we believe that we shall also live with him: Knowing this, that Christ being raised from the dead dieth no more; death hath no more dominion over him. For in that he died, he died unto sin once' – 'once and for ever', 'once and for all', 'once and never to be repeated', 'once and for ever, finally, eternally' – 'but in that he liveth, he liveth unto God'. Then verse 11, 'Likewise reckon ye also yourselves to be dead indeed unto sin'. Exactly as He is dead unto sin, exactly as He has died unto sin once and for all, a death never to be repeated, so you have died unto sin once and for all, a death never to be repeated. Because of that the Apostle would be wasting words if he said to you 'Do not yield yourselves unto sin'. You cannot do so, it is impossible. If you yielded yourselves again unto sin, then you would have to die once more unto sin; but you cannot do that, because you have died once and for all, and once and for ever, unto sin; and it cannot be repeated. It cannot be repeated in you any more than it can be repeated in Him. 'Likewise . . .' So he does not tell us not to yield ourselves unto sin, because there is no need to do so, indeed it would be foolish to do so.

Had you realized that, because you are a Christian, you cannot yield yourself unto sin? You are under the reign of grace, you are in Christ. There are certain things that as Christians we cannot do, and that is one of them. We can never yield ourselves unto sin. We shall find the same truth again, and yet more strongly, in verse 14. But it is already here in what Paul does not say. Incidentally, as we go along, let me exhort you as Bible students to be careful to observe what the Bible does not say almost as much as to observe what it does say.

We can now come to the positive side. The Apostle Paul never stops at a negative; the Gospel never stops at a negative. The negative is absolutely essential, but if the Gospel stopped at negatives it would be morality and not a Gospel; and this is not morality, this is Christianity, this is spirituality. Your moralists, your good men, your good men of the world stop at the negative, they are interested in the negative. They have to be; they would have nothing to say if they could not talk about morality. They can see that man by nature ever tends to produce sheer chaos, so they hold on to their morality; but it is entirely negative.

The difference between Christianity and morality is seen at a point like this. Christianity never stops at the negative, it always goes on to the positive. We are not simply called to be moral; we are called to be holy, we are called to be sanctified. So the Apostle goes on to his positive, and this is how he puts it: 'Present yourselves, therefore, unto God.' Yes – yourselves. This is something you can do. You cannot present yourself to sin, but you can present yourself to God. Why? Because of what has been done for you. It is possible for us as Christians to put ourselves at God's disposal, to yield our wills to God, to allow God to use us. This is because of the work of the Lord Jesus Christ for us. The Apostle puts it in this way. He says, 'Present yourselves unto God as those that are alive from the dead'. None but the Christian can present himself to God; the unbeliever cannot do so, because he is 'dead in trespasses and sins'.

The most terrible thing about the unbeliever is that he can never be used in this vital sense as an instrument of God. God can use him in a mechanical way, but He cannot use him in this living sense in the furtherance of His purposes of righteousness. He could use the Chaldeans, He could use Cyrus, and did so, but only in a negative sense. But in His great scheme and plan of righteousness, He cannot use an unbeliever; the non-Christian is disqualified, he is outside. He is like a man who volunteers to fight in an army, but who after being examined is rejected as unfit. But as Christians we are fit, because we are 'alive from the dead'. We are no longer dead in trespasses and sins. 'You hath he quickened, who were dead in trespasses and sins' – 'quickened together with Christ', 'baptized into him', as we have seen in the first eleven verses. 'Buried with him, risen with him'; alive unto God in Him and with Him! Those are the terms and all the rich content that is included in them. It is Christians alone who have an entry into the presence of God; and in the presence of God we can present ourselves, and all that we have.

'Present' means, as I have been saying on the negative side, 'Put yourselves at His service', 'put yourselves at His disposal'. Have you ever marvelled at the thought of what a privilege it is, that you can put yourself at the disposal of God? Nobody but a

Christian can do that. You must be alive before you can do that. You can enter as it were into God's recruiting office and present yourself; you can enlist and you will be accepted. You have been given the necessary qualifications, and you are taken in, and become a member of this heavenly army; and you begin to engage in this heavenly crusade.

Or to put it in another way, what Paul says here is what he says also in 2 Corinthians 5 : 15 : 'We thus judge', he says, 'that if one died for all, then were all dead, that they which live should no longer live unto themselves, but unto him that died for them, and rose again'. The Bible strikes this note repeatedly. Christians are not to live to themselves, or for themselves; they are to live for God, they are to live for the Lord Jesus Christ. 'Ye are not your own, ye are bought with a price' [1 *Corinthians* 6 : 19, 20]. So the first thing the Christian has to realize is that he must present himself to God. He gives up self-interest. Our Lord had anticipated it all Himself. In Matthew's Gospel chapter 16 He is recorded as saying, 'If any man will come after me, let him deny himself, and take up his cross (daily), and follow me' [verse 24]. That is a call to self-denial, to live no longer to ourselves. We lived to and for ourselves when we were 'dead'; we are 'alive from the dead' now, and we now live, not for self, but for God. 'Yield yourselves, present yourselves, unto God.'

But, again, the Apostle does not stop there, he goes on into the details. 'Present yourselves', he says, 'unto God, and your members as instruments of righteousness unto God'. Frances Ridley Havergal, in her well-known hymn which begins with the words 'Take my life and let it be, consecrated Lord to Thee', does something which is of real value. She gives a list of the various members or parts that we present to God. But she puts these things in the wrong order; she put the details first, and then ends by saying –

> *Take myself, and I will be*
> *Ever, only, all for Thee*

She ends with presenting herself. Paul starts with that, and having started with the self he goes on to the members. It is a great pity that she reversed the order; but there is value in the hymn in that it does remind us that we do not stop at the general action of presenting ourselves to God. Having presented ourselves we go on in detail to present all our members, our every faculty.

This is a most important consideration in the matter of our sanctification. Many a man has drifted into antinomianism because he has not realized the importance of presenting his members as well as presenting himself. He says, 'I have given myself', and then is negligent about his members. Immediately the devil seizes his opportunity. We must present the members, every one of them, all of them, to God, as well as ourselves as such; indeed, all that we are and have and hope to be must be put at His disposal. We are to live altogether for His praise and for His glory. And there is every inducement to do so. God's purposes are righteous. We are to present our members, therefore, as 'instruments of righteousness'. God, the God of all righteousness, is fighting this foul enemy, the world, the flesh, and the devil, sin and all its power, so what the Apostle is saying is this: Give all you have to this other side, enlist in the army of God, let all your powers be used as His weapons to destroy evil and sin and unrighteousness, and to bring in the Kingdom of light and of glory and of truth. That is the Apostle's exhortation, that is his commandment here, that far from doing anything in any way to encourage the success of that old power from which we have been delivered, we should do the exact opposite. Positively and actively, we should be engaged in this mighty crusade of righteousness and of truth which is God's crusade.

Thus we have gone through the details of the commandment, the exhortation. But you notice that in doing that certain great principles have been emerging, and I must note them as I close. There are vital principles concerning the New Testament doctrine of the method of holiness and of sanctification taught in this verse. In the first place, one of the most fatal things we can ever do in connection with sanctification is to start with ourselves; and yet I suspect that if we examined ourselves, and were honest, most of us would have to admit that we have almost invariably done so. Our chief reason for being interested in holiness and sanctification is that we are having a terrible fight and battle with sin. We tend to fall constantly and to go down. What can I do about this problem of sin and evil that is in me? Where can I find relief? Is that not the way we almost invariably start with this matter? It is utterly and entirely wrong. That is not the way in which the Apostle deals with it here or anywhere else. We are subjective, and, so often, holiness teaching meets us on the grounds of our own subjectivity. Here am I thus struggling and striving, defeated and unhappy. Suddenly I look at an advertisement which says, 'Come to the clinic'. I am quoting actual words that are used – 'Come to the clinic'. What you need, we are told, is to come to the clinic, to the spiritual hospital, and here your sickness and your illness can be dealt with. But as I read the verses that we are studying I see no suggestion whatsoever of a clinic. Rather, I find a barracks; not a hospital, but a military centre. What do I need? what do I find? I do not find a doctor here. What we all need is not a doctor, but a sergeant major. Here we are, as it were, slouching about the parade ground, feeling our own pulses, feeling miserable, talking about our weakness. So we say, 'I need a doctor, I need to go to the clinic, I need to see the Medical Officer'. But that is not right. What you need is to listen to the voice of the sergeant major who is there shouting out the commands of God to you – "Let not sin reign in your mortal body'. 'Yield not your members as instruments of unrighteousness unto sin.' 'Yield yourself unto God.' You have no business to be slouching about like that; stand on your feet, realize who and what you are, enlisted in the army of God. 'Present yourself.' This is not a clinic.

The main trouble with the Christian Church today is that she is too much like a clinic, too much like a hospital; that is why the great world is going to hell outside! 'We are all suffering' – to quote Charles Lamb again – 'with the mumps and measles of the soul' and feeling our own pulses and talking about ourselves, and our moods and subjective states. We have lost the concept of the army of God, and the King of righteousness in this fight against the kingdom of evil. 'What can I do to be delivered?' we tend to say. I answer: Look at the great campaign, look at it objectively, look at it from God's standpoint. Forget yourself and your temporary troubles and ills for the moment: fight in the army. It is not a clinic you need; you must realize that we are in a barracks, and that we are involved in a mighty campaign.

In the second place, we must go on to realize that this is a question of service. We persist in thinking of it in terms of 'my feelings' and 'my failure' or 'my success'. But Paul bids us look at it in terms of service! When you fall to that sin, the real trouble is not so much the particular thing you have done, or the badness of the thing. That is important, I agree; but there is something much worse; it is that you, for whom Christ died, have allowed sin to use a faculty that is in you. That is the way to look at it. Holiness is a matter of service, not of feelings and subjective moods and states, not a matter of experiences. We are meant to be serving the living God with the whole of our being; and no part of us is ever meant to be used, and must not be used, in the service of sin. We must not fraternize with the enemy. That is the New Testament way of teaching holiness. What most of us need is not a clinic, but to listen to the sergeant major drilling his troops, commanding them, warning them, threatening them, showing them what to do. The New Testament teaching is altogether different from the sentimentality and subjectivity that have controlled holiness and sanctification teaching for so long, and which tell us that it is 'quite simple'. But it is not easy. 'Fight the good fight of faith' says the New Testament. Play the man. 'Quit yourselves as men'; 'Put on the whole armour of God'; 'stand in the evil day'. Those are all military commands; there is nothing of the clinic about them. We must get rid of that notion of the clinic and the hospital; and we must look at these things more in terms of God and His glory, and the great campaign which He inaugurated through the Son of His love, and which He is going to bring to a triumphant conclusion.

The thought, then, that should be supreme in our minds is that it is the King and His service that matters; and that what I must be concerned about is not so much the condition and state of my soul, as my relationship to Him, and my value to Him, and my value in His Kingdom. Let us get rid of the flabby, sentimental ideas, and this morbid interest in ourselves, and our desire simply for something to help us. Let us get rid of that approach altogether, for it is unscriptural and wrong. Let us look at the position, rather, in this manly, strong, positive manner in which the Apostle puts it here, as indeed he puts it in all his teaching concerning this matter of sanctification everywhere. It is only as we look at it in this way that we shall see the privilege of our position. Sin will then become unthinkable. We shall not allow it to reign in our mortal body, or yield any one of our faculties or members as 'instruments of unrighteousness unto sin', but, positively, we shall 'yield ourselves unto God . . . and our members as instruments of righteousness unto God'.

Fourteen

*

Let not sin therefore reign in your mortal body, that ye should obey it in the lusts thereof. Neither yield ye your members as instruments of unrighteousness unto sin: but yield yourselves unto God, as those that are alive from the dead, and your members as instruments of righteousness unto God. For sin shall not have dominion over you; for ye are not under the law, but under grace.

Romans 6 : 12–14

We have seen that in working out his particular argument the Apostle lays down certain vital principles characteristic of the New Testament teaching concerning holiness and sanctification. The first is this, that in this matter of holiness and sanctification we must never start with ourselves and our problems. Far too many Christians regard the Christian Church merely as a clinic, a hospital, instead of realizing that it is more like a barracks. 'Quit yourselves as men'; 'endure hardness as a good soldier of Jesus Christ'. Those are the phrases, the exhortations, we constantly find in the New Testament.

The second principle is that we must look at this matter always in terms of service to God. If we were but animated by this controlling conception of ourselves as having the privilege of being God's servants and channels and instruments, it would solve the problem of our personal holiness and sanctification. We are all so subjective, we are always thinking about ourselves, examining ourselves, and feeling our spiritual pulse. That is the wrong approach. We must look at the matter in terms of our calling, and think of what God has done for us. Not only that, but we must realize also that He can use us in His great Kingdom. That is the healthy New Testament approach over and against the unhealthy 'clinic,' subjective approach that has been so commonly taught.

But there are two further principles. The New Testament always presents this doctrine of holiness and sanctification by reminding us of who we are and what we are. That is really what the Apostle has been doing in the first eleven verses of this chapter. He has told us that we are free from sin, free from the dominion, the domain, the whole power of sin; indeed that we are dead to it. As the Lord Jesus Christ died unto sin once, so too have we who have believed in Him and who belong to Him. Hence, says the Apostle, you are dead to sin and you are alive unto God. This means that we have a new life. 'Yield yourselves as those that are alive from the dead'. We have new life in us; and we must realize that. We are not in the position of the unbeliever, the sinner, who is not a Christian; he has nothing but his own strength and power. We have new life in us, Christ dwells in us, His Spirit has taken up His abode in us. Because of that, we have the power and the ability to resist sin in our mortal body and outside us. And the New Testament tells us to do so, to do so very boldly.

There is another teaching that puts all the emphasis on the other side, so I emphasize and repeat this point. The New Testament calls upon us to take action; it does not tell us that the work of sanctification is going to be done for us. That is why it does not put us into a clinic or a hospital where the patient is told 'It will be done for you', and 'Allow the Lord Jesus Christ to do it for you'. It calls upon us to take action, and exhorts us to do so. And it tells us and commands us to do so for this reason, that we have been given the ability to do it. If we had not been given the ability, if we had not received the new nature as the result of the new birth, if we had not been given the new life, if the Spirit was not in us, then, of course, we should need someone to do it for us. But as we have been given the power and the ability and the capacity, the New Testament quite logically, and in perfect consistency with itself, calls upon us to do it. 'Do not let sin reign in your mortal body' it says. 'Do not present your members as instruments unto sin or unrighteousness.' Do not do it! This is something that you and I have to do; it is not going to be done for us.

We are in the good 'fight of faith', and we have to do the fighting. But, thank God, we are enabled to do it; for the moment we believe, and are justified by faith, and are born again of the Spirit of God, we have the ability. So the New Testament method of sanctification is to remind us of that; and having reminded us of it, it says, 'Now then, go and do it'.

That, in turn leads to the fourth general principle. Before and above all other considerations we must realize that we should always live entirely to the glory of God. That is the message of the Bible from beginning to end. 'The chief end of man is to glorify God and to enjoy Him forever.' Our first concern should not even be our own holiness. If it is so, that is where we go wrong. Our first concern should be the glory of God. That must always come first. But we all tend to reverse these things. We are so much concerned about ourselves. We say, 'Here am I, struggling with sin, and defeated. Sin is so powerful and I am so weak. Is there any teaching anywhere which will somehow or other give me the victory? That is what I want. I want victorious living, I want to be emancipated and set free, I want this . . .' It is all for myself, all subjective.

You never find this kind of thing in the New Testament; that is not the way it puts it. The first and the supreme consideration must always be the glory of God. We are to live to His glory. It is only as we look at life in that way that we shall see why we are meant to be holy, and why we should be holy. The true reason for being holy is not that we may no longer be miserable, nor that we may have a comfortable feeling within us, nor even that we may be victorious. The one reason for being holy is this, that it is only as we are holy that we can glorify God. 'Be ye holy'. Why? Because you will have a nice comfortable feeling? Because you will no longer be defeated? Not at all! 'Be ye holy, for I am holy' [1 *Peter* 1 : 16]. We are to be holy not for our sakes primarily, but for God's sake. Any teaching with regard to holiness and sanctification which starts with us and our needs, rather than with the glory of God, is unscriptural, and seriously unscriptural. That subjective approach, it seems to me, is what has led so many astray for so many years. 'The Christian's Secret of a Happy Life.' That title in and of itself suggests a wrong approach. 'How can a Christian glorify God?' would be better. Happiness, and everything else, is subordinate to that. We must not think primarily in terms of our happiness or our own states and feelings. All must be controlled by the glory of God. Perhaps the highest point of holiness is reached when a man can say as Job said, 'Though he slay me, yet will I trust in him' [*Job* 13 : 15]. The glory of God! That must always be the first note in our teaching, and the supreme reason for any concern about holiness and sanctification. All that, it seems to me, is clearly implicit in these two important verses, 12 and 13, in this sixth chapter of the Epistle to the Romans.

Now let us move on to verse 14, which is not only an important but also a glorious statement. This verse is the last in the first major section of the chapter. The first section runs from verse 1 to verse 14; the second section from verse 15 to the end. So this verse comes at the end of the first section, and, as is the custom with this great Apostle, it not only ends the section but at the same time gives a summary of the whole statement in the entire section. In other words we have here the final refutation of the monstrous charge that is brought against the Apostle's teaching mentioned in verse 1: 'Shall we continue in sin, that grace may abound?' Here is the final answer to that question, the summing up of the detailed answer he has given in all the preceding verses.

But, as you notice, it is also closely connected with the immediately preceding verse. He says 'For'. In other words it is a continuation from verse 13 as well as the concluding verse of the whole section. What then is the connection between this fourteenth verse and verses 12 and 13? Some say that this is a command. They read in this way, 'Neither yield ye your members as instruments of unrighteousness unto sin; but yield yourselves unto God as those that are alive from the dead, and your members as instruments of righteousness unto God. For sin must not be allowed to have dominion over you'. That, it seems to me, is one of the false expositions of this verse. It is not a command. We have already met with the command in verses 12 and 13; and if it is just a command, then the Apostle is repeating himself; he is guilty of tautology. But he cannot be charged with this fault. Clearly, verse 14, unlike verses 12 and 13, is neither a command nor an exhortation for that reason.

Again – and this is perhaps a still more important negative – Paul is not saying here that, if we do what he has been telling us to do in verses 12 and 13, then sin shall not have dominion over us. There are many who have interpreted it in that way. They read it, therefore, in this way: If you do not allow sin to reign in your mortal body; if you do not yield your members in the way the Apostle is indicating; but if you do yield yourselves unto God, and your members as instruments of righteousness; then the result will be that sin shall not have dominion over you. But, you notice, in order to expound the words in that manner they have to incorporate and add the little word 'then', which is not in the text. A book happened to come into my hands quite recently, a new translation and exposition of this Epistle, and I was interested to observe that the author does this very thing. He slips in the word 'then', and it therefore reads, 'For then, if you do all this, sin shall not have dominion over you'. But that is not only seriously to misunderstand the verse, but also to miss the whole glory of the verse. That is what makes that interpretation so serious an error.

What, then, is the message of this verse? It is not a command, it is not an exhortation, it is not a statement of the consequence of what has gone before; it is an encouragement – an encouragement to do what Paul has already been commanding us to do. Otherwise stated it is the reason which he gives us for carrying out the exhortations and commands of verses 12 and 13. Let me demonstrate my point. You notice that the verse consists really of two statements introduced by the little word 'for' – 'For sin shall not have dominion over you; for ye are not under the law, but under grace'. The repetition of the word 'for' introduces us to the natural divisions of the statement. So let us look at them.

The first 'for' obviously supplies us with the reason why we must have nothing whatsoever to do with sin. Why must I not allow sin to reign in my mortal body? Why must I not yield my members to it? The answer is, because sin shall not have dominion over us. Now this is a grand, positive assertion. It does not merely inform me of the results that will accrue to me if I carry out and apply the exhortations. No, Paul is telling me to do these things because of what is true of me now and will be true of me in the future. He really tells us that this will not happen to us because it will not be allowed to happen. 'Sin', says the Apostle, 'shall not have dominion over you' – it will not be allowed to have dominion over you.

In what sense is this true? We have seen that, as regards the guilt of sin, we have already died to it once and for ever. We have seen also that we are dead to all its rule and its reign and its authority. But the statement goes yet further; we shall be in a condition finally in which we have nothing at all to do with sin, it will simply have nothing to do with us at all. This is the real object and purpose of salvation. God's reason for ever sending His Son into this world to live, and to die on the Cross, and to rise again, was that He might so undo the works of the devil as to destroy him and them. That is the object, that is the motive; it is to deliver those who believe in Christ entirely and completely and utterly from sin. We are going to be 'presented faultless and blameless, without spot or wrinkle or any such thing'. In other words the object is that 'sin shall not have dominion over you'. This is the purpose and determination of God; He will not allow sin to have dominion over us.

The argument which the Apostle is working out runs thus: if that is the avowed object of this great salvation that God has provided for us in the Person of His only begotten Son, it is therefore monstrous to suggest, as people were suggesting, that the effect of his preaching was to drive people to say, 'Let us continue in sin that grace may abound'. But there is something equally monstrous, namely, that we should believe that this is the object of salvation, and that the Son of God came into the world and died on the Cross and rose again, in order that we might be delivered once and forever from sin, but that in the meantime we should allow sin to reign in our mortal bodies or should in any way present our members as instruments for sin's use. It is monstrous, says the Apostle, you must not do that. Why? 'For (because) sin shall not have dominion over you' – you are going to be delivered altogether from it. Well, then, do not be inconsistent and do not in any shape or form allow it to have any influence even in your mortal body. That is the meaning of that first 'for'.

But then we come to the second 'for', and the object of this is to give us an explanation of the first statement, the basis on which the first statement can be made so confidently. It is as if the Apostle imagined someone turning to him and saying, 'Well now, Paul, you are being very dogmatic; you are making a great asseveration; you are asserting that sin shall not have dominion over these people of God; on what grounds are you making that statement?' 'Well', he seems to say, 'my grounds are these. You are not under law, but under grace. Sin shall not have dominion over you, because (for) ye are not under law, but under grace'.

[181]

What does this mean? We must first look at the term 'law'. What does it mean in this particular context? I am very ready to agree with the vast majority of commentators who say that it not only means the Mosaic Law but also law in general, law as a principle. Previously, in chapter 2, the Apostle had said that, in a sense, a man who is not a Christian is 'under law'. The Gentiles who had never heard the Law of Moses were under law, for they were a law unto themselves. There was a law in their hearts, and it was because of that that they were able to 'accuse or else excuse one another' [chapter 2 verses 14, 15]. In other words, the whole of mankind is under law.

There are only two positions, we are either 'under law', or else we are 'under grace'. Being under law means this, that you have got to attempt to justify yourself in the presence of God by your own actions, by your own works, by your own deeds. Law is always something that comes to a man and says, 'Do this and thou shalt live'. It is the exact opposite to justification by faith. The Apostle then is very much concerned to say that we are not under law. Why so? Because that is the only way whereby we can ever see or come to understand the truth which he has already stated, namely, that 'sin shall not have dominion over you'.

How does he demonstrate this? That question is really answered in chapter 7. It is the theme of that chapter, and also of the first four verses of chapter 8. They show us in detail exactly what this fourteenth verse really means. Without going into it in detail, we shall find in chapter 7 certain things which we can say here and now, and indeed must say, in order that we may understand this section clearly. Indeed the Apostle has already been throwing out hints as to what he asserts here.

The fundamental proposition is that law cannot deliver us from sin. Paul works it out like this. 'Sin', he says, 'shall not have dominion over you'. Why? 'Because you are no longer under law'. 'If you were still under law', he says in effect, 'I could not make that statement about you. If you were still under law, then I would say, and have to say, that sin indeed will have very great dominion over you. But you are not under law, you are under grace. Therefore sin shall not have dominion over you'. The proposition is that law, any law of any kind, cannot deliver us from the power and the tyranny and the dominion of sin.

Let me adduce some reasons for this assertion. We have already seen in the twentieth verse of chapter 3 that law was never given in order to deliver us, not even the Law of Moses. The Apostle puts it in this way: 'Therefore by the deeds of the law there shall no flesh be justified in his sight, for by the law is the knowledge of sin'. That is all the law can do. He has already said in verse 19, 'We know that what things soever the law saith, it saith to them who are under the law; that every mouth may be stopped, and all the world may become guilty before God'. He has also said in verse 23 of that same third chapter, 'We have all sinned and come short of the glory of God'; – and in verse 10, 'There is none righteous, no, not one'. In other words law can never deliver us from the bondage of sin, because it was never meant to do so. 'By the law is the knowledge of sin'. Not the delivery from sin, but the knowledge of it! It was never designed to do more. We must go even beyond that. The Apostle says that law, far from delivering us from the tyranny and the bondage of sin, even tends to aggravate sin in us, and the bondage and the tyranny of sin over us. Remember what we saw in chapter 5 verse 20, 'Moreover', he says, 'the law entered that the offence might abound'. We interpreted that as not only meaning that it helped to bring sin out, and to define it, and focus it, but that it even encouraged it. 'The law entered that the offence might abound.'

In chapter 7 the Apostle is yet more explicit. Verse 5: 'For when we were in the flesh, the motions of sin, which were by the law, did work in our members to bring forth fruit unto death.' Verse 6: 'But now we are delivered from the law, that being dead wherein we were held; that we should serve in newness of spirit and not in the oldness of the letter'. Then in verse 8: 'But sin, *taking occasion by the commandment,* wrought in me all manner of concupiscence.' For without the law sin was dead.' Again in verse 10: 'And the commandment, which was ordained to life, I found to be unto death.' Verse 11: 'For sin, *taking occasion by the commandment,* deceived me, and by it slew me.' Sin made use of the commandment to put the Apostle into a worse state even than he was before. And then in verses 13 and 14: 'Was then that which is good made death unto me? God forbid. But sin, that it might appear sin, working death in me by what which is good' – that is to say, the law – 'that sin *by the commandment* might become exceeding sinful. For we know that the law is spiritual: but I am carnal, sold under sin.'

Now all these verses are assertions to the effect that the law, far from delivering men from the power of sin, has the effect in the natural man of aggravating sin within him, making it even worse, and leading to sin all the more, because he is sinful. Sinful man will even pervert the goodness and the holiness of God's Law; he will twist even that. That shows the terrible power of sin. Again look at the verses at the beginning of chapter 8: 'For the law of the Spirit of life in Christ Jesus hath made me free from the law of sin and death. For what the law could not do, in that it was weak through the flesh, God sending his own Son in the likeness of sinful flesh, and for sin, condemned sin in the flesh: that the righteousness of the law might be fulfilled in us, who walk not after the flesh, but after the Spirit' [vv. 2–4] These are tremendous statements.

But in the Scriptures elsewhere there are supporting statements that are even more striking. Take, for instance, the Apostle's tremendous argument at the end of 1 Corinthians 15. He says, 'The sting of death is sin, and the strength of sin is the law'. The law is the strength in sin that produces the sting that produces death. It is the same thing exactly as we have here. Then consider Galatians 3: 21: '. . . for if there had been a law given which could have given life, verily righteousness should have been by the law'. That means, that if it had been possible for us to obtain righteousness by law, God would have given that law, and He would never have sent His Son from heaven to earth, still less to the Cross and to the grave. But law cannot do that, says Paul, it is impossible. Then we have the dogmatic statement of Hebrews 7: 19: 'For the law made nothing perfect'. It could not do so, it was never meant to do so; and it most certainly has not done so.

Let me sum up all this teaching in a number of principles. There is no power in God's Law to deliver us from the power and the tyranny of sin in any respect. It was never meant to do so. The business of the law was to tell us what we had to do, 'by the law is the knowledge of sin'. That is the sole reason why it was ever given. Its effect, Paul says, was to bring out 'the exceeding sinfulness of sin', to help people to see the nature and the character of sin – what a terrible thing it was – and their need of Christ. 'The law is our schoolmaster to bring us to Christ', to show us our helplessness and our terrible need. Yes, but because of our

fallen nature the law actually encourages sin in us. Far from delivering us, it aggravates the problem. If we are under law, that
will be the effect that the law will have upon us; and that, in turn,
will produce a state of utter depression, and a sense of hopelessness. And that makes us yet more susceptible to the power of
sin; for whenever a man is depressed he is more open to temptation. He is discouraged, and so sin gets an opportunity. Further,
the law discourages us because it shows us the holiness of God;
it shows us the deceitfulness of sin within us; it pin-points it;
it brings it out, aggravates it, and so stimulates it in us. It tells
us not to do something, and in telling us that, it introduces us to
it and arouses within us a desire to do it. 'Unto the pure all things
are pure; but unto them that are defiled and unbelieving is nothing
pure, but even their mind and conscience is defiled' [*Titus* 1 : 15].

That is why I have never believed that moral teaching alone
to unbelievers is sufficient. It is sheer nonsense to believe that
you can teach young men in the army and elsewhere not to commit sin by merely telling them about the evil consequences of sin.
What you are probably doing is to introduce them, perhaps for
the first time, to the pleasures of sin. That is the effect that moral
teaching generally produces; because man is corrupt, he will
pervert even the pure. In telling him not to sin you are giving him
a picture of the thing, and at once he desires it. The elementary
passions and lusts are stronger than our minds. That is how sin
works.

Here is a man under law. He is hopeless, depressed and discouraged; and the more the law tells him not to do certain things
the more he desires them. Does not every child do that? Tell
him not to do a thing and immediately he wants to do it. That is
human nature. Sin twists all the commandments and makes us
worse than we were before. It utterly depresses us. 'Very well,'
says Paul in effect, 'I am not telling you that sin shall not have
dominion over you because you are under the law. If you were
under the law, I could not make such a statement; I would have
to say the exact opposite about you. But thank God,' he says,
'that is not our position. I am saying that sin shall not have dominion over you for this reason, that you are no longer under law,
but under grace. The whole situation is entirely transformed;
you are delivered out of the depression and out of the hopelessness and the sense of despair of those who are under the law.'

In other words Paul is saying here again what he had said so wonderfully at the end of the previous chapter, in the words, 'That as sin hath reigned unto death, even so might grace reign through righteousness unto eternal life by Jesus Christ our Lord' [*Romans* 5 : 21]. 'I am saying,' says Paul, 'and I am saying without a shadow of hesitation, that sin shall not have dominion over you. My grounds for saying so are that you are under grace. You are under the reign of grace, and you are going to share in the triumph of grace. The whole purpose of grace is to annul, to destroy the works of the devil in every shape and form; everything about grace is designed to that glorious end.'

How does grace do this? Grace introduces us to a new covenant, a new agreement between God and ourselves. It is not like the old covenant. What is the difference? Here are some of the terms of the new covenant that God has made with man in Jesus Christ. He forgives our sins freely. 'Your sins and iniquities', He says, 'will I remember no more', put aside for ever. 'The Lamb of God that taketh away the sin of the world' has removed them. 'Your sins and iniquities will I remember no more.' He does not stop at that. 'I will be to you a God, and you shall be to me a people.' This is absolutely new, and in an intimate sense. Christians are God's people in this intimate relationship, the special objects of His concern and His solicitude. What is God's purpose for us who are His people? 'This is the will of God, even your sanctification.' It is the will of the Lord Jesus Christ also, says Paul, in the second chapter of the Epistle to Titus: 'Who gave himself for us'. Why? 'That he might redeem us from all iniquity, and purify unto himself a peculiar people, zealous of good works' [*Titus* 2 : 14]. You remember also Christ's last prayer for us before He died. It was this: 'Father, sanctify them through thy truth: thy word is truth' [*John* 17 : 17].

Such is the purpose of God the Father, God the Son, and God the Holy Spirit. How is this purpose carried out in us in this new covenant? Here are some of the answers. We are given a new nature. We are not given new instructions, but otherwise left just as we were. No, we are born again, made anew; we are new creations, with new life, new beginning; we are new men in Christ Jesus. But not only that! The new covenant is unlike the old in another respect. In the old God gave the people His laws on tables of stone, but now, under the new covenant, 'I will put my laws into their mind, and write them in their hearts'. The Christian is not a man who is looking at a code of morals outside himself; he has them inside himself. They are in his mind, and written in his heart, a vital principle of his being, within himself. Not only that! God says, 'Every man shall know me, from the least to the greatest' [*Hebrew* 8 : 7–13]. We have this access to God and this personal knowledge of Him.

Then, too, God puts His power in us. That is why Paul, praying for the Ephesians, says that he not only wants them to 'know what is the hope of his calling, and what the riches of the glory of his inheritance in the saints', but also 'what is the exceeding greatness of his power to us-ward who believe'. Then at the end of chapter 3 of that Epistle he puts it like this: 'Now unto him that is able to do for us exceeding abundantly above all that we ask or think, according to the power that worketh in us'. That is the truth; that is how God deals with us under this new covenant. 'Work out your own salvation with fear and trembling, for' – because – 'it is God that worketh in you both to will and to do of his good pleasure' [*Philippians* 2 : 12, 13]

And yet more! Perfect provision has been made for us in every respect. In Ephesians 1. 2 we read that 'He hath blessed us with all spiritual blessings in heavenly places in Christ'. There is nothing beyond that; everything you need has been done. Listen also to 2 Peter 1, verses 3 and 4: 'According as his divine power hath given unto us all things that pertain unto life and godliness, through the knowledge of him that hath called us to glory and virtue: Whereby are given unto us exceeding great and precious promises; that by these ye might be partakers of the divine nature, having escaped the corruption that is in the world through lust'. Everything that you need for life and godliness is already provided in all these blessings with which He has blessed us in the heavenly places in Christ Jesus.

What more do you want? We are under grace, and because of these things, sin shall not have dominion over us. That is absolutely certain, as we are assured in the prophecy of Jeremiah. God gave this word to Jeremiah, 'I will make an everlasting covenant with them, that I will not turn away from them, to do them good; but I will put my fear in their hearts, that they shall not depart from me' [32 : 40]. God is not going to allow us to depart. 'Sin shall not have dominion over you'. 'You shall not depart from me', He says. 'I am going to keep you. 'I will make an everlasting covenant with you, that I will not turn away from you, to do you good; but I will put my fear in your hearts, that you shall not depart from me'. Indeed, we have already had a magnificent statement to the same effect in this very Epistle in chapter 4, verse 16: 'Therefore it is of faith, that it might be by grace; to the end the promise might be sure to all the seed'. What a statement! 'It is of faith, that it might be by grace', with this end and object, 'that the promise might be sure (that it might never fail) to all the seed'. It is as certain as that.

But I have been quoting the servants, Jeremiah and the Apostle Paul. Let me end by quoting the Master, the Lord Himself. This is what He says in John 6: 39: 'And this is the Father's will which hath sent me, that of all which he hath given me I should lose nothing, but should raise it up again at the last day'. The Father has given Him a people; He is going to raise us, every one of us. There will be nothing missing, there will be nothing lost. And it is certain that He will do it. 'Sin shall not have dominion over you.' Finally in John 10.28: 'And I give unto them eternal life; and they shall never perish, neither shall any man pluck them out of my hand'. This is certain and sure. 'Sin shall not have dominion over you; for ye are not under law, but under grace' – the grace of God and the grace of the Lord Jesus Christ. It is invincible, it is everlasting, it is final. Nothing is to be lost; we shall all be delivered entirely from sin, we shall all be raised perfect, spotless, blameless, in a glorified condition.

It is the realization of this truth according to the New Testament that constitutes the greatest incentive to holiness; and that is the New Testament way of producing holiness in us. It does not say or teach that we have nothing to do, that Christ will do it for us. It says to us: Realize these truths, and realizing them, stand against sin. Do not let it reign in your mortal body. Do not offer your members to it: you are under grace, and sin shall not have dominion over you.

There is nothing that is so encouraging to holiness, so stimulating, so uplifting, as to know the certainty of my final salvation and glorification. Because I am certain of it I join the Apostle John as he says, 'He that hath this hope in him, purifieth himself even as he is pure' [1 *John* 3 : 3]. You do not need a hospital, or a clinic, you need this instruction, this information, this command,

'Reckon ye also yourselves to be dead indeed unto sin, but alive unto God, through Jesus Christ our Lord'. Remember this, 'Sin shall not have dominion over you' – never – 'for you are not under the law, but under grace'. Realize, then, all that grace means; read again the terms of the new covenant; and live as a man who has read the title-deeds, and who is proud of them, who has lost all his depression and all his hopelessness and despair, and who, looking at the glory which is coming, says to himself, 'I have no time to waste, I am longing for glory, I am looking forward to it. I must press on, I must purify myself "even as he is pure"; I must prepare for the great day that is coming, so that when I stand before Him I shall not be ashamed'. If this is not the greatest encouragement to holiness and to sanctification that you have ever heard, then I despair of you. This is the New Testament method. Realize these things. They are true of you as a Christian. You, such as you are, are going to stand in His presence. You will see Him, you will be like Him; your very body will be glorified. And as you realize these things, you will hate sin and all that belongs to it; you will turn your back upon it; you will resist it, you will 'resist the devil, and he will flee from you'. Your motto will be, 'Blessed are they that do hunger and thirst after righteousness, for they shall be filled'.

Fifteen

*

What then? shall we sin, because we are not under the law, but under grace? God forbid. Know ye not, that to whom ye yield yourselves servants to obey, his servants ye are to whom ye obey, whether of sin unto death, or of obedience unto righteousness?
Romans 6 : 15, 16

We come here to the second section of the sixth chapter of this Epistle. But before we proceed to the study of it, it is surely appropriate that we should ask ourselves certain questions concerning what has gone before. Have we a thorough understanding of the doctrine of justification by faith? Do we realize that if we truly understand the doctrine of justification by faith we have already grasped the essence and nerve of the New Testament teaching about holiness and sanctification? Have we realized that to be justified by faith guarantees our sanctification, and that therefore we must never think of sanctification as a separate and subsequent experience? The Apostle's entire argument has been this, that if we truly realize what is meant by justification, we realize that it inevitably means that we are 'in Christ' also, and that that guarantees our deliverance from sin and our final glorification. As the Apostle will put it later in chapter 8, 'Whom he (God) justified, them he also glorified' [verse 30]. It has already happened, it is already complete, in the sight of God.

But I can put it in a still more practical manner. We have been considering the first fourteen verses of this chapter in detail. The way to discover whether their message is clear to you or not is this. Has the effect of this teaching been to make you hate sin more than you have ever hated it before? Has it given you a new confidence as you face the world, the flesh, and the devil? Has the effect of this teaching been to advance your growth in grace and in the knowledge of the Lord? For that is the way in which we are 'sanctified by the truth'. As we have been working out the teaching and understanding it, it should have affected our whole attitude towards the problem of sin. We are delivered from sin as it attacks us and threatens to get us down, and are able to conquer it and master it by an understanding of this truth. So if we are not conscious that we are in a position in which we can resist sin as it still remains in the mortal body, and confronts us in the world outside us and in the devil, with greater confidence and assurance, greater certainty and a greater sense of triumph, we have misunderstood the teaching. This teaching is a teaching that puts a man on his feet, as it were, and enables him to realize who he is, and what he is, and what is being done to him under the power of the reign of grace. So it should lead him to triumph and to rejoicing in his victory. So we ask ourselves these questions as we now move on to the second sub-section.

At first one almost feels that the Apostle is virtually repeating himself. 'What then? shall we sin because we are not under the law, but under grace?' But you will notice that this, while very similar to the question put in verse 1, is at the same time not identical; it makes the same general point but it is expressed in a slightly different way. Before, it was this: 'In view of the fact that grace superabounds where sin abounds, shall we not therefore continue in sin?' But now it is put in a different form: 'In view of the fact that we are not under the law, but under grace, does it not follow that we can live as we like, that it does not matter what we do because there is no longer any law and we are under grace?' That is the form in which the Apostle now puts the question; and what he proceeds to do in the remainder of the chapter is to show once again the utter absurdity of such a deduction, indicating, as it does, a complete failure to understand the truth and the doctrine. But he is not content to leave it like that; he goes on, positively, to show that the whole purpose of the Gospel is designed to do the exact opposite; and that in actual practice it does so.

Let us first of all make a general analysis of verses 15 to 23 before we turn to the particulars. Verse 16 deals with this objection in the form of a general principle which ought to commend itself to the mind of any thinking, reasonable person. It is not a directly spiritual argument, as we shall see, but a general argument.

Verses 17 and 18 show the particular application of this general argument to every person who is a Christian in his daily life and living. Verse 19 then goes on to make a general appeal to us in the light of that argument. Verses 20 to 23 are really nothing but an enforcing of the appeal of verse 19, but they are couched in such a way as to be a remarkable exposition of the latter part of verse 16.

This may sound complicated, but actually it is not. The Apostle is simply following his common practice. He states a truth briefly and tersely; then he seems to have forgotten it, but he later comes back to it and takes it up and works it out. Thus verses 20-23 are really an exposition of the statement, 'whether of sin unto death, or of obedience unto righteousness', at the end of verse 16. And he uses his exposition of that phrase to enforce the argument of verse 19, where he says, '. . . as ye have yielded your members servants to uncleanness, and to iniquity unto iniquity; even so now yield your servants members to righteousness unto holiness'.

There, then, is a general analysis to show us the main thread of the statement of this particular paragraph; so coming to our detailed consideration, we start with verse 15. 'What then?' Here, once more, the objector breaks in: 'In the light of what you have just been saying, that sin shall not have dominion over us because we are not under the law but under grace, shall we continue to sin, and do so freely?' Now this is not an imaginary question, as we indicated with respect to the question in verse 1. Sometimes writers and teachers anticipate questions; they imagine difficulties, and they therefore put them in the form of rhetorical questions in order that they may deal with them. That may be partly the case here, but it is not entirely so. It is not merely an imaginary question, for history shows that this kind of question was being asked by people in Paul's day. Indeed, not only was the question being asked, but the Apostle was very definitely being attacked along this line. He was a man who had to face many opponents. Any teacher worth his salt will meet with opposition. 'Woe unto you', said our Lord, 'when all men speak well of you'; and this Apostle, because he was loyal to truth, and preached the doctrine that had been delivered to him, had to confront terrible and grievous opposition. There were people who went about charging him with the most grievous offences. He has already referred to this in chapter 3 verse 8.

There were two main types of persons who were criticizing the Apostle for his teaching, and the same two groups are still to be found amongst us, both in the church and outside it. The first group consisted of those Jewish legalists sometimes called Judaisers. They are represented today by people who are primarily moralists, and whose interest in the Christian faith is exclusively moral and ethical. Their objection to this teaching about justification, and these resounding phrases which say 'Sin shall not have dominion over you, because you are under the reign and the rule of grace' is this. They say, 'If you in that way remove the law, then there will be nothing left to tell us what to do. Not only will there be nothing left to tell us what to do, there will be nothing to restrain us from doing that which is wrong.' They say that this is therefore highly dangerous teaching. They grant that it sounds wonderful to say to people, 'You are no longer under the law, but under grace', but they are concerned about the effect it is likely to have upon them. How will anyone know what is right and what is wrong? And what will there be to restrain us? The law restrains because 'by the law is the knowledge of sin'. It pronounces its judgments and its punishments, and so keeps people in order. That is the function of law. 'Well now', they say, 'if you are going to dismiss law, if you say you are no longer under law, you are guilty of encouraging licence and lawlessness. The result will be that the whole state of morals and of ethics will undergo a sad decline'.

That is the first objection. There are many people who argue in that manner today. Their view of the Christian faith is purely moral and ethical. You find the view frequently in the newspapers. There are statesmen who really seem to think that the main function of the Christian Church is to help the state in this way to maintain law and order. Another form in which it is found is sometimes called 'Public School Religion', which teaches that Christianity is just that which teaches you how to be 'a good little gentleman', teaches you what not to do and what to do. Thomas Arnold, the famous headmaster of Rugby School, certainly perverted the Christian faith into that very teaching over a hundred years ago. And it persists to this day. Such moralists always feel that when you talk about justification by faith only, and say that you are no longer under law but under grace, you are teaching something that is extremely dangerous, for in their view, Christianity is a moral and ethical system which is meant to improve the state of society.

The second objection put forward by a second group is almost the exact opposite of that. These are the people who are guilty of antinomianism. They are the people who say that it really does not matter what you do, because you are under grace. If you are saved you are saved, and therefore what you may or may not do is utterly unimportant. 'Sin shall not have dominion over you, because you are no longer under law, but you are under grace.' 'Very well', they say, 'I can do anything I may choose.' There were people who spoke in that way in the early Church; and there are such people, alas, today. They pervert the Gospel of Christ 'turning the grace of our God into lasciviousness' [*Jude* 4]. There are many warnings against such an attitude in the various epistles in the New Testament. They warn people who abuse and misuse the grace and the freedom of the Gospel, who twist this teaching into assertions that if you are in Christ, what you do does not matter, and therefore you can freely indulge in sin.

As those were the two main objections then, they remain the two main objections today. I therefore would make two practical observations at this point. The first is that the true preaching of the gospel always exposes us to these two misunderstandings and to this particular charge. I say that mainly for the benefit of preachers. If our preaching is not such as to expose us to this particular charge, then there is something wrong with it. There are many preachers who never preach justification by faith at all, because they do not believe it. They regard the New Testament message as no more than an ethical system, and they are always exhorting people to live better lives, and to stop doing this and that. They apply this in a more general sphere, and so are always making protests to Governments and other powers. They talk unceasingly about applying the Christian ethic. No one could ever charge such preachers with inciting people to sin; no one could ever bring the charge against their preaching that they say 'Let us sin because we are not under the law, but under grace'. That is one reason why we can say without any hesitation that such men are not preaching the Gospel. The Apostle Paul preached the true Christian faith, and because he preached it, people began to ask and to say, 'What then?' True preaching of the Gospel always exposes itself to this misunderstanding, to this particular charge. That is my first general observation, and by it we must always test our preaching. There is always something that sounds dangerous in the preaching of justification by faith only; so if our preaching does not sound dangerous in this respect, probably the Gospel is not being truly preached.

My second observation is that true preaching of the Gospel, while it exposes us to this danger, should nevertheless also safeguard us against this danger. That is what the Apostle is determined to prove. He says in effect: 'God forbid that you should say that kind of thing! If you do, it means that you have not understood what I have been saying'. So he says it again in a clearer and in a more detailed way, in order that all who listen carefully will not be able to misunderstand the teaching. Similarly, true preaching of the Gospel, while it exposes us to these charges among those who lack a clear understanding, at the same time safeguards us against these charges. I therefore draw this general deduction, that it is vitally important that our evangelistic message should be a full message, and that it should not merely call for decision or a vague indication of some kind of nebulous belief. The Apostle himself is quite clear because he always preached a full message. If he had not done so he could not have argued as he argues in this sixth chapter. The message preached in evangelism must be essentially a simple message, but it must also be a full message. It must have content; it must never give people the impression that all they have to do is to say that they believe in Christ, and all is well. That is an incomplete message, ultimately a non-ethical message. True evangelism is always ethical; true evangelism should always enable people to see the consequences of what they are saying, and what they are proposing to do. It must not be so simple as to leave out this vital element which the Apostle now proceeds to work out. With those two thoughts in our minds let us look at his actual terms.

The first statement is, 'Shall we sin because we are not under the law, but under grace?' It is important that we should get the right meaning of 'sin' as the word is used here. It means deliberate and persistent sin; it means continuance in a state of sin, a persistence in the habit of sin. It does not mean a fall occasionally and unawares, as it were, into sin; it means a settled life of sin as we have seen earlier in a reference to the First Epistle of John, chapter 3, verses 8 and 9. Many a poor, troubled, untaught

Christian, after falling into an act of sin says, 'I have never been a Christian at all; I cannot have been born again, because the Apostle John says there that he that committeth sin is of the devil: And if I am of the devil, I am not in Christ.'

The answer to all such reasoning and fallacies is found when a man discovers the meaning of the terms employed. 'To sin', in all these instances, means 'a going on with sin' 'a settling down in it', 'a continuing in it' – deliberate and persistent sin. If it does not mean that, but means 'any single act of sin', then there is no such thing as a Christian at all. But that makes the position absurd and ridiculous: so, clearly, the Apostle was not saying any such thing. What John teaches is that a man who is born of God does not go on living or abiding in a state and a condition of sin. And the word 'sin' has exactly the same meaning in this fifteenth verse of Romans 6. This is a vital distinction. I sometimes think that there has been nothing which has tripped and trapped so many Christians, and has caused so much misery and dejection in the Christian life, as the failure to realize the meaning of this word 'sin' here, and in 1 John chapter 3.

Look next at this other statement – 'under law'. 'What then? Shall we sin because we are not under law?' We have already defined the term 'law'. It obviously means, not the ceremonial Law, but the demands of the moral Law. In particular it means that we are no longer under the Law in the sense that our salvation depends upon our keeping and observing the Law; we are no longer under the Law in the sense that the Law is a system which says, 'Do this, and thou shalt live'. That, of course, is the position of all who are not Christians. If a man is not a Christian, that is his position; he is 'under law'. He claims that he can justify himself by his works, and the Law meets him and says, 'Very well, if you do this you shall live'. So it gives its precepts and commandments. The Apostle says that we are no longer under that law, we are no longer in the position that our salvation is determined by our actions and by our works. Our salvation is entirely of grace and by grace. He is saying that, and he is saying no more than that.

So much then for the two main terms. Next we come to his strong rejection of this whole suggestion, in the words 'God forbid!' or 'May it not be'. He has already used that expression in verse 2 and he repeats it here. The very suggestion is utterly unthinkable, is monstrous; and this should be patent to everyone. But I ask the question again. Is it patent and clear to us? Do we feel that his suggested argument is a plausible one? Do we find difficulty in rebutting it? It is good for us to ask ourselves these questions before we go on to the Apostle's answer. Would you be troubled by a man who came to you and said, 'Your teaching means that, because you are no longer under law but under grace, you can go on sinning'. Would you be troubled by him? Can you answer him, and rebut the suggestion, and dismiss it?

But let us now look at Paul's refutation of this charge, and his exposure of it as a complete failure to understand his teaching concerning justification by faith only, and the assurance to which it leads. He does this mainly in verses 16, 17, and 18. In verse 16 he starts by saying, 'Know ye not?' I would remind you again of the Apostle's fondness for this expression. All of us who preach have favourite expressions which seem at times to amuse and delight our hearers. We are in good company. Paul has used this mode of address before in verse 3. 'Know ye not that so many of us as were baptized . . . ?' It was his characteristic way of dealing with a difficulty or problem. 'Knowing this', he says in verse 6. And in verse 9, 'Knowing that Christ. . . . '

What is Paul's object in using it there? He is appealing to general knowledge, to reason, to logic, and to common sense. The Apostle's way of dealing with a difficulty such as this is not just to say, 'Well now, don't be worried about things like that; all you have to do is to look to Christ and to abide in Him; do not be bothered about anything else'. The Apostle does not just appeal to them to surrender themselves and not be worried. No! he says, rather, in effect: 'Face this as an argument. I want to show you what a monstrous thing it is to raise such a plea against the truth of the Gospel; and I can do so on general principles. I can deal with this, to start with, apart from Christianity. The trouble with a man who argues like that is that he really does not know how to argue.'

I am concerned about this use of argument for the following reason. There are some people who seem to think that it is unspiritual to argue at all; but the Apostle not only argues, he argues by means of that particular method. If you can show a man that, leaving Christianity aside for the moment, he really does not know how to argue on his own ground, you gain something. The Apostle does not disdain to do that. He was not too spiritual to show people the utter fallacy of their reasoning processes. That is exactly what he is doing here. Yet how often is this kind of teaching entirely ignored! How often do you hear these arguments of the Apostle worked out and presented? It is thought to be more spiritual not to do this kind of thing. But to adopt such an outlook is to depart from the method and the example of this mighty, holy man of God. There is a grave danger of our being much more supposedly holy than the Apostle was, or than the New Testament is! But it is a false kind of piety, it is a sentimental view of Christianity that does untold harm. Thank God for the strength, for the manliness, for the virility of the New Testament teaching and this particular working out of it here.

What then is the Apostle's general principle? Let us start with his terms. 'Know ye not', he says, 'that to whom ye yield yourselves. . . .' The meaning of the term 'yield', you remember, is 'to present', 'to hand yourself over'. The next term is the word 'servants'. 'Know ye not that to whom ye yield yourselves servants to obey.' Unfortunately the Authorized Version has given us a poor translation here; it is much too weak, and is really misleading. The word the Apostle used and wrote means 'slaves', not 'servants'. 'Know ye not that to whom ye present yourselves as slaves to obey.' There is a difference between a servant and a slave, is there not? There are many servants today who say, 'We do not object to being servants, and we are ready to hire ourselves out as servants; but we are not going to be slaves'. That is a valid and important distinction. There is a voluntary element about service; but there is none in slavery. I emphasize the importance of this word 'slaves' because the Apostle's whole argument depends upon it. He is really saying that a man is either a slave to sin, or else he is a slave to grace. The whole argument of this sixth chapter is about the 'reign of grace', the 'power of grace'; and it is a power such as is exercised by a slave-owner, a slave-master. Sin exercises such a power; so does grace. The word here, therefore, is 'slaves'.

Sin, you notice, the Apostle personifies once more – 'whether of sin unto death, or of obedience unto righteousness'. Still more interesting is it to observe that he should have put over against

sin as a slave-owner the term 'obedience'. Why did he choose this
particular term? When we come to verse 17 we shall make a
great deal of this word 'obedience', but I must just emphasize
here that it is most interesting that he should have chosen this
particular word to represent the position of the believer. What he
puts over against 'sin' is 'obedience'. He does not put 'faith' only,
he puts it in the form of obedience, and he does so very deliberately. His object is to show how utterly ridiculous and monstrous
it is to suggest even for a moment that there is anything about the
Christian faith and the Christian message which should ever
lead a man to live a life of sin. That is what he is really concerned
to say.

When we say that we are not 'under law', it does not mean that
we are lawless, or that we are a law unto ourselves. Were we to
argue, 'Oh, if we are not under law, then we are free, we can do
what we like, we can do what we choose', we should be making a
false deduction. The reply to that is, that to say that you are not
under the Law does not mean that you are lawless; it means,
rather, that you are under obedience. Take a parallel statement of
this by the same Apostle in 1 Corinthians 9: 21. There he is describing himself as a preacher, and he says, 'To them that are
without law, I am become as without law'; then, in brackets,
('being not without law to God, but under the law to Christ').
As a Christian I am never lawless, I am not under the Law in that
old sense, but that does not mean that I am absolutely free and
antinomian and do not recognize law at all. No, I am 'under the
law to Christ'. I am always under one law or another. All this is
suggested by the word 'obedience', the term which the Apostle
uses as the opposite of sin in verse 16.

His other term is the word 'righteousness'. Is not this an interesting point again? How would you have expected the Apostle
to conclude this verse? Would you not have expected this, 'Know
ye not that to whom ye yield yourselves servants to obey, his
servants ye are to whom ye obey, whether of sin unto death or of
obedience unto life'? Is not 'life' the opposite of 'death'? But the
Apostle says 'righteousness'. Why did he choose the word 'righteousness'? It is not accidental, but very deliberate. If the Apostle
had put the word 'life' here instead of 'righteousness', he would
have contradicted his own teaching, and he would have taught a
lie. He would have been teaching that obedience leads to life;

and if you say that obedience leads to life, then you are teaching justification by works. But that is never true. As he says in the last verse of this chapter, 'The wages of sin is death, but the gift of God is eternal life'. Eternal life is not the result of obedience; eternal life is the gift of God. So he could not say here that obedience leads to life. Very rightly he says that it leads to righteousness, it leads to the kind of righteous life which God would have His people live.

In other words, as Paul puts it again also perfectly in Ephesians 2. 10; 'We are his workmanship, created anew in Christ Jesus unto good works, which God hath before appointed that we should walk in them'. That is the righteousness to which obedience leads. How important it is when you are reading the Scriptures to watch every word! Think as you read, and reason, and say to yourself, 'This is strange. I would have thought the parallel to 'death' on that side is 'life' on this side; but it is not. Why not?' Ask questions, and you will find that Bible study will become a most thrilling and exciting occupation. How wonderful was the mind of this man of God! And how wonderful is divine inspiration!

Let me now sum up the Apostle's argument. Look first at the general argument, then consider it in the form of propositions. Here is the argument: 'Don't you know, don't you realize, don't you understand that to whom you yield yourselves slaves to obey, his slave you are to whom you obey, whether it be sin unto death, or obedience unto righteousness?'

Now look at it reduced to propositions. If we present ourselves as slaves to any power, then we become the slaves of that power. That sounds very obvious; nevertheless people frequently forget it, as the Apostle shows here. If I sell myself to a power I then become the slave of that power; and the power that it has over me is the power of a slave-owner over his slave. But the characteristic of the power of a slave-owner is that it is a totalitarian and exclusive power. If I hand myself over to be a slave to such a power, then I am nothing but the slave of that power. I am in his hands, in his grip, under his authority. It is a totalitarian power and I am no longer a free man; the power decides what I do and what I am.

Secondly, there are only two ultimate totalitarian powers.

The one is sin, the other is obedience. That is the great theme of the Apostle; he began working it out in chapter 5 at verse 12. We have seen how, all along, he keeps on saying in effect: 'It is no use talking or arguing; there are only two positions – a man is either in Adam, or else he is in Christ'. In verse 21 of chapter 5 he says; 'One is either under the reign of sin which reigns unto death, or else under the reign of grace which leads to righteousness and to eternal life by Jesus Christ our Lord'. There is no middle position; it is either the one or the other; and every human being is either a slave to sin or else a slave to obedience.

Thirdly, these two powers, sin and obedience, are entirely different and are utterly opposed to each another. This is a most important part of the argument. They are complete antitheses. They are both slave-owners and masters; but (I repeat) they are bitterly and violently and eternally opposed to each another. The difference between sin and obedience is the difference between the devil and God; it is the difference between hell and heaven, it is the difference between lawlessness and rebellion on the one side, and the holiness and the righteousness and the truth of God on the other side. They are eternal opposites in their very nature. They are also eternal opposites in the results they produce. The one produces the death that always results from a life of sin, as we shall find in verses 20–23; the other produces righteousness, which is an attribute of God Himself.

That brings us to the fourth point. In the light of the three foregoing points it is obviously impossible to be slaves to both these masters at one and the same time. We are either the slave of the one or the other, and as they are bitterly and violently and eternally opposed, it is a sheer impossibility for any man to be a slave to both at the same time. He cannot be a slave to grace and yet live in sin; it is utterly impossible. They are mutually exclusive, mutually contradictory. Our Lord has put this perfectly once and for ever in Matthew 6: 24: 'No man can be slave to two masters' – the Authorized Version says 'serve' – 'for either he will hate the one, and love the other; or else he will hold to the one, and despise the other'. Then He goes on, 'Ye cannot serve God and mammon'. That is an utter impossibility, because they are eternal opposites. This, then, is a vital part of the Apostle's argument. So far, you notice, the argument is entirely on the plane of general logic, of general common sense. You cannot at

[201]

one and the same time be the slave of two masters who are everlastingly different and fighting each other.

A fifth principle is that we finally proclaim who our master is, and what our whole position is, by what we do. Not by what we say, but by what we do! That is the very thing the Apostle is concerned to emphasize. He is being charged with saying, 'We are now under grace, therefore we can sin'. 'That is utterly impossible', says the Apostle. 'I have proved to you that it is impossible'. Therefore, if you show me a man who is living in sin, I say that that man is not under grace. He cannot be; he could not go on living in sin if he were under grace. His manner of life shows that he is under sin and under the power of sin. We proclaim what we are, finally, not by what we say, but by what we do. Christian people, let us never forget this. Let us who talk of justification by faith only, who extol the glories of grace, be careful. Let us remember words such as these in Matthew 7.15: 'Beware of false prophets, which come to you in sheep's clothing'. They look very attractive, they look like sheep, and they produce a sound which is remarkably like the bleating of sheep. But 'inwardly they are ravening wolves'. How are we to judge men? Not by what they say, but 'by their fruits'. 'Do men gather grapes of thorns, or figs of thistles? Even so every good tree bringeth forth good fruit.' The way to judge the tree is to examine the fruit; and the 'corrupt tree bringeth forth evil fruit'. Then observe particularly, 'A good tree cannot bring forth evil fruit, neither can a corrupt tree bring forth good fruit. Every tree that bringeth not forth good fruit is hewn down, and cast into the fire. Wherefore by their fruits ye shall know them. Not every one that saith unto me, Lord, Lord, shall enter into the kingdom of heaven; but he that doeth the will of my Father which is in heaven. Many will say to me in that day, Lord, Lord, have we not prophesied in thy name? and in thy name cast out devils? and in thy name done many wonderful works? And then will I profess unto them, I never knew you: depart from me, ye that work iniquity' [*Matthew* 7 : 16–23]. That is exactly what the Apostle is saying here. I do not care what a man's profession may be, says Paul; if he is continuing in sin he is not under grace, but under sin. He is under the devil, whatever he may say. Good and evil do not mix, they cannot mix. There is always this essential glorious consistency in the teaching of the Scriptures.

Or look at the matter as our Lord put it in the eighth chapter of John's Gospel. Our Lord turned to certain men who seemed to believe what He had been teaching, and He said to them, 'If ye continue in my word, then are ye my disciples indeed, and ye shall know the truth, and the truth shall·make you free' [verses 30–32]. Instead of shouting 'Hallelujah!' they said, 'We be Abraham's seed, and were never in bondage to any man: how sayest thou, ye shall be made free?' 'Jesus answered them, Verily, verily, I say unto you' – it is as simple as that, the logic is inevitable – 'Whosoever committeth sin' – goes on committing sin – 'is the slave of sin'. What matters is not what a man says. He may boast of being one of Abraham's children. 'But', says our Lord, 'if you were Abraham's children you would not treat me as you do; Abraham would not have treated me like this.' But they said, 'We are not born of fornication, we are God's children'. Christ replied, 'If God were your Father, you would love me' [verse 42]. The nature expresses itself in the actions; and to be a Christian does not merely mean that you say that you believe in the Lord Jesus Christ. It means that you are born again, it means that you are in Christ; there is a new nature in you, and that new nature must show itself. It shows itself in obedience and righteousness and holy living; it does not show itself by continuing in sin. So the Apostle urges his readers to pull themselves together, to gird up the loins of their minds, to try to think straightly. He warns them against being muddled in their logic; they must realize that if a man 'commits' sin he is the servant of sin.

Finally, here is a quotation from the First Epistle of John, chapter 1, verse 6: 'If we say that we have fellowship with him (the Lord), and walk in darkness, we lie, and do not the truth.' In chapter 2, verse 4 John is even more outspoken, and says, 'He that saith, I know him, and keepeth not his commandments, is a liar, and the truth is not in him'. That is the way in which the New Testament teaches holiness and sanctification. It does not come to us and say, 'Come to the clinic, and let me comfort you; let me soothe you by telling you how it all can be taken out of you'. Not at all! The New Testament says, 'You are telling me that you are a Christian, that you are a believer in the Lord Jesus Christ, that you are born again. At the same time you are living in sin'. All I have to say to you, says the Apostle John in effect, is not 'Come, let me put you to bed, and treat you, and give you ease'. 'No!' says John. 'You are a liar, you are a barefaced liar, that is all I have to say to you. You cannot do these two things at the same time. Whosoever is born of God doth not commit sin.'

That is precisely what the Apostle Paul is saying here – you are either a slave to sin, or else you are a slave to obedience. Whatever your profession may be, whatever your knowledge and understanding may be, if it is not producing the fruit of righteousness, it is a mockery, it is a lie, and it is of no value at all. That is the argument; that is the way in which the Apostle rebuffs and refutes this false charge that is being brought against him. 'God forbid!' 'Don't you know that a man proclaims whose slave he is by the way in which he lives and behaves?' The slave-owner, Sin, commands and insists upon a certain type of life; and the other slave-owner, Obedience, Grace – call it what you will – also insists upon a very different kind of conduct and behaviour. 'By their fruits you shall know them.' This is not justification by works. It is the announcement that the man who has been born again by the grace of God has a principle in him that produces good fruit, not evil fruit. It is not the 'sheep's clothing' on the man that matters, it is what is inside, what comes out of him; it is in the man himself. If we are truly slaves of grace, and of obedience, and of God, it will show itself, it must show itself, in obedient conduct and holy behaviour. 'Sin shall not have dominion over you', because grace now has dominion over you and it will bring its own set purposes to pass, and above all, the fruit of obedience and righteousness.

Sixteen

*

*But God be thanked, that ye were the servants of sin, but ye have
obeyed from the heart that form of doctrine which was delivered you.*
Romans 6 : 17

We come here to one of the great striking and outstanding verses
in the Bible. Every verse in the Scripture, of course, is of supreme
importance, but the history of the Church shows clearly that there
are some verses which have been used by the Spirit in an unusual
and extraordinary manner. It is not that I have proof that this
verse has been used in that way, but I venture to say that it is one
of the most important and pivotal verses. That is so because it
contains one of the clearest definitions found in the New Testament as to what exactly it means to be a Christian.

Those who have followed the argument of this chapter will
realize that what the Apostle is doing here is to apply to all who
are Christians the truth he had stated in verse 16 as a general
proposition. You recall that he had laid down that general principle in verse 16 in order to rebut and refute the question which he
records in verse 15 – 'What then? Shall we sin because we are
not under the law, but under grace? God forbid'. Then came the
general principle in verse 16, 'Know ye not that to whom ye
yield yourselves servants to obey, his servants ye are to whom
ye obey, whether of sin unto death, or of obedience unto righteousness'. That is the general principle which we have already
worked out, and of which the main conclusions are: first, that
there are two great powers anxious to possess us and to dominate
our lives. There are only two, and they are diametrically opposed
to each other. Second, it is a sheer impossibility for anyone to be
under both of these powers at one and the same time. The final

[205]

point, we saw, was that we all proclaim whose slaves we are by
the way in which we live. The slave-owner insists upon a certain
type of conduct; therefore if you look at a man's conduct you
can tell who his master is. 'Know ye not that to whom ye yield
yourselves servants to obey, his servants ye are to whom ye obey'.

These being the general principles, the Apostle in this seventeenth verse applies them to the case of all Christians. He says in
effect, 'In your case, you Christians in Rome, I am in a happy
position. God be thanked', he says. None need trip over this
expression. When you first read the verse you may well think that
the Apostle is thanking God that these people were once the servants of sin. But, of course, he could not possibly thank God for
that which is the tragedy of mankind. What he is saying is, 'I
thank God that you, who were once servants of sin, are no longer
of that character, but you have now obeyed from the heart that
form of doctrine which was delivered you'. In putting it in that
way the Apostle really tells us what is true of a Christian. He is
looking at these Roman Christians and he says, 'God be thanked,
I know that you are all right. You are no longer in the wrong
position, as you once were; you are in an entirely new position'.
Thus speaking, he throws out one of the most wonderful definitions of the Christian to be found anywhere in the Bible. Let me
expound it in terms of three principles, which the Apostle teaches
very clearly.

The first is this. A Christian is a person who has undergone a
great change. 'Ye were': 'that is what was once true of you; but
it is no longer true of you. You are now in an entirely different
position.' 'Ye were'; but 'ye have'. We cannot stay with this now
but it is obviously of crucial importance. Nobody is born a Christian; something has to happen to us before we become Christians.
Those who are familiar with the argument of the first five chapters
of this epistle do not need to be convinced of that truth. In chapter
5 from verse 12 to verse 21 the Apostle has proved to us beyond
any doubt that we are all born the children of Adam, and that we
inherit Adam's nature. We were guilty of the sin that Adam committed; we sinned with him. 'Wherefore, as by one man sin entered into the world, and death by sin; and so death passed upon
all men, for that all have sinned'. That is what we are by nature;
nobody is born a Christian. So to become a Christian it is obviously necessary that we should undergo some great change.

All the New Testament terminology about salvation puts it in that way. Here are the terms: 'Ye must be born again' – not that you must be improved a little in your journey; not that you need a little encouragement in your fight. 'Ye must be born again.' Regeneration, new creation is essential. 'If any man be in Christ, he is a new creature (a new creation).' The change is as great as that. This is the typical and characteristic New Testament terminology with regard to salvation. A Christian is a man who has undergone a change that can only be described by such terminology. 'Ye were' – now, 'Ye have'. Something has happened and you are entirely different. Paul thanks God for it.

What I desire to emphasize at the moment is the greatness of this change. It is not enough for us merely to know that we have been changed, or that a Christian is a man who must undergo a change; we must have some adequate conception of the greatness of the change which is undergone. We see the greatness in this way, that it is a change which affects the whole of a man's personality. Look at it again. 'Ye have obeyed' – there is your will. 'From the heart' – there is your emotion. What have you obeyed from the heart? 'The form of doctrine delivered you'. How do you apprehend doctrine? You do so with your mind. So the change a man undergoes to become a Christian is a change that affects him in his mind, in his heart, and in his will; the entire personality is involved.

Christianity does not merely deal with one part of us. That is where it differs from the cults and many false religions and movements. Their characteristic always is that they only deal with a part of man. There are philosophers that interest and excite and intrigue the intellect and the mind; they take up a man's mind, but do not touch his heart at all, and they have no effect upon his conduct. They are partial. There are many such teachings at the present time; their appeal is only to the intellect. This is the position of your so-called intellectuals. They are concerned about the whole problem of life, but their interest never goes beyond the intellect, the mind and the understanding. That is one reason why it is finally of no value. Then there are other movements which interest us and move us only in the realm of our emotions and affections. There are many things that can move us to tears, but they are of no ultimate value to us. This applies to most forms of entertainment, and to many books which are read. They may move

you, but they do not give you any understanding; they have
nothing to say to your mind, and they do not lead you to anything of value. Music of a certain type can do this. Great music, of
course, goes much further; it takes in your mind as well. But
there is a type of music that makes a direct appeal to the emotions
and to nothing else – the sloppy, sentimental type. The Gospel
is not like that, says the Apostle; it is not only an appeal to the
emotions.

We must be careful about these things. There is no charge that
is brought so frequently against the Christian faith and message,
as that it is nothing but some kind of emotionalism. And, indeed,
there are Christian people, Christians by profession, who certainly give the impression that all they have is something which
moves them emotionally. They say, 'I do not understand; I
cannot give you any reason or explanation; all I know is that I
have felt something'. They cannot tell you what that something
is. They have been moved solely in the realm of the emotions;
and that is not Christianity.

In the same way, there are teachings and movements that
make a direct appeal to the will only. That is true of morality and
an ethical interest. It goes straight to the will, and it stops there.
It is not so much concerned about the understanding, and not
interested at all in the emotions; but it is interested in practical
results, so it concentrates on the will. There is a form of preaching that specializes in appeals to the will. It possesses little intellectual and doctrinal content, and there is nothing about it that
ever moves the emotions; but tremendous pressure is brought
to bear on people in the realm of their wills. They are made to
'decide', and to do something – all the pressure is on the will.
The point I am making is that any of these partial emphases is
unworthy of the name of the Gospel, this Gospel which the
Apostle describes elsewhere as 'the glorious gospel of the blessed
God' [1 *Timothy* 1 : 11]. It is so big, it is so great, that it takes in
the whole man, it engages the entire personality. If our minds and
hearts and wills are not engaged we are not Christians. 'Thank
God', says the Apostle, 'ye have obeyed from the heart that form
of doctrine that was delivered you'. The whole personality of
these Romans was involved in this change. You cannot be converted in your mind only, you cannot be converted in your
heart only, you cannot be converted in your will only; if you are

truly converted and born again, the three are involved, the whole man is involved.

The second way in which the Apostle puts the matter is to say that this change is so great that it involves a complete change of ownership. This is highly important in the argument of the Apostle at this particular point. He is really stressing the application of the principle laid down in verse 16. He says to the Christians of Rome, 'You have undergone a complete change of ownership'. Let us work that out a little.

The first thing he tells us is that man by nature, man before he is converted and becomes a Christian, is a slave of sin. 'God be thanked', he says, 'that you who were' – What were they? 'The servants', says the Authorized Version weakly; but it is actually, 'the slaves of sin', as we have seen. Man is a slave of sin by nature. Man is not born neutral, as so many seem to think, with the possibility of deciding to which of the two masters he will yield himself and sell himself. Not at all! He is 'born a slave of sin'. We need not prove that again, as the Apostle has done so thoroughly in chapter 5 verses 12–21. 'In sin did my mother conceive me', says the Psalmist. We are 'born in sin, shapen in iniquity'. Man is never free; he is always a slave. He is born a slave of sin. The Lord Jesus Christ put it thus, 'The strong man armed keepeth his goods in peace'; and that 'strong man', the devil, will go on doing that until 'a stronger than he shall come upon him and overcome him and take from him all his armour wherein he trusted, and divide his spoils' [*Luke* 11 : 21, 22]. That is our Lord's picture of humanity. He Himself is the One Who comes and who masters the strong man armed, robs him of his armour and sets free this people whom he has held in bondage and in captivity. These are the New Testament terms: 'We are all by nature the children of wrath, even as others' [*Ephesians* 2 : 3]. We are said to be 'under the dominion of Satan'. We are 'in the kingdom of darkness' by birth. Or as Paul puts it in chapter 5 verse 21 of this Epistle, 'Sin hath reigned unto death'. In other words, there is nothing which is quite so foolish and pathetic as to talk about the natural man's freedom. There is no such thing; we are born the slaves of sin. 'God be thanked, that you were once the slaves of sin . . . ' They did not make themselves that; they were born like that, that is man by nature. That is the doctrine of Original Sin, with original guilt and original pollution included.

Many find it difficult to believe this. They say, 'But I know a number of very good people who are not Christians but are nevertheless very moral people. I cannot point a finger at them'. They argue, therefore, that these people are free, and ask, 'How can you say of such people that they are slaves of sin?' You see the fallacy. It is to identify sin with some of its manifestations only. But all manifestations of sin are sin. The slavery of sin is sometimes shown by violent sinning – drunkenness, murder, adultery, living to lust and passion and desire – and anyone can see clearly the obvious slavery of sin.

But that is not the only form which the slavery of sin takes. The same slavery can be seen in many nice and polite people who are never guilty of such violent sins. But what do they live for? For the pleasures of this world. They are quite respectable pleasures, and such people are living entirely for them. They are harnessed to 'the thing to do', they are slaves of custom, and of society; they just follow the habits of their fellows. There is nothing more obvious than the slavery of non-Christian society today in its politest forms. You can read about it in your newspapers – I refer not only to the reports of what is said in law courts – in the gossip columns and the doings of 'high society'. The one is as much slavery as the other. It is seen in the way they observe the niceties, and are punctilious about falling into line with 'the done thing'. They are careful to speak in the right way, and to eat and drink in the right way. It is sheer slavery. Respectable in some forms, not respectable in others; but always slavery. The devil is not concerned about the appearance as long as we are slaves.

The real proof of the slavery of the whole of mankind is ultimately found, not so much in what men do, as in what they omit to do. Look at the people I have been describing, many of whom are intellectual, moral people who do a lot of good. They give their money to, and belong to good causes; they are active in trying to improve the condition of the whole of mankind. So you may ask, 'How can you say that they are slaves of sin?' There is a very simple proof. Why do they not believe in God? Why do they not believe in the Lord Jesus Christ? Why do they not believe in His atoning death? The answer is that they are not allowed to believe. 'If our gospel be hid', says Paul, 'it is hid to them that are lost; in whom the god of this world hath blinded the minds of them which believe not, lest the light of the glorious gospel of Christ, who is the image of God, should shine unto them' [2 *Corinthians* 4 : 3, 4]. They are not violent sinners, there is nothing openly reprobate about them; but the proof of the slavery is that they are not allowed to believe in God, and in His Son, and in the glorious Gospel, because their slave-owner prohibits it. They are 'blinded' by him. There is no slavery more terrible! We must never be misled into regarding sin as having only one kind of manifestation. The whole world is born in slavery to sin: 'There is none righteous, no, not one'. We are all 'born in sin, shapen in iniquity'; we are all 'even as others, the children of wrath'.

Such is mankind by nature; such is the continuing position of all who do not believe the Gospel. They are the utter slaves of sin, slaves of the devil, slaves of the kingdom of darkness. And as such, and if they remain such, and die as such, they will go to hell and to the darkness outside God to all eternity. That is the most terrible aspect of sin. It is not so much the actions as this slavery to evil and to all that is opposed to God. That, then, is one side of the matter.

But look at the other side. 'God be thanked' the Apostle says in effect; 'you were that', but 'you are no longer that. You are now slaves to Jesus Christ'. In verse 18 he says, 'Being then made free from sin' – from the slavery of sin – 'you became the servants (the slaves) of righteousness'. The Apostle was so concerned about this that he says it again in verse 22. 'But now being made free from sin, and become slaves of God, ye have your fruit unto holiness and the end everlasting life'. Man, I repeat, is always a slave; he is born a slave of sin, by second birth he becomes the bondslave of Jesus Christ. Observe how the Apostle describes himself in that way at the beginning of so many of his epistles. 'Paul, a bondslave of Jesus Christ' – that is his favourite way of describing himself. He reminds the Corinthians, 'You are not your own, you have been bought with a price' [1 *Corinthians* 6 : 19, 20]. They were the slaves of sin and of Satan, but they have been bought out of it by another Master who owns them. 'You are not your own.'

Man is never free; he is either a slave of sin and Satan or he is a slave of God and of the Lord Jesus Christ. The believer was in that old kingdom of darkness and of death, but now he is in a new kingdom of light; and he is subject to all its laws and powers. He was mastered by evil before, he is now mastered by righteousness, and obedience, and all that is on the other side.

That is the first thing, therefore, the Apostle tells us about the Christian. The Christian is a man who has undergone this great change. And obviously, a man who has undergone such a change knows it and is aware of it. He knows to whom he belongs, and who is his master, and in whose kingdom he lives and acts. Are we quite certain where we belong? Can we say 'I was'; 'I am no longer'; 'I am now'? 'I was a slave of sin; I am now a slave of God, and of Christ, and of righteousness and holiness.' That is what makes us Christian, nothing less than that. It is the profoundest, the greatest change that is conceivable.

The second matter which the Apostle puts before us is that he tells us how this great change comes about. What are the agencies that bring about our transfer from slavery to sin on the one hand, to slavery to God on the other? There is first of all, he says, an immediate agency, which he describes as 'that form of doctrine'. 'Ye were the servants of sin, but ye have obeyed from the heart'. What? 'that form of doctrine that was delivered you'. The phrase can be translated as 'that pattern of doctrine', 'that mode of doctrine'.

What does the Apostle mean by this? Here again is a subject which is not only of theoretical interest, but of great practical interest also. I know of nothing that is more important from the standpoint of evangelism than this very statement. I have a suspicion that many of our troubles in the church today, and perhaps one of the major reasons why revival tarries, is that we are not clear about the true note of evangelism as it is defined here. What is this 'form of doctrine' that is to be used as the immediate agency to produce this great change? The very results that follow from the change gives us a shrewd idea as to the nature of the 'form of doctrine'. If the change produced is as great as I have been describing, and as I shall yet draw it out, what is the content of this 'form of doctrine?' Another aid we have to the understanding of it is that the Apostle tells us that the Romans had already believed it. Paul had not preached to them himself, but this 'form of doctrine' had been delivered to them, and they had believed it. What then is it?

We must start with a negative. From what I have been saying, and from what the Apostle puts so clearly here, it is obvious that the form of doctrine is not merely a message of forgiveness only. There are people who think that forgiveness is the sole message of evangelism. All you do in evangelism, they say, is to call people to 'Come to Christ', and you offer them forgiveness. You call upon them to 'decide for Christ'. They generally go on to say that if you afterwards go to other meetings you will learn a deeper doctrine, a profounder truth; but in an evangelistic meeting there is only a simple message – it is 'Come to Jesus; come to Christ, decide for Him. If you want forgiveness, here it is'. Now as I understand this verse, such teaching is not only dangerous, but also utterly un-scriptural. That is why this matter is of such tremendous importance.

That is not the message the Roman Christians had believed, otherwise Paul could not have drawn these great deductions from it. What then is it? 'The form of doctrine delivered them' was the full doctrine has been elaborating hitherto in this Epistle – nothing less. The message of evangelism is a message that starts with man in sin under the wrath of a holy God. Paul starts with that away back in chapter 1, in verses 16, 17, and 18. 'I am not ashamed of the gospel of Christ, for it is the power of God unto salvation to everyone that believeth; to the Jew first and also to the Greek. For therein is the righteousness of God revealed from faith to faith; as it is written, The just shall live by faith. For (because) the wrath of God is (already) revealed from heaven against all ungodliness and unrighteousness of men who hold (down) the truth in unrighteousness.' That is an essential part of the message. You do not skate lightly over and around sin in evangelism, and say to people 'Do not bother about repentance now. Come to Christ first, you can repent afterwards'. No! The doctrine of sin is a vital part of this 'form of doctrine' that produces the amazing result. We all have to see ourselves under condemnation, bound for hell, hopeless and helpless in sin and under the wrath of God. We have to see the foul, terrible nature of such a condition, its slavery to sin and Satan, and the terrible end to which it inevitably leads. That is a part of the message.

Then comes the utter hopelessness of all human striving and effort to achieve salvation. It took Paul most of chapters 1, 2, and 3 to unfold this aspect of the doctrine. The Gentiles with their philosophy cannot deliver themselves, neither can the Jew, the man who boasted that because he had the Law a happy future was assured to him. 'No', says Paul, 'you are no better than the Gentile. Knowledge of the Law does not save; you have to keep the Law.' So he concludes 'that there is no difference; all have sinned and come short of the glory of God'. The whole human race has failed. You cannot save yourself. It matters not at all how good and moral and excellent and religious you may be. This counts for nothing. Whether you have been circumcised or not does not matter; and all morality is useless in and of itself. Man by his own effort cannot save himself. Paul elaborates the teaching to remind them of it, and to confirm them in it.

This is all a part of evangelism. Evangelism does not consist in telling stories and playing on people's emotions, and then pressing them to a decision at the end without any true knowledge on their part of what they are doing. No, but it is the outlining of this 'form of doctrine', this message, this truth. Then you go on to tell them that from this complete hopelessness and helplessness and despair God has provided a way of escape: 'Being justified freely by his grace through the redemption that is in Christ Jesus, whom God hath set forth to be a propitiation through faith in his blood'. That is the message, that is the 'form of doctrine that has been delivered'. That is the immediate agency that produces this great change.

But what is the ultimate agency? 'The form of doctrine' is the message used; but what uses it, who uses it? The Apostle answers the question, 'But God be thanked, that ye were the servants of sin, but ye have obeyed from the heart that form of doctrine which was delivered you', says the Authorized Version. Alas, it is a wrong translation. All the other translations are agreed about this, as are the commentators. The expression used by the Apostle does not mean 'the form of doctrine delivered unto you'. The Revised Version reminds us that the verb is passive, not active. It should read, 'Ye became obedient from the heart to that form of teaching whereunto ye were delivered'. That is the Revised Version. The Revised Standard Version says, 'the standard of teaching to which you were committed'. What it really means is, 'You have obeyed from the heart the form of doctrine to which you have been delivered over'. These Roman Christians had been 'handed over', 'delivered over' to this form of doctrine.

Some authorities would have us believe that the picture the Apostle had in his mind here was one suggested by the word he deliberately chose. Think of a great mould. A man comes along and pours molten metal into that mould. Because the metal is molten it now takes the form of the mould, so that when it cools he can lift it out in its solid form. It will be exactly the same shape as the mould into which he put it. That is the idea conveyed by the Apostle. 'You', he says, 'who have become believers, have been delivered over, you have been poured into the mould of this form of doctrine.' 'That is why you are what you are.'

But that at once raises the question, Who has delivered them over to this? Who delivers any man over to this? How can a man who is a slave of Satan be fashioned according to this form of doctrine. Who can put him into this new mould? There is only one answer. It must be the work of another. He cannot perform the work upon himself. That is to say, you cannot make yourself a Christian, it is a sheer impossibility. You have been 'delivered over unto'. Who does it? Again there is only one answer. It is God! That is what we read in the second chapter of the Epistle to the Ephesians. 'You hath he quickened, who were dead in trespasses and sins' [verse 1]. We were hopeless, we were dead; but He has quickened us, He has raised us, and caused us to be 'seated in the heavenly places' [verse 6]. 'We are his workmanship', says the Apostle, [verse 10]; 'not of (our) works, lest any man should boast'. 'By grace are ye saved.' It is all of God. It is God who delivers us over, and pours us into this new mould.

Observe the Apostle saying a similar thing in Colossians chapter 1: 'Giving thanks unto the Father, who hath made us meet to be partakers of the inheritance of the saints in light: who hath delivered us from the power of darkness, and hath translated us into the kingdom of his dear Son' (verses 12 and 13). It is God who has done it all. This is how the great change comes about. The Holy Spirit of God takes this word, this message, this 'form of doctrine', and He puts us into it and it works upon us. It fashions us, it puts us into shape, as it were. The word of Scripture, of the Gospel, is the immediate agency, the instrument used; but the One who is using the instrument is the blessed Holy Spirit. So it is not surprising that the Apostle began this statement in the way he did. How does it start? 'God be thanked . . .' Of course! There is nobody else to thank. 'He that glorieth, let him glory in the Lord.' Every mouth has been stopped; there is no room for boasting. Man has done nothing; man can do nothing. Who has moulded us anew? God! 'He that glorieth, let him glory in the Lord.' Yes, God be thanked, 'I am what I am by the grace of God'.

Do you resent this teaching? If you do I can tell you why. You have never realized that you are an utter, absolute slave to sin. That is the reason. You do not realize that you are a slave of Satan, that you cannot move, that you cannot overcome that 'strong man armed'. It is impossible for man to overcome him, Christ tells us. It takes a stronger than he to do so. The patriarchs could not do it; but the Son of God has done it. I am always amazed that any should be so foolish as to object to this teaching, and especially if they claim to be Christians. Why? For this reason, that this is the basis and the foundation of the most glorious assurance and certainty a man can ever have. My assurance, and my confidence concerning my final salvation is just this, that I am in the hands of God, that He took me from that old sin mould and put me into this new mould. It is His mould; and He is going to keep me in it until I am perfect. When God starts on the work, and begins to fashion us, He does not leave it half done, He goes on with it. 'He which hath begun a good work in you will perform it until the day of Jesus Christ' [*Philippians* 1 : 6]. I shall come out of that mould at the end 'without spot or wrinkle or any such thing'. I shall be perfect, I shall be entire, I shall be holy, completely holy. I shall be like Him. Thank God it is He who puts me into His own mould and fashions me according to His own eternal will and purpose in Christ Jesus. That, then, is the way in which the change takes place, that is how it comes to pass.

A word next about the third and the last principle which is equally important. It is about the evidence of the fact that the great change has taken place in us. We are all concerned about this. How can we know to a certainty whether this great change has taken place in us? It follows of necessity from what Paul has already said. This is not a matter of dispute; it is as certain as everything I have just been saying. And it is only because of the certainty of this that the Apostle can refute and rebut the ridiculous argument that he quotes in verse 15. What is the result of being put into this mould, into this 'form of doctrine' to which God delivered us? To what does it lead? Here is the answer – Obedience! 'God be thanked, that ye were the slaves of sin, but ye have obeyed . . . ' Note that he does not merely say, 'You have believed'; he says 'you have obeyed the form of doctrine'.

What a vital point! It is not belief only. There is, alas, such a thing as giving intellectual assent alone to the truth of the Gospel. That does not save anyone. There are men who are still the slaves of sin, and utterly carnal, who enjoy reading the Scriptures and playing with its doctrines as others do with crossword puzzles. If you happen to have been brought up in such circles it can be a highly intellectual occupation. Such men are interested in their minds, they believe the teaching intellectually; but it has never led to anything in their lives. What of them? They are not Christians. I emphasized at the beginning that the whole person is involved in salvation. If the will is not involved you are not a Christian. Let me say again that it is not belief in forgiveness only. There are people who believe that God forgives them in Christ, but they go on sinning. That is no true belief; that is of no value at all. That is why I must say once more that there is nothing that is so unscriptural, so utterly wrong, as to place or create a division between justification and sanctification. No such thing is possible. But that has been popular teaching. 'Now that you have taken your justification by faith, come along and take your sanctification by faith. You were saved by your justification when you believed at that evangelistic meeting; you took it by faith.' 'But', they say, 'you have spent too many years in that position. Come now and take your sanctification by faith.'

That, to me, is a denial of the Scripture, it is a lie. I am not speaking violently or too strongly; I am interpreting Scripture. What makes a man a Christian is the 'obedience' that he gives to 'the form of doctrine delivered unto him'. That is what these Roman Christians had done. The Apostle's whole argument depends upon this. If he granted for a moment that a man could be justified without the process of sanctification starting at exactly the same time, he would not be able to answer the objection voiced in the words, 'What then? Shall we sin because we are not under law, but under grace?' If you could stop at justification that objection would be valid. Here is a man who believes that he is forgiven, but it has not led to any change in his life; he is not sanctified. So the critic of Paul says, 'Ah, I see, justification means that you believe your sins are forgiven but that you may go on living as you did before'. Thus the Apostle's argument would fall to the ground. But he says that that position is impossible, because to 'believe' in the true sense of the word means that it is not your mind only that is involved but your heart and your will also. It is an obedience from the heart.

So I say that it is not only wrong to separate justification and sanctification, and to put them in separate compartments, it is equally wrong to put evangelistic meetings and holiness meetings into separate watertight compartments. But there has been much of that. I know many Christian people who never attend a Sunday evening service. 'Ah', they say, 'that is an evangelistic service. I am saved, and of course that type of service is for unbelievers' – as if there is nothing for a believer in an evangelistic service! Their view is that they could derive no benefit at all. Some attend because they believe they can help the preacher and also pray for the unbelievers who may come in. But the idea is, 'Of course, I have passed beyond that; that is the first department'. But there are no such departments in the Church of God and in the Gospel; and there is no essential difference between these two messages. The message of evangelism includes all this, and you cannot be justified without being partially sanctified.

We must beware, then, of these unscriptural and artificial divisions in thought and in practice. According to the New Testament, faith always includes the element of obedience. There is no value whatsoever in a supposed faith that does not lead inevitably to a changed life. James agrees with what the Apostle Paul says here. 'Faith without works is dead', he says; it is not faith, it is an intellectual assent only. You cannot believe in Christ in portions and in parts. He is one and indivisible. If you see the truth at all, you see something of its wholeness.

Why is this of necessity true? Let me suggest some answers. The prime object of God in instituting salvation for us in Christ Jesus is not simply that we might be forgiven. This is how Paul puts it in his letter to the Ephesians, 'We are his workmanship, created in Christ Jesus'. What for? '. . . unto good works, which God hath before ordained that we should walk in them' [2 : 10]. Or again, in his Epistle to Titus: 'Who gave himself for us'. Why did He do it? '. . . that he might redeem us from all iniquity,

and purify unto himself a peculiar people zealous of good works'
[2 : 14]' You cannot stop at forgiveness. Christ died to do all
this; and all this must be stated in our evangelism. It must also
become apparent at once in the life of the believer. Indeed everything about the Gospel inevitably leads to this end.

What does this 'form of doctrine' tell us? It tells us about the
terrible character of sin, about our appalling position as slaves
of sin, and under the wrath of God, as hell-bound sinners. That
immediately produces a hatred of sin, a horror of sin, an alarm
about the results of sin, and a desire to get away from sin. Let the
Epistle to Titus speak to us again: 'The grace of God that bringeth
salvation, hath appeared to all men, teaching us' – What? 'that
denying ungodliness and worldly lusts, we should live soberly,
righteously, and godly, in this present world' [2 : 11–12]. That
is what it teaches us. Such obedience is inevitable. The message
of the Gospel makes it inevitable.

I sum up the Apostle's teaching about 'the form of doctrine'
in this way. The essence of sin is disobedience of God, His Word
and His way; and therefore the essence of the opposite, which is
faith, is obedience to God. The Christian man is a man who obeys
God. How? He obeys God's Word, he obeys God's Gospel,
he obeys everything that God has said. That is why in the first
chapter in the fifth verse the Apostle talks about 'the obedience of
faith'. And in the last chapter of this Epistle he says it again in
verses 18, 19, and 26. 'For they that are such *serve not* the Lord
Jesus Christ.' 'I beseech you, brethren', he says, 'mark them which
cause divisions and offences contrary to the doctrine which you
have learned: and avoid them. For they that are such *serve not*
our Lord Jesus Christ, but their own belly; and by good words
and fair speeches deceive the hearts of the simple. For *your obedience* is come abroad unto all men. I am glad therefore on your
behalf.' And then at the end in verse 26: 'But now', he says, talking about this mystery of the Gospel, 'But now is made manifest,
and by the Scriptures of the prophets, according to the commandment of the everlasting God, made known to all nations'. What
for? 'For the *obedience* of faith'. Faith is obedience.

This is not only Paul's teaching. Peter, in his first Epistle,
chapter 1, verse 22, says, 'Seeing ye have purified your hearts in
obeying the truth through the Spirit'. To believe the Gospel
means to obey God. To what does God call us? Is it just to

[219]

believe, or to 'Come to Christ', or to 'Decide for Christ?' No! His command is to 'Repent'. 'God commandeth all men everywhere to repent', says the Apostle Paul to the Athenians [*Acts* 17 : 30]. John the Baptist preached the same message of repentance.

Faith is obedience; any so-called faith that does not put its emphasis on obedience is unworthy of the term. And the Christian not only obeys, he obeys from the heart – 'ye have obeyed from the heart'. The obedience is not grudging or hesitant. The Christian rejoices in serving God; he lives to His praise. 'Whose service', the Prayer Book puts it, 'is perfect freedom'. Philip Doddridge gives us a wonderful description of true Christianity –

> *My gracious Lord, I own Thy right*
> *To every service I can pay;*
> *And call it my supreme delight*
> *To hear Thy dictates and obey*

Not grudging, not feeling that it is narrow, not trying to live as near as you can to the world, and to that old life of sin, and feeling it is a pity that the Gospel is so stringent in its demands! No, that is not Christianity! A man who feels like that is a man who is not saved.

The man who is saved is a man who has undergone this profound change. He is in the 'mould', shaped by the doctrine. What does it teach him? To repent, to leave sin, to 'flee from the wrath to come', to give himself entirely to God and His obedience. And he does so not merely with his will; his whole heart is in it. He has seen the truth with his mind, but it has also moved him. He is melted and he wants to thank God, he wants to show his gratitude.

> *I call it my supreme delight*
> *To hear thy dictates and obey.*

The Christian is a willing slave, a happy slave, the bondslave of Jesus Christ, and his supreme desire is to live to the praise of the glory of God and of His dear Son who came into the world on account of our sins, that we might be rescued and redeemed. God be thanked, that we, who were the slaves of sin, have been taken up by God and put into the divine mould, 'the form of doctrine', with the result that we now obey from the heart His every dictate, and it is our 'supreme delight' to do so.

Seventeen

*

Being then made free from sin, ye became the servants of righteousness.   Romans 6 : 18

This is one of those verses, of which we have come across previous instances in this very chapter, in which the Apostle, as it were, after working out his argument, sums up the position of the Christian. That is, of course, of the very essence of true teaching. Here, having worked out his argument in verses 16 and 17, he sums it up and arrives at a fundamental conclusion about the Christian man, and particularly in terms of the objection which was being brought forward against his teaching by certain people, to the effect that his teaching was one which encouraged people to continue in sin.

This eighteenth verse is, therefore, in many ways a parallel to verse 11; it merely does for this second section of the Chapter what verse 11 did for the first section. Having worked out his argument in verses 1 to 10 Paul says, 'Likewise reckon ye also yourselves to be dead indeed unto sin, but alive unto God, through Jesus Christ our Lord.' That is the truth about the Christian. Here he states it again, the same truth in substance, but he states it this time in terms of the illustration about slavery which he has been using in his argument in verses 16 and 17.

It is important that we should recognize the Apostle's characteristic method. Another characteristic of the method is that he gives us one of these summaries of the Christian's position before he goes on to make an appeal or a practical exhortation. He did that in verse 11. Having told us that we are to 'reckon ourselves' – because it is true – 'as dead indeed unto sin, but alive unto God, through Jesus Christ our Lord', he then goes on to the appeal in verses 12 and 13, 'Let not sin therefore reign in your

[221]

mortal body', and so on. He does exactly the same thing here. He makes a statement about the Christian in verse 18; then, continuing, he says, 'I speak after the manner of men because of the infirmity of your flesh: for as ye have yielded your members servants to uncleanness and to iniquity unto iniquity; even so now yield your members servants to righteousness unto holiness'. In other words, because what he says in verse 18 is true of believers, he has a right to make the appeal of verse 19 and the following verses. Indeed, because of what is true of them in verse 18, it follows inevitably that he must make the appeal of verse 19. Thus in every way he proves the utterly foolish and futile character of the charge which is made against him, and which he has put before us in verse 15.

There, then, are what we may call the mechanics of this most important verse. Having seen how the Apostle came to make the statement, we can now proceed to consider it. We start with certain general remarks. This is a statement of fact; it is not an exhortation. He is not exhorting us to free ourselves from sin, he is telling us that we are free from sin. This is the position of, and the truth about the Christian.

Secondly, I would emphasize again that this is true of all Christians. It is not merely true of some Christians who have gone on to have a second experience; it is true of all Christians. This is a vital part of the Apostle's entire argument at this point. It is not only true of certain 'special' Christians who have something which the ordinary Christian lacks. We can put it in another way. You cannot be a Christian at all except this be true of you. Let us work this out.

What, then, according to the Apostle is true of every one of us who is a Christian? You notice he starts with a negative. In the Authorized Version it is, 'Being then made free from sin'. But a better translation is, 'Having been freed from sin'. That is the negative that is true of us. Let me add some more negatives. It does not mean sinless perfection. It does not mean that we are now entirely free from sin in every respect, that there is no sin left in us at all, and that we have finished once and for ever with sin itself or sin as such. It does not mean that. The Apostle is not teaching sinless perfection. The whole context proves that, and especially the exhortation in verse 19 which follows. So we must not interpret 'being free from sin' as meaning that literally there is no sin left in us in any shape or form whatsoever, and that we have finished completely and absolutely with it.

Secondly, it does not mean that we are free from our sinful nature. It does not mean that the sinful nature has been taken right out of us. You remember we have drawn a distinction between the 'old man' and the sinful nature. The old man has gone, he is dead, and we have finished with him once and for ever. But that is not true of the sinful nature; the sinful nature remains, as we have been reminded in verse 12, in our 'mortal bodies'. So it does not mean that we are free altogether from the sinful nature. It means less than that, but at the same time it means more than that. Let me explain myself. It means less in this way, that if we say that we are entirely free from the sinful nature, we are claiming sinless perfection, which Paul is certainly not teaching here, and never teaches anywhere else. But then, on the other hand, it means more in this sense, that we are free from sin as a power, free not only from the tyranny of the sinful nature but also from the tyranny of the devil and all his forces, and even hell itself. So we must be careful to differentiate here and to realize that Paul is not simply saying that we are free from the sinful nature.

My last negative is to indicate that Paul is not saying that we are free from temptations, that we shall never again be tempted, that we shall never again be worried by an evil thought which the devil may throw at us, or that we shall never again be troubled by the motions of sin which remain in the sinful body, 'the body of sin' or 'the mortal body', as he calls it.

I introduce these negatives because there are many good Christian people who are troubled about this matter. They seem to think that the mere fact that they are tempted somehow means that these great statements of the Scriptures do not apply to them. It is important, therefore, that we should not interpret 'free' and 'being freed from sin' as meaning that we no longer are subject to temptation, or that we shall never be worried by what Paul calls in chapter 7 'the motions of sin' that are in the sinful body.

What then do the Apostle's words mean positively? They mean, clearly, the opposite of what he says in the rest of the verse. There is a kind of parallel which he has used previously. 'Being then made free from sin'. Well, what is the opposite of being 'free from sin'? It is to be 'servants of righteousness';

and remember that the word 'servants' here, as in all these verses, means 'slaves'. So as the positive means to be 'slaves of righteousness', the negative means that we are no longer 'slaves to sin'. That is the parallel. We are slaves to righteousness, but we are no longer slaves to sin. We have been freed from sin's slavery, we have been delivered from it, we are no longer in that position of bondage.

Let me use the terms I have used before. As Christians – and you cannot be a Christian without this being true of you – you are no longer under the slavery and the tyranny and the dominion and the whole bondage of sin. You notice that the Apostle is virtually repeating what he has already said several times in this chapter. Take verse 2: 'God forbid. How shall we that died to sin live any longer therein?' As we have seen previously, this means that we have died to the reign of sin, to the rule of sin, to the dominion of sin, to sin personified and sin as represented by the devil with all his powers and subtlety. Paul says the same thing again in verse 6. 'Knowing this, that our old man was crucified with him'. Remember that that means 'once and for ever'. It occurs again in verse 7. 'He that is dead is freed from sin'. It is also present by implication in verse 10, where the Apostle says of our Lord, 'In that he died, he died unto sin once'. He says that the same is true of us in verse 11: 'Likewise reckon ye also yourselves to be dead indeed unto sin'. You have died unto it. What we have here is clearly just a repetition of the truth. In a sense Paul even says it in verse 14: 'For sin shall not have dominion over you'. Why? 'Because you are not under the law, but under grace'. And as we have seen, it is the whole implication of verse 17. 'God be thanked, that ye were the servants of sin (the slaves of sin), but ye have obeyed from the heart that form of doctrine into which you were delivered', or 'to which you were committed'.

Here, then, is a most important statement that is true of us as Christians. The very fact that we believe the Gospel at all is proof positive that this is true of us. No man can believe the Gospel of Christ while he is a slave to sin; it is impossible. The Apostle says that clearly and explicitly, as we have seen, in 2 Corinthians 4, verses 3 and 4: 'If our gospel be hid, it is hid to them that are lost, in whom the god of this world hath blinded the minds of them which believe not, lest the light of the glorious gospel of

Christ should shine unto them'. The man who is a slave of sin and all its powers cannot believe; so the very fact that a man believes the Gospel is proof that he has been 'freed from sin'. This is, obviously, a great and crucial statement; it is the argument of the whole of this chapter, and therefore we must be clear about it. This is a fundamental statement of the New Testament about the Christian man; he is no longer the slave of sin as a power, as a reigning force; he has been set free from that by a greater power. That is the negative aspect of the matter.

The positive aspect is found in the words, 'Being then made free from sin, ye became the servants of righteousness'. That is how the Authorized Version puts it. But it is not adequate, it is not strong enough. What it says is true, but it might be misinterpreted. A better translation is, 'Ye were enslaved to righteousness'; that is exactly what the Apostle says. Not only have we 'become' the slaves; but we have been 'enslaved to righteousness'. We were before 'enslaved to sin', we have now become 'enslaved to righteousness'. We were 'delivered over unto the form of doctrine', Paul has said, and now he puts the matter in a different way by saying that we have become 'enslaved to righteousness', where by 'righteousness' he does not mean morality only, but the original righteousness which God gave man. He means uprightness in the highest moral sense; indeed, as he will put it specifically at the close of verse 19, he means 'holiness'.

Our position, as Christians, is that we have been 'enslaved to righteousness'. This does not mean that we admire righteousness, nor that we desire to be righteous; it does not mean that we are attempting to be righteous, or attempting to practise righteousness in our daily life. It includes all these things but has a much wider content. What the Apostle says is, that we have become 'slaves to righteousness' – nothing less. Not 'servants', but 'slaves' of righteousness! That means that we have come under the power and control and influence of righteousness. As once we were tyrannized over and ruled by, and governed by sin, we are now, we may say, tyrannized over and governed and ruled by righteousness itself. Furthermore, this is something that is true of every one of us from the moment of our regeneration. The Apostle is talking about Christians – any Christian. From the moment we are regenerate it is true to say of us that we are no longer slaves of sin; we are the slaves of righteousness. How utterly wrong and

unscriptural it is, therefore, to separate justification and sanctification, and to say that a man can be justified apart from sanctification, or to say that a man can receive his justification and
perhaps years later go on and receive his sanctification. According
to the Apostle's argument, that is not only wrong, it is utterly
impossible. From the moment we cease to be the slaves of sin
we are the slaves of righteousness. There is no interval in between,
no such thing as a spiritual 'No man's land', no neutral position.
You are either the slave of sin or else you are the slave of righteousness. The moment you are delivered from the one you are
in the other.

I repeat, there is no gap between justification and sanctification. Sanctification starts from the moment of our re-birth. I
go further; there is really no choice in this matter of sanctification. The moment we believe, the moment we are made regenerate, the process begins. You remember how the same Apostle
puts it in the First Epistle to the Corinthians, chapter 1 and verse
30: 'But of him are ye in Christ Jesus, who of God is made unto
us wisdom, and righteousness, and sanctification, and redemption'. If you are 'in Christ' all these things become true of you
immediately.

How does this work out? What does it mean to say that we
are enslaved to righteousness?' To be born again means that a
principle of new life is put into us. It is a principle of righteousness, for we are made 'partakers of the divine nature'. And it is a
principle that begins to work at once in us, and it works with
divine power. The Apostle puts it in a different form in Philippians 2: 12 – 13: 'Work out your own salvation with fear and
trembling; for it is God that worketh in you both to will and to
do . . . ' The New Testament teaching is that it is the Holy Spirit
in particular that does this. Take for instance Galatians 5 : 17:
'The flesh lusteth against the Spirit, and the Spirit against the
flesh'. You notice that the same is said of the two powers. The
flesh 'lusteth', and so does the Spirit. The moment a man becomes
a Christian the Holy Spirit of God is in him, and the Holy Spirit
of God lusts within him to win him wholly to the Lord.

There is a very interesting parallel statement in the Epistle of
James in the fourth chapter and the fifth verse. The Authorized
Version puts it like this, 'The Spirit that dwelleth in us lusteth

to envy'. But a very interesting and better translation is found in the margin of some of the Bibles: 'The Spirit which he made to dwell in us yearneth for us even unto jealous envy'. The Christian is subject to two forces which are anxious to possess him, and to govern him. On the one side there is the power of evil and of sin. But the Spirit that God has given to us is lusting on the other side 'even unto jealous envy'. What for? To win us to God, to win us to righteousness, to make us what God would have us be. So you have these two forces. This is how the Spirit that is en-slaving us to righteousness works. We are under this power that is lusting for us 'even to jealous envy' in order that we might be finally perfect in the presence of God. 'For this is the will of God, even your sanctification' [1 *Thessalonians* 4 : 2]. So we can con-fidently say this, that the work which God has begun in us will be continued until it is perfected. 'He which hath begun a good work in you will perform it until the day of Jesus Christ' [*Philip-pians* 1 : 6].

God puts the principle of life in us, and it is a principle of righte-ousness. It works in us, and the Spirit works on it; and so the process will go on until we shall be finally faultless and blameless before Him in glory. He has many ways of doing this. In a sense it is a terrifying thing to be a Christian! The moment we become Christians we must be very careful as to what we do. If you do not obey the Gospel of Jesus Christ you can expect chastisement, you can expect punishment, you can expect to find yourself in positions of difficulty; and you will be bewildered. This is all a part of the divine work within you. It means that God is perfect-ing you, God is sanctifying you; and if we will not allow Him to sanctify us through the Truth, He takes these other measures. If it is God's will for us to be sanctified we shall be sanctified. In other words, we are under the slavery of righteousness, and thus it is that He brings it to pass. That is now our position. We were the slaves of sin. That is no longer true as regards the tyranny and the reign of sin. We are free men in that respect because we are now the slaves of righteousness.

That, then, is what the Apostle is concerned to say at this point in order to establish his argument that it is monstrous and foolish to suggest that any man who believes this doctrine will then go on to say, 'Shall we continue in sin because we are not under the law, but under grace?' But we cannot leave the matter without indicating that we must still carry in our minds the way in which all this happens to us. Nowhere should we be more careful not to take a statement out of its context than in the case of this verse. Imagine certain people picking out this verse and saying, 'Being then made free from sin ye became the servants of righteousness', and beginning to work it out after their own imagination. They might say, 'Oh well, we can see it was our belief and our obedience that did this'. But it is not our obedience that does this, it is not our believing that does this. It is the same power that does this that does everything that the Apostle is dealing with in the entire chapter. And what is that? It is our union with the Lord Jesus Christ; being baptised into Him we are baptised into His death and into His resurrection. It is the result of all that He has done for us. That was the great argument of verses 3 to 10. We cannot deliver ourselves from slavery, we cannot make ourselves slaves of righteousness. This is done to us, this happens to us. Because we were in Adam, because of Adam's original transgression, we were all enslaved to sin. We did not choose to be slaves to sin, we were born slaves to sin. In the same way a man does not 'decide' to be enslaved to righteousness; he is enslaved to it; it is done to him. He is put into this 'mould' as we have seen. So we must continue to bear in mind that what produces this result in every one of us who is a Christian, is the fact that grace has taken hold of us, has delivered us from the bondage and the reign of sin, and has brought us into a glorious captivity to Christ. It has fettered us to Him, it has enslaved us to righteousness.

That is the teaching, and that is why I was so careful over this matter of translation. It is not enough merely to say that we have 'become' the servants of righteousness; we have been 'enslaved' to it; it is the power of grace, it is the 'reign of grace' that has laid hold upon us, and we are in its mighty and its firm grip. 'If the Son shall make you free, you shall be free indeed'; and He makes us free from sin by making us His own slaves. He has bought us out of the old market; we belong to Him; we are now the bondslaves of Jesus Christ. Paul's argument, therefore, is that to continue in sin is something which is a sheer impossibility.

Having thus expounded the eighteenth verse, I now proceed to make a comment upon it. This is in many ways a crucial verse in the whole question of the Christian man and his ethical behaviour. It is therefore a strikingly up-to-date verse. It is the subject of much popular discussion at this moment. I do not normally refer to topical matters, but I hold strongly that the Gospel of Jesus Christ should not merely be expounded as such, and then left as it were in the air. It must be applied to our present condition, and our every-day circumstances. Having heard of a discussion in a programme on the BBC television, I listened to the repeat of its sound track. It struck me as being extremely interesting. The question that was put was this. Lord Birkett, a very distinguished lawyer, a retired judge, had apparently said on some other programme, when asked about his religious position, that once he had been a Christian, and not only that, he had also been a Methodist lay-preacher, but that now his position had changed. He said that he still held to the Christian ethic but that he no longer believed the Christian doctrine and the Christian dogma. Indeed, he said that he rather liked to describe himself as a Christian agnostic. So the question raised in the programme to which I listened was therefore put in this form. 'Is it possible for a man to hold on to the Christian ethic, to believe it and to practise it, without the Christian doctrine?' Now this is the very question that is dealt with in the eighteenth verse of this chapter. Let me summarize what was said, three chief points being made.

The first point was that you can have the Christian qualities without believing the Christian doctrine; that you can hold on to the Christian ethic but reject the Christian dogma, the Christian doctrine. That was the case with Lord Birkett himself, of course; he held on to the ethic, he said, but rejected the doctrine.

The second was, that any thought of compulsion in the realm of morals is wrong, and that the very idea of authority in such a realm is alien to the whole concept of morality. Morality, said one speaker, means your responsibility for yourself. He would not have any idea of compulsion or indeed of any authority or sanction. Morality, he said, is your responsibility for yourself, and it is therefore something self-contained.

But there was a third statement, and I am here quoting the exact words that were spoken. 'Belief in redemption is antithetical to morality'. That is not my statement, it was that of a speaker on the programme. He explained what he meant by this. 'The idea of something being done for you; the idea of your being delivered without your doing anything, does away with the sense of individual responsibility; it is the negation of all moral effort and striving'. The speaker said that this preaching of redemption, this idea that you can be delivered, that it is something done for you, had been the curse in the past. 'Why', he said, 'it is the death of moral effort and moral endeavour and any moral striving; and therefore', he added, 'the Christian redemption is actually antithetical to and opposed to morality.'

Let me try to show how the Apostle's words in this eighteenth verse answer this argument. We start by agreeing that moral teaching is not confined to the Bible; there is much moral teaching outside the Bible. We are well aware of that. The ancient Greek philosophers taught their ethics and morality. Certain men have made lists of the teachings of some of these great Greek philosophers. They have put that on one side of the ledger, and then put the teaching of the Sermon on the Mount and the ethical teaching of the Bible on the other. It is astounding to notice the similarity between the two. We agree then that moral and ethical teaching is not peculiarly Christian; you can meet with it altogether outside Christianity.

Further, we do know as a matter of fact that there have been many men, and many systems of thought, in the past, which have admired the teaching and the ethic of the New Testament, and have borrowed from it, and incorporated it into their own systems. They have also done their utmost to live and to practise it.

Up to this point we are in agreement with what has been said. But to say that, in the light of all this, you can hold on to the Christian ethic, the Christian way of life, the Christian qualities, without the Christian doctrine, is to reveal an utterly inadequate view of what the Christian ethic and the Christian qualities really are. In defining the Christian ethic and the Christian qualities the speakers talked about 'kindliness', 'consideration for other people' a 'desire to help', about 'avoiding moral evil, and trying to live a good, clean, straight and moral life'. They confined their definition of the Christian qualities and the Christian ethic entirely to that. That is, of course, where they go hopelessly astray, for the Christian life, the Christian qualities, the Christian ethic cannot be confined to that. It goes entirely beyond that. Into what realm? It goes into the realm, for instance, of the Beatitudes – 'Blessed are the poor in spirit; blessed are the meek;

blessed are they that mourn; blessed are they that hunger and thirst after righteousness'. They did not say a word about these things, but confined themselves to kindness, brotherliness, friendliness, philanthropy, and the avoidance of gross sin. But these moral qualities do not describe the truly Christian qualities, they are not the end of the Christian ethic. The Christian ethic goes on to the Beatitudes, it goes on to 1 Corinthians 13. Not a word was said about that – the great principle of love, and how you can know everything, perform many noble deeds, and even give your body to be burned; but if you have not got 'love' it is all of no value. Not a word was said about that – about that quality of love controlling one's actions and thoughts and motives and everything else.

Indeed, humanists at their best have no conception as to the meaning of the Christian word 'righteousness'. I have already reminded you that to be righteous in the New Testament sense means that you live to the glory of God, that you live to please Him. It includes your motives, it includes your desires. Indeed our Lord Himself put it like this: 'Be ye therefore perfect, even as your Father which is in heaven is perfect' [*Matthew* 5 : 48]. What is the Christian ethic, what are the Christian qualities? I can put it in one word: it is 'holiness', and holiness means to be like God. 'Be ye holy, for I am holy' [1 *Peter* 1 : 15–16]. It is not merely being nice and gentlemanly and affable and friendly and doing good turns. It goes infinitely above that; it includes this quality of holiness which makes us, I say, like God. Listen again to what our Lord said when He was asked by a lawyer, 'What is the first and the greatest commandment?' His reply was this – not that you must be kind and brotherly and friendly, but 'Thou shalt love the Lord thy God with all thy heart, and with all thy soul, and with all thy mind, and with all thy strength; that is the first and great commandment'. And He went on to say, 'The second is like unto it, Thou shalt love thy neighbour as thyself' [*Matthew* 22 : 36–39].

That is a summary of Christian ethics and a summary of the Christian qualities. Is it possible for a man to attain to that, and at the same time shed the Christian doctrine? Let us listen to the answer of the Apostle Paul. This is what he says: 'There is none righteous, no, not one'. But these men claim that they can do it. Paul goes on to say, 'All have sinned and have come short of the glory of God'. Paul says, 'O wretched man that I am! who shall deliver me?' 'The evil that I would not, that I do . . . ' He then adds, 'What the law could not do, in that it was weak through the flesh' [*Romans* 8 : 3]. The law could not do it. In Philippians Chapter 3 he looks back at his old life when he thought he was doing so well, and when he thought that as regards the demands of the law he was perfect, and he says, 'I count it as dung'. In other words, the Apostle says, 'I once thought that I could do all this, but I found that I could not.' When did he discover his inability? He tells us in the seventh chapter of this Epistle in verse 9, that as long as he was looking only at the letter of the Law he thought all was well with him. 'I was alive without the law once: but when the commandment came, sin revived, and I died'. In the light of such an experience, he found that he was a complete and an utter and an absolute failure.

That is the reply of the Apostle Paul. But he is not alone. Listen to Charles Wesley –

> *Just and holy is Thy name,*
> *I am all unrighteousness;*
> *Foul and full of sin I am,*
> *Thou art full of truth and grace.*

Listen to Toplady confirming Wesley's words –

> *Not the labours of my hands*
> *Can fulfil Thy law's demands;*
> *Could my zeal no respite know,*
> *Could my tears for ever flow,*
> *All for sin could not atone;*
> *Thou must save, and Thou alone*

What are we to conclude? I sum it up in this way. Let us not be misled by the distinguished character of these humanists; that has nothing to do with the argument. What we have to say about these men is just this, that they are nothing better than Pharisees. 'But surely', says someone, 'you cannot call them Pharisees!' What else can you call them? Here is the position. These are men who claim that in their own strength and power, without any of the aid of the Christian Gospel, they can practise and live the Christian ethic. They maintain that they can do it. We have seen what the Apostle Paul said, we have seen what two great saints of the centuries have said; but here are men who claim that they can do it. They are represented to perfection, surely, in our Lord's parable of the Pharisee and the Publican who went up into the temple to pray. The Pharisee prayed with himself and said, 'God, I thank thee that I am not like other men are, and especially like this publican. I fast twice in the week, I give tithes of all that I possess. . . .' He does not ask for forgiveness, he does not need it, for he is an eminently good man. He thinks he is carrying out the ethic; he is a moral man, and he just thanks God that he is as he is.

I am not being unfair to these humanists, for that is precisely what they are claiming. If a man says that he can carry out and practise the Christian ethic without Christian doctrine, he is virtually copying the language and the ethic of the Pharisee. I therefore say that the ultimate verdict upon such persons, and such a view, is that it is Pharisaism of the worst type. It is the same as the error of Saul of Tarsus before his conversion. How do such men fall into this error? In this way. What the Pharisees did, you remember, was to pick out certain of the dictates of the Law, and as long as they were not guilty of particular prescribed sins they thought they were perfect. They took the letter of the Law, they never understood anything about the spirit of the Law at all. But having defined the Law in their own terms, not in God's terms, they carried it out, and they thought themselves perfect. Their mistake was that they had never understood the spirit of the Law, and the real purpose of the Law. This is how Paul puts it in chapter 10 of this Epistle; 'For they', he says, speaking about such people, 'being ignorant of God's righteousness, and going about to establish their own righteousness, have not submitted themselves unto the righteousness of God'. They had never seen their need of a Saviour, and chiefly because their view of God's Law was inadequate. Their law was not God's Law, it was a law of their own devising. They called it God's Law, but it reflected their own self-righteousness, not the righteousness of God. They had never had the experience which Paul knew, and which makes him say, in effect, 'I was alive without the law once, but when the commandment came, when I learned what the law spoke about coveting and all else, then I saw myself condemned; sin revived, and I died'.

That is my answer on the first count, The Pharisaism of the humanist is based upon a terrible and a tragic failure to understand the real meaning of God's law.

But come to the second matter: this idea that a man is responsible for himself alone, that morality means a man's responsibility for his own self, and that there must be no sanctions. What of this? I have a number of questions to ask here. What is it that determines a man's view of himself? What is 'myself?' Is there any objective standard whereby I can know that my view of myself is right? If morality is simply my own responsibility for myself, the first thing I want to know is, What am I? What should I be? What is the true idea of the self? According to what was said by these authorities, every man decides that for himself. So you arrive at this position, that whatever I say is right for me is right. Another man says the exact opposite, and there is a clash immediately. What do you then decide about these differing views and these differing standards? The position you arrive at is one of complete anarchy and chaos; you are back in the position of the Book of Judges, when 'there was no king in Israel; every man did that which was right in his own eyes'. Even the most primitive societies denounce such a view; the most primitive tribes have their tribal laws, their tribal rules. They have their taboos; for instance, you cannot dress as you like amongst them. Why do they have their rules? Sheer necessity has forced them to do so. You cannot live in society without having definitions, laws, rules, and orders. The most primitive societies have found them to be essential; the most advanced forms of society have found them equally essential. A police force is as necessary in Great Britain today as it has ever been; the magistrates and the courts are as necessary as they have ever been. Why? Because you cannot leave questions of law and order to a man himself. When man is a law unto himself the result is nothing but anarchy and chaos.

But not only that; humanism is not only wrong, it is also entirely selfish. I mean this, that the Christian ethic and the Christian way of life says that a man must not be content with doing merely what he thinks is right, he must also consider other people. He must love his neighbour as himself. 'Conscience', says the Apostle, 'not thine own, but of the other' [1 *Corinthians* 10 : 29]. I must not say that, because this thing is right for me, I am therefore going to do it. What about my weaker brother? What about the other man and his welfare? The pharisaical academic view of morality that was propounded in that discussion had no concern at all about the weaker brother, about the other man. It is hard, intellectual, self-contained, and entirely lacking in sympathy for the underdog, the person who is accounted a failure. It has nothing to say to him; and therefore it is selfish in addition to being wrong.

I go yet further. Our own consciences within us tell us not only that there is need of an external standard and authority, but that there is one. That is why we have remorse, that is why we are miserable when we have done wrong; we know we are wrong. We do not welcome such feelings, but we cannot hold them back; the voice of conscience compels us to recognize an objective standard beside ourselves. Experience adds to this. Have we not all known this? There were things we were told not to do when we were young; but we disliked the prohibition and rebelled. We thought we knew better, and we said, 'Why shouldn't I do what I want to do?' As we have grown older and more experienced, and have more learning, we have come to see that our objection then was quite wrong, and that we needed to be taught and to be trained and to be instructed. Then we draw this inevitable deduction – I still am in that position, I still need more light. So the very fact that I recognize my fallibility and the possibility of my being wrong, and the need of training and learning and instruction is in and of itself a proof of the need of an objective standard and of some sanction behind our morality.

I clinch that argument in this way. The history of the human race makes it abundantly clear that religion of any sort, with its ultimate sanctions and its threat of punishment for wrong doing, has always been the greatest moral and moralizing force, the strongest keeper of law and order that the world has ever known.

I still have one further point. The objection was raised that the doctrine of redemption is antithetical to morality. It is very difficult to control one's self as one deals with these things. I almost wish that I could be a politician for five minutes in order to deal with this argument. With glibness and pomposity it was stated that redemption is actually antithetical to morality. It was said with a sneer and with an element of derision. Could anything be more ridiculous than that, particularly when the man who said that happens to be a professor of History?

The Professor of History says that redemption is actually antithetical to morality. What is our answer to him? First of all there is the evidence of history. The ages which have been most deeply convinced of the truth of the doctrine of redemption have been the greatest ages that this country has ever known. That is sheer fact, found in the secular history of this country. Which have been the periods when you have had most law and order, and concern about morality, good conduct and behaviour? I name first the Elizabethan period. That was the period that followed the Protestant Reformation, when the great doctrines of the Christian faith were understood and realized afresh, and especially the doctrine of redemption. They produced a higher level of morality as contrasted with the period before the Reformation. And what of the Puritan period? That was the period in which the acts of parliament were passed which these authorities object to so much, concerning observing the Sabbath, and the opening of theatres and other places of amusement on Sunday.

But what made the Puritans pass such acts? Why was morality such a great concern in the Puritan period? The answer is simply this – they believed in the doctrine of redemption, they were governed and controlled by the very doctrines that these men want to throw overboard. When you come to the eighteenth century, you find exactly the same thing. Read a book like *England Before and After Wesley* by J. Wesley Bready. See the moral condition of this country before the great Evangelical Awakening, and look at it afterwards. What produced the change? What led to the so-called Victorianism and Victorian morality? The answer is the doctrine of grace, and especially the doctrine of redemption. I can quote another Professor of History – Lecky. He says quite categorically that what saved this country from a revolution similar to the one they had in France in 1789 was nothing but the Evangelical Awakening in which these very doctrines were preached and were believed by the people. That is the answer of history.

I have stated the case in general; let me state it also in particular. We can produce exactly the same evidence with regard to individuals. Is not this the great testimony of the Church, that men who have been slaves to sin, and who were utterly foul and vile and immoral, have been completely changed and have lived a new life? What has led to that? Is it that they have decided to adopt the Christian ethic? No, it is the doctrine of redemption which they believed, and which has been powerful in their lives.

In other words, the answer to this contention is that not only is redemption not antithetical to morality, redemption is essential to morality. Redemption is essential to morality because man is, as this verse in Romans tells us, a 'slave to sin' by nature. He is not neutral, he is not detached, he does not merely take an intellectual view of things; he is the creature of powerful drives, controlled by this tremendous energy of sin; he is under the dominion of sin, he is under the reign of sin. But intellectual humanists know nothing about that; they sit back and take a detached, intellectual view of life. I do not know these particular men whose words I have quoted, but I know others like them, who can say similar things very glibly and intellectually; but when you get to know the facts about their lives you find that they are not quite as moral as they would have you believe, and are themselves slaves to lust and sin and passions. How easy it is to talk about the Christian ethic and about adopting it! It comes very easily to these men. But there are other types of persons of whom they seem to know very little. They have nothing to say to the man who is born with a hatred of morality and a vile nature.

They do not seem to realize that, as men and women, we differ in exactly the same way as all the creatures and the animals do. There are some dogs that by nature are friendly and kind and obedient; you have no trouble with them at all. But there is another type of dog that is the exact opposite. He will bite you and snarl at you. The same is true of cats and all other types of animals. And it is the same with human beings. There is the sort of man who is born with a pleasant, affable nature, and he has a natural intellectual interest in morality and ethics. He says, 'I am going to live the Christian ethic without your Christian doctrine'. But I ask, What about the other man who is altogether and entirely different? Where does he come in? What have they to say to him? Nothing at all! In other words, they do not understand the doctrine of sin. Sin is a terrible power that is working within us all by birth and nature. The problem with men is not that they need more information about truth and morality and light and right. Our Lord said that the problem is this, that 'they love darkness rather than light because their deeds are evil' [*John* 3 : 19]. That is part of the slavery and the power of sin; it is not merely a matter of deciding calmly to adopt an ethic. Man by nature loves the darkness, he hates the light in his heart of hearts. This is true of every one of us. In other words, man as he is by nature, is completely helpless; what he needs is not good advice, not good teaching; he needs someone to save him, he needs deliverance. It is his nature that is wrong, not his mind only; and his fundamental need is the need of power to do that which is good.

Now it is at this point that all these clever gentlemen fail so completely. Intellectually and academically they are interested in ethics, and they claim that they can live the good life. I have shown what a small ethic it is. But let us confront them suddenly with a helpless, hopeless drunkard; let us confront them with a man who has taken so many drugs that he has lost his will power; let us face them with a man who has striven with all his might to live a better life but who has gone down repeatedly in failure. What have they to say to him? Nothing at all except that he ought to be practising this excellent ethic! They have no power to give him. They do not even understand him. They have no hope to give him.

Is there then no hope for the hopeless? There is; but where is it? It is in the doctrine of redemption, and there alone. The only power that can deliver this hopeless failure – moral and ethical – is redemption power. I mean that God alone can help him. The trouble with this man is that he is estranged from God, and nothing will avail him until God delivers him. The chief doctrines of the New Testament – these doctrines that they want to throw overboard, and about which they are agnostic – are the very doctrines which tell us how God brings salvation to the lost. How has He done it? By sending His own Son, Jesus of Nazareth into the world – the doctrine of the Incarnation. He not only came and taught and lived; but He died on the Cross. It is His dying once and for ever for sin that enables us also to die to it, and to be freed from it. That is the doctrine of redemption, of substitutionary atonement. Christ bore our sins; He has conquered; He has delivered us. He is the way. Likewise with His resurrection, and also with the doctrine which teaches that He gives us a new nature and a new birth and a new start, and that He puts His Spirit to dwell within us, the Spirit who works in us and gives us power. This is the way in which a man is delivered and set upon his feet.

How do I know this? I know it only by these Christian doctrines. There is no deliverance, there is no morality apart from this. 'All have sinned and come short of the glory of God.' Even by the Law given by God you have nothing but 'the knowledge of sin'. But now this new thing has entered in, this redemption, this grace of God, this righteousness as a free gift from God the Father. And this saves us, because by working in us, it creates within us desires after morality and holiness. The pundit says that redemption is antithetical to morality; the New Testament says redemption creates within men a hunger and thirst after righteousness, it creates longings after morality and holiness. Not only so, it provides us also with a supreme motive for living the moral life, namely a sense of gratitude and of love. The Christian realizes that Christ has done all this for him, and he wants to show his gratitude. The greatest incentive to morality and holiness is the desire to please Him who has died for us and given Himself in our place. And above all, God's redemption provides us with the necessary power. Far from producing a lazy, immoral, irresponsible creature who is indolent and who does not apply himself to the tasks of life, the doctrine of redemption does the exact opposite, as the lives of all the saints testify, and as the death of all the martyrs proves to the very hilt. Redemption antithetical to morality? No, says Isaac Watts –

> *Love so amazing, so divine,*
> *Demands my soul, my life, my all.*

This is not compulsion, this is joyous freedom. We are no longer slaves to sin, we are slaves of Jesus Christ. That is not serfdom, for His service is 'perfect freedom'. 'The joy of the Lord is your strength', and nothing gives a man the joy of the Lord so much as an understanding of the doctrine of redemption, and a living experience of its power.

Eighteen

*

I speak after the manner of men because of the infirmity of your flesh: for as ye have yielded your members servants to uncleanness and to iniquity unto iniquity; even so now yield your members servants to righteousness unto holiness.   Romans 6 : 19

This verse, as I have already suggested, corresponds in many respects to verses 12 and 13 in this chapter. The Apostle in a sense says the same thing twice over in this chapter, but in a slightly different manner. His first argument ran from verse 1 to verse 14, and the second from verse 15 to the end of the chapter. Verse 18 corresponds to verse 11, and in the same way this nineteenth verse corresponds to verses 12 and 13.

His method is to lay down a doctrine and then to make an appeal on the basis of that doctrine. Having stated in verse 11, 'Likewise reckon ye also yourselves to be dead indeed unto sin, but alive unto God through Jesus Christ our Lord', he makes the appeal, 'Let not sin therefore reign in your mortal body, that ye should obey it in the lusts thereof', and so on. In the same way, having said in verse 18, 'Being then made free from sin, ye became the servants of righteousness', he now goes on to make the exhortation and appeal found in this nineteenth verse. He will go on to support this by additional arguments in verses 20 to 23.

As we come to this verse we are struck at once by the preliminary statement the Apostle makes before he proceeds to address his appeal or exhortation to these Roman Christians. What he does here is rather unusual. He says, 'I speak after the manner of men because of the infirmity of your flesh'. He is referring to the way in which he has been using an illustration or an analogy. He began to do this in verse 16. 'Know ye not', he says, 'that to whom ye yield yourselves servants to obey, his servants ye are to whom ye obey?' There, he begins to use an illustration from the realm of slavery; and he has kept it up. We have seen that in verse 18 he says that, 'being made free from sin ye became enslaved to righteousness', or 'became the slaves of righteousness'. That is a continuation of the same illustration; and when he comes to his practical exhortation he still goes on using it. He says, '. . . for as ye have yielded your members, or presented your members, slaves to uncleanness; even so now present your members slaves to righteousness unto holiness'.

In the extraordinary phrase at the beginning of this verse, he is referring to his use of this illustration. He says, 'I speak after the manner of men'. That does not mean that he was speaking as a man, or using human language because he could not speak in any other way. As a man he could only speak in human terms and in human language. What he means by 'after the manner of men' is that he is using a familiar illustration taken from ordinary life. He is not referring to the terminology, to the words as such, but to the fact that he has been using a familiar illustration.

Why does he use this particular phrase and call attention to what he is doing? Why did he not just go on with his illustration? Why turn aside to make a comment on his own procedure? This is an extremely interesting point, and especially so because it is rather unusual in this Apostle's writings. It therefore demands examination.

There are those who have thought that the Apostle was apologising for using an illustration, that he felt that there is a sense in which a preacher of the Gospel should not use an illustration at all; or that he was apologizing for the particular illustration he had used. That, surely, is an entirely false explanation of what the Apostle is saying. There is nothing here that calls for an apology. It is not that he has temporarily forgotten himself, and has been speaking after the manner of men in that way. He is not apologizing for it, but explaining why he did it. This is a matter that is of significance and importance as regards teaching methods. It is very important for all preachers in particular, but also for anyone who ever uses an illustration or a figure in an attempt to elucidate and to make plain the truth of Scripture.

Let us try to see the reasons which led the Apostle to use his illustration about slavery. He gives us the explanation himself.

The first reason is that he has done so in order to make the subject matter clear. He says in effect: 'I am speaking to you in this
way, and using this illustration from the familiar fact of slavery,
because you are all familiar with slavery.' Until this point in his
Epistle the Apostle has not employed this method; it is the first
time he does so. The Apostle Paul does not tell stories in his
letters; he does not use illustrations freely. He does so here, and
he seems to feel the need of explaining why he has done so.
Thus, his not apologizing, but giving an explanation.

The business of preaching and teaching is always to make the
meaning and the matter plain and clear. That is a rule from which
I imagine no one would dissent. Holding that in our minds, it
seems to me, therefore, that there are two extremes that we must
always avoid, two dangers of which we must be constantly aware.
One is the danger of being childish. That is a very real danger today – if I may say so with temerity – in evangelical circles. The
great word is the word 'simple'. 'Oh, it is so marvellously simple' is a favourite comment. Well, to be simple, of course, is
right as long as we mean by that, that the meaning is plain and
clear. But we should never be childish; we should never treat
people as children. If we merely tell them stories, and spoon-feed
them, we are really treating them as children. Do we realize the
significance of this?

In order to explain let me do what the Apostle does at this
very point; and I do so solely to make this point quite clear. I
remember how, when preaching on one occasion, a man came to
me at the end and said, 'You only gave us one illustration this
evening. The last time I remember there were several'. I immediately examined that man in my mind. He was a bit of a poet, and
in my opinion was really only interested in the stories and illustrations in a sermon. That was what appealed to him. There is no
doubt that this has become a very real danger in the Christian
Church. We must never be guilty of using stories and pictures,
analogies and illustrations, as a means of entertainment.

There is, however, the other extreme. This is not so common a
danger today as it was in the last century, and particularly in
certain circles. I am thinking, for instance, of what is said to be a
perfectly true story, of people going out of a service in Edin-
burgh one Sunday morning. The preacher, a great 'pulpiteer',
had been delivering a tremendous sermon. As the congregation

was walking out of the church, a poor woman amongst them was asked by someone, 'Well, did you enjoy the sermon?' She replied, 'Yes, it was wonderful'. 'Well', said the other, 'Were you able to follow the argument?' She answered, 'Far be it from me to presume to be able to follow and to understand the mind of such a great preacher'. That is the other extreme. It was a real danger a hundred years ago. I mention it for this reason, that I am convinced that it is one of the explanations of the state of the Christian Church today. Those 'great' preachers went into the pulpit with their academic sermons, which were often read, and the majority of the congregation had no idea what they were talking about. Why then did they attend such services? Somehow they had the feeling that it was wonderful to be listening to discourses which were so great that they could not understand them, entirely forgetting that the business of a preacher and of a sermon, as I am emphasizing, is to make the meaning plain.

I am using this analogy, says the Apostle, in order that you may the better understand what I am talking about; and that is the only reason for using illustrations or analogies. They must never be used to entertain, or to bring glory to the man who has told a good story. The very nadir in this respect is reached when you hear of men who keep notebooks in which they enter tales or stories they may hear, in order to use them later in their own sermons. Thus congregations are amazed and entertained by stories and illustrations for the sake of stories and illustrations. The great Apostle never did that. He is not defending himself; he is saying that the only reason for using such an analogy is that it does help to make the meaning plain and clear.

We can look at this matter from another standpoint. The Apostle uses his analogy because he is anxious to avoid, and prevent, a serious misunderstanding of what he is saying. Not only does he want to make his doctrine plain and clear, he realizes that there is the possibility of a serious misunderstanding of what he is saying, or, to use a Scriptural phrase, he was afraid that they might 'wrest the truth unto their own destruction'. Those are the words of the Apostle Peter in his Second Epistle. He is referring to the writings of his 'beloved brother Paul', 'in which', he says, 'there are some things hard to be understood, which they that are unlearned and unstable wrest, as they do also the other Scriptures, unto their own destruction' [3 : 15–16]. The

Apostle Paul realized that there was a danger that what he was saying might be misunderstood, so he uses this analogy of slavery in order to safeguard the truth.

What is he safeguarding? Surely it is this! He has said in verse 14, 'For sin shall not have dominion over you, because you are not under the Law, but under grace'. At once he realizes the danger that some of these people might say, 'Very well, as we are not under the law we need not be bothered about our conduct and behaviour any longer; we need have no concern now about righteousness; we are free, absolutely free'. No, says Paul, 'It is not so, you are now slaves to righteousness, you are enslaved to righteousness'. He has said that at the end of verse 18. In other words he is anxious that they should see that the man who is no longer under the Law is now under law to Christ. He is not free from righteousness; he is free to righteousness, he is set free for the practice of righteousness. Paul is so anxious that none should imagine that not being under the Law means that a Christian is completely free, that he says that while Christians are no longer slaves to sin they are nevertheless slaves to righteousness. 'Now', he says in effect, 'I have put it like that in terms of this analogy of slavery – and of a man being a slave of one master, and then another coming and buying him and delivering him from his former master, and making him his own slave – I have put it like that, in order that nobody might wrest my statement about being no longer under the Law, to his own destruction.' That is why he used the analogy. He saw that he must put it as plainly and clearly as possible so that no-one could be in any kind of misapprehension or uncertainty with regard to his teaching.

I go on to a third reason for his use of the analogy. He says, 'I speak after the manner of men, because of the infirmity of your flesh'. In other words: 'Do not be mistaken about this, there are limits to an illustration, even when it is of value. It helps to make the meaning plain and clear; it helps to safeguard against misinterpretation; but, after all I am coming down to a lower level as it were, in using an illustration, because no illustration is perfect, and no illustration must be pressed too far. I have used an analogy', he seems to say, 'but do not press this absolutely, otherwise you will have the truth in its wrong proportions. There is a kind of slavery in the Christian life; but it is not like that old slavery. The new form of slavery is not completely identical with the other', says the Apostle. 'Because I have just used this term about your being "enslaved to righteousness", do not be mechanical in your interpretation and say that this slavery is identical in every respect with the other slavery; for it is not.'

There is a similarity, and yet there is a difference. Under sin, the slavery came with the domination exercised by 'the strong man armed'. You remember our Lord's statement, 'The strong man armed keepeth his goods at peace'. That is a picture of mankind in sin under the tyranny and the dominion and the rule and the sovereignty of the devil and of evil. It is a totalitarian tyranny of the worst type. That is the one form of slavery. There is no freedom there at all. But, says Paul, this other slavery in which the Christian is enslaved to righteousness, to God and to Christ, is different. This is where the analogy tends to break down. In other words, it does not take us far enough. Paul had to put it in this form in order to safeguard the truth; but it is not completely adequate. Let me further explain.

There is a unique and wonderful quality about our relationship to righteousness. At one and the same time it combines the elements of slavery and freedom. In this new slavery there is a kind of compulsion, but it is not comparable to the compulsion that preceded it. A Christian is, in a sense, a slave; but he is not a slave in the same sense as he was before. There is a difference. It is that he is now a slave to love. The element of love comes in, and that changes the entire situation. A man who is in love is, of course, a slave. He lives for the other, for the object of his love; and the one whom he loves really controls him in a totalitarian sense. But what a difference there is between that and the slavery imposed by some terrible potentate or tyrant! There is a sense in which it is right to say that both are conditions of slavery, and yet you cannot leave it at that; you have to explain the difference in the slavery. In the second case it is a willing slavery.

We can use another statement made by the Apostle to show exactly what he means. Formerly the compulsion of which we were aware was the compulsion of the tyranny of Satan and of sin. It was black and terrible and awful. What is the position of the Christian? He says, 'The love of Christ constraineth us' [2 *Corinthians* 5 : 14]. The Apostle says that he is like a man in a vice, and the vice is being tightened up more and more. He is under pressure, there is a tremendous sense of compulsion; but what produces the pressure? It is the love of Christ. It is no longer a horrible tyranny, it is love; it is the tyranny of love. This is a paradox, the paradox of the Christian faith and the entire Christian position. The Christian is not a free man, he is a man who is, so to speak, under the tyranny of love. He says, 'The love of Christ constraineth' me. 'Woe is unto me if I preach not the gospel'! He is a bondslave of Jesus Christ, but that is all the time within the relationship of love.

It seems to me that the Apostle is explaining this paradox to us at this point. What he was concerned to bring out was that there is compulsion in both cases. The certainty of obedience is secured in both cases; but the moment you have said that, everything else is different. The Christian is under the power of righteousness. He was formerly under the power of sin; he is now under the power of righteousness. His position must not be thought of as one of detachment; he is not a man who is free and detached, and who may do what he pleases because righteousness is a controlling power. We are 'under grace', says the Apostle, and because of that, there is an element of certainty in the result, as there was an element of certainty in the old life. The man who has been delivered from a bondage 'under the law' is a man who will never be in the position of saying 'What then? Shall we sin because we are not under the law, but under grace?' That is quite impossible, because now he is under this compelling, constraining power of love and of righteousness. That question is therefore quite unthinkable and utterly impossible. In saying, 'I speak after the manner of men because of the infirmity of your flesh', the Apostle is warning us to be careful, and especially of the way in which we make use of his illustration, which only helps us up to a certain point.

That brings us to yet another meaning of this extraordinarily illuminating phrase. The ultimate reason for his using his illustration and analogy, he tells us, was because of 'the infirmity of your flesh' – 'I speak after the manner of men because of the infirmity of your flesh'. Here again is a statement which throws great light upon the whole question of our approach to the New Testament. Note that Paul does not say, 'I speak after the manner of men because of the infirmity of your intellect, or your mind'. He says 'because of the infirmity of your flesh'. That is a central, vital, point in the New Testament teaching. He does not say 'intellect'; and I emphasize that for this good reason, that if he had said 'intellect' he would be putting a premium on intellect. He would have been saying, 'Of course, if you only had better brains and greater intellects, and more penetrating understanding I need not have used my illustration at all. You would have understood the complete truth as I stated it in my doctrine'. But he is not saying that, and he never says anything of that kind. The New Testament as a whole, thank God, never says any such thing. No, what he says is, 'because of the infirmity of your flesh'.

What is 'the flesh'? The 'flesh' means all the faculties of man as influenced by, and perverted by, and controlled by sin. It does not mean the physical body. We have come across that term 'the body' before. But here the Apostle is not thinking of or referring to the body; he speaks of 'the flesh', which means the natural human faculties without the aid of the Spirit. 'The flesh' means the faculties of the body as dominated, perverted, and misused by sin, and it is that, not the mind and intellect alone, that makes it necessary for him to use his illustration.

Why do I assert that this is so vitally important? For this reason, that according to the biblical teaching man's trouble by nature is not that he merely lacks intellect. What he lacks is spiritual understanding. Man's trouble is not in his mind alone, but in his lack of the capacity and ability to understand, and to believe and to follow, spiritual truth. Here we have the essential biblical doctrine of sin, and of man in sin as the result of the fall. What is the most devastating result of the fall? It is undoubtedly this, that man since the fall has lost the capacity for spiritual apprehension. Before the fall he possessed it. Before the fall Adam was able to commune freely with God and to have fellowship with Him. The moment he fell, and sin came in, man lost that capacity of spiritual apprehension and understanding.

This is a crucial matter in biblical doctrine. It is worked out at great length in the first three chapters of Paul's First Epistle to the Corinthians. He begins to deal with it in verse 12 of chapter 1, and continues with it as far as the end of chapter 3. That is the most extended treatment of this particular aspect of truth. The most devastating thing that sin does to man is to rob him of his power of spiritual apprehension. Let me put it in this way. The whole problem of becoming a Christian, of believing the Christian truth, of accepting the Christian faith, is not primarily a matter of intellect at all. I say again, thank God for that! The Apostle argues that men may have great natural capacity, great intellects, great minds, great brains, great knowledge, and great natural understanding, and at the same time see nothing whatsoever in Christianity. Indeed, as he says, they may see nothing in it but utter folly. The Jews regarded it as a stumbling block, and the Greeks regarded it as foolishness. He says, further, 'The natural man receiveth not the things of the Spirit of God, for they are foolishness unto him; neither can he know them, because they are spiritually discerned' [1 *Corinthians* 2 : 14]. These men have great brains, and great intellects; but when you bring them face to face with this truth they see nothing in it at all. Speak to them about the Lord Jesus Christ, tell them about the Incarnation, about the two natures in the one Person, and they dismiss it as nonsense and folly. Hold before them the doctrine of the atonement and the meaning of the death upon the Cross, and they say that it is rubbish, and immoral. They denounce it, they laugh at it, they ridicule it. Why? Because they are lacking in this faculty of spiritual apprehension, spiritual understanding. This is not a matter of intellect.

We can put it from the other side in this way. There are simple people, ordinary people with poor brains, very little intellect and understanding, who are yet able to receive these things and to rejoice in them, and revel in them. How are they enabled to do so? The Apostle giving an extended answer in 1 Corinthians, Chapter 2 says that it is solely the result of the work of the Holy Spirit upon them. When the Son of God was in this world, 'the princes of this world did not know him, for had they known him, they would not have crucified the Lord of glory'. How then can anyone be a Christian? The answer is, he says, 'God hath revealed them (the truths of the gospel) unto us by his Spirit; for the Spirit searcheth all things, yea, the deep things of God' [1 *Corinthians* 2 : 10]. 'For we have received, not the spirit that is of the world, but the Spirit that is of God, that we might know the things that are freely given to us of God' [verse 12]. It is entirely a matter of the illumination of the Spirit.

The Apostle glories in this. In the first chapter of the same Epistle he says – and remember that Paul is one of the greatest intellects the world has ever know – 'Ye see your calling, brethren, how that not many wise men after the flesh, not many mighty, not many noble, are called: But God hath chosen the foolish things of the world to confound the wise; and God hath chosen the weak things of the world to confound the things that are mighty; and base things of the world, and things which are despised, hath God chosen, yea, and things which are not, to bring to nought things that are: that no flesh should glory in his presence' [verses 26–29]. Being a Christian has nothing to do with intellect and natural ability and understanding; and the Apostle glories in that fact. Does this put a premium, then, upon ignorance? Not at all! It only goes to show that intellect is not the determining factor. A man should not boast of his knowledge; neither should he boast of his ignorance. A man should not boast of his great brain and intellect; neither should he boast of the fact that he may not have a great intellect. It is essential that we should say that on both sides. The temptation to some people is to boast about their great brains; but never forget that others are equally tempted to say, 'I am just an ordinary man, you know', with a feeling of self-righteousness and pride. That is just another form of the same unhealthy pride. We must not put a premium either on brains or on the lack of brains, on knowledge or lack of knowledge. Neither of them matters. It is the illumination of the Spirit alone that counts.

What an important truth this is! I do not propose to go on mentioning the discussion to which I listened on the Radio, but I must refer to it once more. Another question that was put to the learned participators was this. 'Why does it seem to be the case that intellectual people seem to be able to answer, and to discuss with ease and freedom and intelligence, the questions which are put to them on subjects which happen to be right out of their own particular field of interest and of study?' If that is possible to them, then why is it that when a question of theology arises they do not seem to be able to deal with it in the same way? For instance, literary people are able to talk about scientific matters though they do not know much about science, and are not specialists in science in any sense of the term. Yet they seem to be able to talk about science quite freely and in an intelligent manner. 'But', said the questioner, 'I have noticed that, when it comes to questions of theology, they do not seem to be able to do so'.

The learned members of the panel seemed to be quite incapable of answering that question. They were trying to say that if you did not know the terminology, or if you were not well versed in theology, you would not be able to take part. In connection with theology such knowledge seemed to be necessary; but not with other subjects. But that is a complete fallacy. There is only one explanation of the failure of the learned members of the panel to speak freely about these matters; it is that they are matters that are 'spiritually discerned'. The greatest natural mind and brain is useless here, as is prolonged study also.

Matters of spiritual discernment belong to a realm which can only be introduced, and into which one can only be introduced, as the result of the operation of the Holy Spirit Himself. It is the realm of the spiritual. Art, and music, and science, and politics, and all such things belong ultimately to the same realm. But Christian truth does not belong to that realm; and any man is completely ill at ease here, and beyond his depth, until he has been given the illumination of the Spirit, and has the spiritual faculty belonging to the new man. This is indeed something to glory in. Face to face with Christian truth we are all on the same level. That is what proves, ultimately, that it is God's way of salvation. Were it man's way of salvation it would depend upon our minds and intellects and intelligence; and then, of course, some would have a great advantage over others. But God has contrived a way of salvation in which no one has an advantage over anybody else. We are every one of us reduced to the same level of complete helplessness and absolute impotence. No brain is of value, no lack of brain is of value; we are all in the same position, we are all on the same level. We all fail to the same degree; we are all equally helpless.

On the other hand there is therefore a corresponding hope of salvation for all types. What a wonderful salvation this is! That is why I say again, that it makes no difference at all to the preacher, in this evangelistic sense, whether he knows the character of the people who are sitting in front of him or not, because he knows that they are already sinners. He is not interested to know whether they have great brains or little brains, he is not at all interested as to whether they are the most cultured people in the world, or the most ignorant people in the world; he knows that they are all sinners. He knows that they all have a blind spot where God and spiritual truth are concerned; and that they can do nothing about that; they need the illumination of the Spirit – every one of them. But he knows also and for the same reason, that there is an equal hope for all. What a Gospel! It has baffled the greatest philosophers the world has ever known; and yet it can save in a moment a man in the heart of Africa who cannot even read or write. That is the Gospel! What a glorious Gospel it is!

The Apostle says that the difficulty about understanding the truth lies in 'the infirmity of your flesh'. It is not our minds; it is this fallen nature, which leads to the loss of the spiritual power of apprehension. It is in the flesh, not the mind, not the intellect; and that is why Paul says he has had to use his illustration.

But let us make the statement complete. Notice this, that though we are born again and illumined by the Spirit, we are still imperfect in this respect. Do not misinterpret what I have just been saying to mean that, because this understanding is the result of the illumination of the Spirit, and because we must all have that illumination, and because all who are Christians have had that illumination, therefore every Christian is identical with every other, and is permanently in exactly the same position as others with regard to understanding and comprehension. That does not follow at all.

This again is an important matter. We know nothing of spiritual truth at all apart from the illumination of the Spirit, but after we have had the illumination of the Spirit, there are all kinds and possibilities of variation in the degree of understanding. I mean by that that the faculty that is given to us by the Holy Spirit can be developed by us. The Apostle makes that quite clear to the Corinthians. He says, 'I could not speak unto you (hitherto) as unto spiritual, but as unto carnal, even as unto babes in Christ', [1 *Corinthians* 3 : 1]. He goes on to say that this was so because 'ye are yet carnal' [verse 3]. He says, 'I have fed you with milk, and not with meat: for hitherto ye were not able to bear it . . .' [verse 2]. 'Howbeit', he also says, 'we speak wisdom among them that are perfect' [1 *Corinthians* 2 : 6]. That which makes the difference and accounts for the various gradations among Christians is the extent to which they have used, or have failed to use, this power, this faculty, that has been given to them by the Holy Spirit.

The author of the Epistle to the Hebrews supports and confirms what the Apostle Paul has been saying. In chapter 5 he says

[251]

that he desired to tell them a great deal more about the doctrine of our Lord and Saviour as 'high Priest after the order of Melchisedec'. He says he has 'many things to say, and hard to be uttered, seeing ye are dull of hearing'. He continues, 'For when for the time ye ought to be teachers (in these matters), ye have need that one teach you again which be the first principles of the oracles of God; and are become such as have need of milk and not of strong meat'. All this was true of them because they had not been 'exercising their senses to discern both good and evil'. They had been content to remain babes, and the result was that he could not give them that deeper teaching, that higher doctrine he was so anxious to give them.

There are many Christians who undoubtedly forget all this at the present time. There are Christians who say, 'I am saved, and all is right with me; I am not interested in anything else. I am not a theologian, I do not want to read great books on theology'. But no Christian has a right to remain a babe in that way, he has no right not to exercise his senses. 'But I am a practical man', you say, 'I am a great worker'. But you have no right to divide yourself up in that way. It should be the ambition of every Christian to 'grow in grace and in the knowledge of the Lord'. You should study your Scriptures, read all the best books you can, get knowledge that is as deep and profound as is possible, and 'exercise your senses,' because according to inspired authors, if you do not, you cannot receive the whole truth. If you remain a babe, and do not grow and develop, you will have to continue being spoon-fed with milk, and you will never know anything about 'the strong meat' of the Word of God, and of the doctrine of salvation.

Thus it is possible for the Apostle, at one and the same time, to say two things about these Roman Christians that seem to be contradictory. In chapter 15 verse 14 he says, 'I myself also am persuaded of you, my brethren, that ye also are full of goodness, filled with all knowledge, able also to admonish one another'. Yet here he says, 'I speak to you after the manner of men, because of the infirmity of your flesh'. But there is no contradiction at all. They had received the light, they had got spiritual understanding, but on the other hand, he says that they had not got sufficient as yet to follow this profound and deep doctrine he was putting before them. These two things are perfectly compatible the one with the other.

Our blessed Lord Himself once put this clearly. He was talking about listening to the Gospel, and said, 'Unto him that hath shall be given, and he shall have more abundance'. 'Take heed therefore', He says, 'how ye hear; for whosoever hath, to him shall be given.' The more you understand of this doctrine the more you will understand; and the more you understand the more you will get, and the more you get, the more you will understand, and on and on and on it goes. You have to be a strong man before you can take strong meat. So our business is to grow and develop, to exercise our senses; and if we do so, and as we do so, the use of analogies and illustrations will become less and less necessary. We shall not then be listening to the same simple Gospel messages, with the same sort of stories and illustrations, fifty years hence as we are doing now. We shall desire something more solid, and we shall be able to take more. Is there anything so tragic as to observe Christian people remaining exactly the same at the end of a long life as they were at the beginning – never growing, never developing. No, says our Lord, 'Unto him that hath shall be given, and he shall have more abundance'.

I end with this question. What kind of food can we take? Are we still only capable of taking milk, or are we beginning to develop a taste for meat? Are illustrations and analogies still essential, or do we know that our minds are expanding under the illumination of the Spirit, and rejoicing in the deep things of God? 'The Spirit searcheth all things, yea, the deep things of God.' I must confess that there is nothing which ever happens in my experience which depresses me more than the following. Sometimes when I am preaching away from home, and have preached what I would have thought were the mere elements and beginnings of the Christian faith, people come to me and say, 'You were making rather heavy demands upon us this evening'. They add, 'We are not accustomed to these deep things'. Deep things! and I thought I was being elementary! That occurs among Christians, and evangelical people!

Let us realise, then, these fundamental principles. Though we are in Christ, the fundamental principles of growth remain. We must fight against indolence. We must read, we must study, we must meditate, we must exercise our faculties, we must grapple with these immensities. 'Hard to be understood' says Peter, and we can agree; but apply your minds therefore, struggle with truth, insist upon getting an understanding of truth. If you have a willing heart, and a true desire, you can be certain that the Spirit will always come to your aid. You will grow, not only in grace, but 'in the knowledge of the Lord'.

'I speak after the manner of men because of the infirmity of your flesh' says Paul. Watch every word this Apostle writes. You will often find gems of deep truth in what on the surface appears to be nothing but a casual passing remark.

Nineteen

I speak after the manner of men because of the infirmity of your flesh: for as ye have yielded your members servants to uncleanness and to iniquity unto iniquity; even so now yield your members servants to righteousness unto holiness.   Romans 6 : 19

As we have seen, the Apostle continues here with his illustration, showing that the Christian is a slave to righteousness and the Lord Jesus Christ. Having explained why he is using his illustration, he now continues by giving the practical exhortation that follows from the doctrine that he laid down in verse 18. We might therefore read it like this. 'Being then made free from sin, ye became the servants of righteousness'. Then, 'For (because) as you have yielded your members servants to uncleanness and to iniquity unto iniquity, even so now yield your members servants to righteousness unto holiness'.

This exhortation follows logically from the doctrine of verse 18. It is because verse 18 is true that he can now make this exhortation which we are to consider. With regard to the actual exhortation itself there should be no difficulty, for we have already met the terms in verse 13. There we read, 'Neither yield ye your members as instruments of unrighteousness unto sin, but yield yourselves unto God as those that are alive from the dead, and your members as instruments of righteousness unto God'.

We recall that the meaning of that term 'members' covers all the various faculties and propensities that we have, and through which we express ourselves. So the term 'members' includes the actual parts and portions of one's physical body; but it does not stop at that; it includes the mind and the imagination and the heart, the feelings, and the susceptibilities. The term 'members' can be considered, therefore, as meaning the ways in which we express ourselves. The Apostle's command therefore is that we yield our all as servants to righteousness and to holiness.

The terms 'as' and 'even so' with respect to the members call our attention to a very important point, namely, that while it is true to say that as the result of the Fall everything in us has suffered, there is a sense in which the 'members' are more or less neutral. What Paul is saying is, 'As you presented these members of yours before in the realm of sin, even so now present the same members as servants of righteousness unto holiness'. The important point here is that we do not need new members or new faculties when we become Christian; and we do not receive them. What a man is in the matter of abilities and powers and propensities before conversion, he still is after conversion. He is not given natural powers that he did not have before. He has the same powers exactly. Take as a convenient example, the very man who wrote these words, the Apostle Paul. As a personality he was the same when he was Paul the Apostle as he was as Saul of Tarsus. As Saul of Tarsus, as a persecutor, and an injurious person, and a blasphemer, he was a man who did things very thoroughly, with great vigour and with great feeling. Saul of Tarsus never did a thing by halves. Whatever he believed in, and whatever he did, he did with all his might. He was a vehement persecutor, and when he was converted and became the Apostle Paul, those precise qualities stand out still. He did not suddenly become a quiet man, or a quiet preacher! We are aware of the passion and the power and the vehemence as we read his epistles. In other words, 'the members', the total way in which a man expresses himself, are the same after conversion as before conversion.

This is important for this reason, that there are people who seem to think that as Christians we should all be identical; that because we are new men in Christ we must all be exactly the same in every respect. Of course that is simply not true; we are not meant to be the same. What the Apostle is urging upon the Roman Christians is, in effect this: 'You have your members, your powers and propensities and faculties; as you have used them in the past in the wrong direction, so you must use them now in the new direction.' He does not say that Christians are to use other people's gifts, he is saying in effect that they are always to be themselves.

This becomes important in the modern scene, for it is one of the characteristics of cults that they tend to make an assault upon a man's essential personality. The Gospel of Jesus Christ does not do that. So, if we find that what passes as Christianity is producing a standard type of personality, we should at once become suspicious. The Gospel does not work in that way. Observe the variation in the characters of the various disciples – the difference between John and Peter and the others – and here in the case of this great Apostle something quite different again. And as you read the history of the Church throughout the centuries you find that the same truth comes out clearly; a man's essential personality is not changed by his conversion. And it is not meant to be changed. A man who was vehement, and who tended to be violent in sin, does not suddenly become a quiet and docile man when he becomes a Christian. He is not meant to do; and he is doing damage to God's original gift to him of his particular personality if he tries in any way to make it conform to an unnatural pattern. 'As' – 'so'. We are not given new members.

In other words, if a man before his conversion was rather backward intellectually you have no right to expect him suddenly to become a genius because he has become a Christian; and he will most certainly not become a genius. We should not penalize him, we should not make him feel that he is a defective Christian. The amount of ability he had before his conversion is the amount he will have after conversion. The one difference Christianity does make is this, that it should make a man use his powers and his faculties and propensities in a better and a more diligent manner than he did before. So the man who was comparatively slow before should be a little less slow now; he will never become quick, he is never meant to be. In other words, the ruling is that we are all of us responsible for the powers, the faculties, the members that we have been given individually by God. We are not all meant to be preachers, we are not all meant to be any one thing in the Christian life. God has distributed these gifts in mankind exactly as he has in nature. No two flowers, no two animals, are identical. There are all kinds of variations; and God displays the wonders of His works in the very variations. We are never meant to be the same. It is machines that produce results that are always identical. God does not work like that. So let us beware of this very subtle snare of thinking that because we have become Christians we are somehow to do violence to our personality; it is not so. We are not to let it run away with us, of course, but we are never meant to crucify our personality. What we are to do is to apply it in the new life as we applied it in the old. That is the teaching here on the very surface of this statement – 'As – so'. The Apostle was a zealous persecutor, he became a zealous preacher. Thank God for this, that here we have a protest in this mechanized world against the attempt to make us all like peas in a pod. Christianity protests against that, and it always has done so throughout the running centuries. It is a proof that we are God's work; and not the work of men.

Having looked in general at our statement we can now consider it more particularly. The exhortation runs thus: 'As you have yielded your members servants to uncleanness and to iniquity unto iniquity, even so yield them now as servants to righteousness and to holiness'. That is a characteristic New Testament way of dealing with this doctrine of holiness and sanctification. Certain things stand out quite clearly. We have already met them in this chapter, but as the Apostle repeats them I have to repeat them. He repeated them, of course, because people were so liable to misunderstand them. I repeat them now for exactly the same reason. We cannot repeat these things too frequently. There is no chapter, as we have seen, which has been more misinterpreted than this particular chapter, and always in the interests of a certain type of holiness and sanctification teaching.

What, then, are the principles concerning the teaching of sanctification and holiness that we derive from this particular statement? First of all, we notice that this is an exhortation; indeed it is a command. The Apostle says, 'yield' – 'as you yielded, now yield'. You remember that we saw in verses 12 and 13 that this means 'to present things', 'to put them at the service of' – as in the case of a man joining the army. All his powers and faculties and propensities are now at the service of his commander and his country. He 'presents them' in that sense. Not that he can hand them over, he is presenting himself and his capacity with himself. You notice, I say, that it is an exhortation, a command. The New Testament way of handling holiness and sanctification is always a command; it is never an appeal, it is a command. That is a most important point.

Then that leads to the second principle, which I put in this form. As it is a command, it is obviously something that we have to do; and therefore it is something that we can do. There is no command in the Scripture to Christians which does not carry that kind of implication with it. But what I am anxious to stress is that here we are commanded to do something, we are commanded to live in a certain given manner. It is not an announcement of a message which tells us how this can be done for us. You realize the significance of that negative. The Apostle is not telling us here that, because we are now Christians, all we have to do is to realize that if we but surrender ourselves all this will be done for us. He is not saying that at all; he is commanding us to do something. He is not just saying; 'You are Christians, but you are having trouble in your daily life and living; you are tending to fall to sin and to temptation, and your life is up and down. Now I am happy to tell you that if you surrender yourselves to the Lord, and maintain this position of surrender, you will find that you will be given victory. It will be done for you, and you will be delivered from all your troubles'. The Apostle is not saying anything of the kind; he does not say that anywhere in this chapter, nor does he say it anywhere else!

The New Testament has no such teaching. Indeed the very parallel Paul uses here proves this. 'In the old life', he as it were says, 'you sinned actively by using your members; therefore', he says, 'as you were active in the old life, be active in the new life. You did not sin passively, it was not something that was done for you. No, you did it because you liked it and wanted to do it; and so you did it. Very well', says Paul, 'you have to live your Christian life in the same way. You yourself have to do these things; you have to use your faculties, your members, your instruments.' He is not just telling them that there is a marvellous way to which he can introduce them, in which somehow all their problems will be removed, and all will be done for them. There is no such teaching here. Instead, there is a command; it is something that you and I have to do. I am emphasizing this for this reason, that there are many Christians who spend the whole of their lives trying to get hold of this marvellous way in which all is done for you, and you have nothing to do but to rest and abide in Christ and the victory is given to you. The answer to that is, that this is a command, an exhortation, a call to us to do something, and to produce a result by using our faculties.

The third principle is that this is an exhortation or a command which is based on what has already happened to us, not on what may or can yet happen to us. That is why I emphasized at the beginning that this command is based upon the statement of verse 18: 'Being then made free from sin', or 'having been made free from sin', 'ye became the slaves of righteousness'. Now that has happened. I say, therefore, that the exhortation and the command are based upon what has already happened to us. The Apostle is not telling us about something marvellous that can happen to us if we only decide to go in for it. He is giving us a command because of what has already happened to us. This is the crucial point, of course. We have already been made free from sin and the reign of sin. Many times he has said that in this sixth chapter. He says in verse 2, 'How shall we that are dead to sin' – 'that died to sin' – 'live any longer therein?' The aorist! It has happened, it has happened once and for ever, it is in the past. That was our conversion. He is not telling us about another experience we may have; he says that we have had the vital experience, and 'Therefore . . . ' Not only have we been made free from sin, the reign of righteousness has already begun in us, and its power and its might are already working in us.

The Apostle is not telling us of another possible experience which we can have, and which will transform our daily life and living, especially in this practical matter of holiness. How often holiness and sanctification is presented in that way! 'Ah', we are told, 'of course you are failing, and have not got victory in your life. Why not? Because you have been trying to do it yourself, exerting yourself. You do not realize that there is another experience possible for you, virtually a second conversion. You can be delivered from all that striving, you can have another experience which will deliver you from all effort and striving, and you will no longer be living a defeated life. You will begin to live a victorious life'. 'Another experience'! But there is not a word here about another experience. What the Apostle says is that we have already had that one vital experience. 'You have been made free from sin, you have become servants of righteousness'. That has happened to us once and for ever. The moment you were justified, the moment you believed in Christ, you were 'in Christ', you were joined to Him. That is the experience, that you have died with Him, and you are alive unto God in Him.

Very well, you have the experience; and because you have had it, 'present your members as servants to righteousness unto holiness.' There is not a syllable, not the faintest suggestion, nothing whatsoever here about some further experience that is going to make all the difference to us. Indeed it is the exact opposite. Paul tells these people that they have had the experience, everything that is necessary they have already had; their business now is to act upon it.

This is a teaching which runs right through the New Testament. Take the Apostle's way of putting it in Philippians 2, 'Work out your own salvation with fear and trembling, for (because) it is God that worketh in you both to will and to do' [verses 12–13]. It is because God is working in you that you are to work it out. Or take it as it is found in the first chapter of the Second Epistle of Peter. He reminds those Christians to whom he was writing, that they 'have obtained like precious faith with us (the Apostles) through the righteousness of God and our Saviour Jesus Christ'. That is justification. Then he goes on to say, 'According as his divine power hath given unto us all things that pertain unto life and godliness'. He says it 'hath been given', he is not referring to some further experience. It has been given already 'through the knowledge of him that hath called us to glory and virtue: Whereby are given unto us exceeding great and precious promises: that by these ye might be partakers of the divine nature, having escaped the corruption that is in the world through lust' [verses 3–4]. He then goes on to say, 'Beside this, giving all diligence', do this and that. He is not inviting them to receive some higher experience – 'giving all diligence, add to your faith virtue and to virtue knowledge' [verses 5–7]. We have to go on adding these various other elements.

But Peter not only says this positively; he puts it negatively as well: 'If these things be in you and abound, they make you that ye shall neither be barren nor unfruitful in the knowledge of our Lord Jesus Christ; but he that lacketh these things' – the man who is not doing all this – 'is blind, and cannot see afar off, and hath forgotten that he was purged from his old sins' [verse 9]. Then back again to the positive, 'Wherefore the rather, brethren, give diligence to make your calling and election sure: for if ye do these things ye shall never fall' [verse 10]. It should be clear, therefore, that the third principle taught in this nineteenth verse of Romans chapter 6, is that the exhortation, the command, is based upon what has already happened to us, the experience we have already undergone, and not upon some other possible experience we may yet have.

That brings us to the fourth principle. The New Testament method and way of sanctification, therefore, is to get us to realize our position and standing, and to act accordingly. That is the New Testament way of teaching sanctification and holiness. In other words, 'Be what you are'. It does not tell us what we can become. No, no, its message is 'Be what you are'. Because you have been set free from sin and become servants to righteousness, therefore, be what you are. It does not offer something further, something higher, some additional experience; instead, 'be what you are'. I cannot find anywhere in the New Testament, teaching which says, 'Christ has been crucified for you; what remains now is that you should be crucified with Christ'. That has been popular teaching; but it is not in the New Testament. Every man who is a Christian has already been crucified with Christ. You cannot be a Christian at all unless you have been crucified with Christ. There is no appeal to the Christian anywhere in the New Testament to become crucified with Christ, because it has already happened. The fact that he is a Christian means that of necessity. You cannot be a Christian without being 'in Christ', baptized into Him and His death, His resurrection, His everything. That is the argument of verses 1–10 in this chapter. Yet how often are we told that we need something further and that in order to have it we have to become crucified with Christ. But there is no indication of that anywhere here. It is because that has already happened, it is because that is true of us, that this command, this exhortation is addressed to us.

The fifth principle is that this demand is utterly reasonable. So the Apostle puts it in this way, 'For as ye have yielded (you have presented) your members to uncleanness and to iniquity unto iniquity, even so. . . .' 'As . . . even so'. We responded to the old and we gave obedience to it, did we not? Why not make the same response now to the new? says the Apostle. You gave yourself to that, now give yourself to this. That, again, is New Testament holiness teaching. It is based upon the reasonableness of what is put before us, it is an address to our logical faculty. It is not sentimental, it is not an offer made of some wonderful experience; it is a reasonable argument that is presented to us.

We are simply told to apply the logic and to be teachable.

So when the New Testament meets a Christian who is falling into sin and failing, it does not say, 'Ah, you have been struggling. What a pity! That has been your great mistake. You need not go on struggling like that. All you have to do is to surrender yourself and the fight and everything, and you will find that you will be delivered – let go and let God'. That teaching is simply not here at all. What the Apostle says to such a man is this: 'Do you say that you are a Christian? Do you say that you believe in the Lord Jesus Christ as the Son of God, that you believe He came from heaven to earth to take your sins upon Him on the Cross, and that He literally died and bore that horrible punishment for you, and for your sins? Do you say that you believe in Him, that He has done all that for you that He might "redeem you from all iniquity and purify you unto Himself as a peculiar person zealous of good works"? Is that what you say? Well, if it is, then the kind of life you are living is utterly inconsistent with your belief; you are being illogical, you are unreasonable. Why do you not think, why do you not face the truth? Your kind of life makes me doubt whether you are a Christian at all.' That is how the New Testament speaks. What are you, what is the value of this belief of which you speak? What is the value of the experience you say you have?

That is how the New Testament speaks to us. I have already quoted the strong language of the Apostle John in his First Epistle, chapter 2 verse 4: 'He that saith, I know him, and keepeth not his commandments, is a liar'. He is a liar! There is no suspicion or suggestion of some magic formula introduced thus: 'Now I am going to tell you of an experience which can make all the difference to you. You have merely to let go, to stop struggling, to rest, and all will be done for you.' Instead he is told that he is a liar. He is told that his life contradicts his profession of faith. Be reasonable, says the Apostle. You responded to the old, respond therefore to the new, and do so in the same sort of way. Our slavery and obedience to Christ, he says, indeed ought to be much greater than our former slavery and obedience to sin. 'As. . . even so' – yes, but even more so because of Him, because of the new Master, and because of what He has done for us! It is an appeal to us to rouse ourselves, to shake ourselves, to act; certainly not to rest. I do not like to use slang expressions but

I am more and more convinced that most people get into trouble
in the living of the Christian life because of their molly-coddling
of themselves spiritually. And certain teachings encourage
them to do just that. But here, and everywhere in the New Testament, I say again, we are much more in the atmosphere of the
barracks, where we are called upon to pull ourselves together,
to 'quit ourselves like men', and to cease to be sentimental.

Let us be practical. Do we not all realize the need of this exhortation, this command? How do we come out of the test of 'As
. . . even so'? What a contrast we so often present to the men and
women of the world in the use of our members! There is no difficulty about the way in which they use them. But how are we using
them? Let me suggest a few tests. Take, for instance, the question
of time. Look at the time men and women of the world give to
sin, the hours they spend at it. They believe in what they do, so
they give their week-ends to it. How do many Christians apply
the 'As . . . even so' in that respect? In the old life they gave up
most of their leisure time to their pleasures; then when they become Christians they tend to say, 'Of course, I live a very busy
life and have not much leisure time; one service on Sunday is
quite enough'. They did not behave like that when they were in
the world; they were not content then with but one session;
they were not content with the minimum; they wanted the
maximum. Is that not pathetic? Claiming vast blessings as the
slaves of Christ, and claiming to know what He has done for us
in His eternal love, the exhortation we need is surely this – 'As
. . . even so'. Be honourable, be consistent, be logical. You have
at least the same amount of time to use; and if you only knew Him
truly you would devote much more of it to Him.

Then take the question of energy. What an extraordinary
amount of energy the unbelievers have! Glance at the people we
read of in the newspapers – big business men, small business
men, and others. There they are in their offices or in their works
all day, but then you read about the hours they spend in dinners
at night, and after the dinner they often seem to be dancing most
of the night. But they are back at business by 9 o'clock the next
morning. What energy these people have! But when some of
them become Christians they seem to lose their energy, they
become tired. There are many Christians who say that they are

much too tired to attend evening meetings at their churches, and other activities. Yet when they were in the world, after they had left the office they would go to a dinner and a dance, or a cinema or theatre a number of nights each week. They obviously know nothing of the 'As . . . even so'. Thus they deny what they profess to believe. At the same time it shows that the Apostle's exhortation is a fair demand, a legitimate demand, an utterly reasonable demand.

Think of it also in terms of application and perseverance. Christian people often fail to persevere in the reading of Scripture and in reading commentaries and other Christian books. They say that they find it rather difficult and they are tired. What a contrast with the way in which they persevered in that old life of sin, and the application they gave to it! Think of young boys persevering in trying to be men in the matter of smoking or something else; how they persevere with it, how they want to do it! But, often, when they become Christians, they fail to show the same diligence. Similarly, think of the same matter in terms of money.

The Apostle's contention is that whatever you can put under the heading of 'members' – the use of your faculties, powers, possessions, and all you have and all you are – should be subject to the argument of 'As . . . even so'. That is the New Testament way of holiness. It is an address to our intellects and wills, to our manliness. We have to do this, and we are cads if we fail to do so. That is the way in which the New Testament preaches holiness and sanctification. There is nothing sentimental and weak about it, nothing suggesting a psychological short-cut. You do not find anything of that kind in the New Testament; instead there is this stern and strong truth addressed to us in terms of what we claim to believe.

So we come to my last principle, the sixth, which is, that our difficulties and failures in connection with holy living are due to our failure to realize the truth about ourselves. That is the whole trouble with regard to difficulties about living the Christian life, difficulties about sin, difficulties about holiness. All these matters are ultimately to be traced to one cause only, and that is our failure to realize the truth about ourselves. That is what we need; and there is nothing but the understanding of the truth that can put us right. 'Sanctify them through thy truth', says our Lord in His prayer, 'thy word is truth'. It is still the same.

The New Man

If you are experiencing trouble in your Christian life, if you find yourself falling into sin and yielding to temptation, the New Testament tells you that what you need is not a new method or a new system, and that there are no patent remedies in the spiritual realm. Many are being offered, but they do not work. They are not based on truth; they are quack remedies. You cannot, as it were, take a dose of medicine and suddenly feel perfectly well. No, you have to pull yourself up and do your exercises – 'As . . . even so'. You have to take these 'members' of yours and apply them to the task, and use them. There are no short-cuts to health in the spiritual realm.

The first and vital thing is that we are to realize the truth about ourselves – what we were, and what we are. The Apostle introduces this in verse 19, but in verses 20 to 23 he works it out; it is the very subject with which he deals. His teaching is that if you do not realize who and what you are – which means that you also realize what you were – you will never be right on this subject. That is the essence of his teaching.

He give us hints of it in the nineteenth verse. What were we? Slaves! he tells us. 'As ye have yielded your members (slaves) to uncleanness'. Your members were in bondage. To what were they enslaved? Notice the terms – two things, 'uncleanness' and 'iniquity'. What is uncleanness? It really tells us everything about itself. It is the term Paul uses here and elsewhere to describe sin as defilement and pollution, something vile in itself and which makes us vile. He says that that is how we were – we yielded our members to uncleanness. This was true of all believers.

'Wait a moment', says someone, 'are you saying that every unbeliever is vile and unclean?' I am not saying that they are all equally unclean in practice; it would be monstrous to say so. Every sinner is not guilty of adultery and utter foulness. There is a variation in practice, but at the same time it is true to say that every man who is a sinner and an unbeliever is unclean. Sin is essentially unclean. Of course the ancient world in which the Gentiles lived was particularly foul. I do not know that it was much worse than today, or what today is becoming; but it was terribly foul. Read the second half of chapter 1 of this epistle, read Ephesians chapter 4 verse 17 to the end, and there you will see something of conditions then. Peter also mentions the matter in the first chapter of his Second Epistle. He says that Christians

[266]

'have escaped the corruption that is in the world through lust'. He does not mean merely corruption in the matter of money; he means that the worldly life, the sinful life, is essentially morally corrupt, it is unclean. Sin is always unclean, and the most respectable man has to admit that he knows something about unclean thoughts and 'vile affections'. I have often said that nothing shocked me more when I was a young man than to hear men who were prominent and great in their professions, telling, and obviously enjoying, unclean stories at dinner parties. They were highly respectable men, I know, but still they enjoyed unclean stories. Man in sin is unclean at his best. It is Charles Wesley, a man who had been brought up in a very godly home, and who had never done anything outrageous in his life, a man who was always religious and who always tried to be highly moral, it is he who says –

> *Just and holy is Thy name,*
> *I am all unrighteousness;*
> *Foul (or vile) and full of sin I am,*
> *Thou art full of truth and grace.*

Sin is unclean, and our 'members' were slaves to uncleanness. And not only uncleanness, but also 'iniquity'. This means lawlessness. Sin is lawlessness. It means a lack of conformity to law, both human law and divine law; it means sin as guilt. Sin is unclean and lawless, it is ugly and foul, and it leads to guilt. It is interesting to notice the order in which the Apostle puts these terms. He puts the uncleanness before the iniquity, he puts the vileness before the lawlessness. In doing so he is not only right, but he is following the example of our blessed Lord and Master. It is unclean desires and thoughts that lead to unclean actions. Why does a man ever break the Law of God? Because of desire! That is where the devil was so subtle in tempting Eve. She was perfect, she had never fallen, and had never broken God's Law. How did the devil persuade her to break God's Law? He implanted a desire in her heart – 'You shall be as gods' – desire! 'And look at the fruit, what good fruit it is.' It starts in the heart, it starts in the realm of desires; and our actions are unclean because our thoughts are unclean. It is uncleanness within that leads us to break the Law. We like something; but the Law says 'You must not'. But we like it so much that we say, 'I do not care what the Law says, I will break the Law'. Uncleanness is thus followed by iniquity or lawlessness.

Our Lord puts it in the following way in Mark 7: 'There is nothing from without a man, that entering into him can defile him; but the things which come out of him, those are they that defile the man. For from within, out of the heart of men, proceed evil thoughts, adulteries, fornications, murders, thefts, covetousness, wickedness, deceit, lasciviousness, an evil eye, blasphemy, pride, foolishness: All these evil things come from within, and defile the man' [*Mark* 7: 15–23]. Uncleanness and iniquity were the powers to which we were slaves.

To what did that lead? It led 'unto iniquity', which is again, of course, lawlessness. The Apostle means that in the old life the members had been presented to 'uncleanness and to iniquity', and that led on to a state of 'iniquity unto iniquity'. In other words they had become lawless altogether, their whole life was lawless and they were getting worse and worse, they were becoming iniquitous. It is a kind of vicious circle; once you start you get worse and worse. There is a time when you are comparatively innocent; but when you do a thing once, it is easier to do it the second time. And you go on and on until you become its utter and absolute slave – 'iniquity unto iniquity' – a state of hopeless vileness and lawlessness.

That is what you were, says Paul; but you are no longer in that state. What are you now? You are still slaves. So 'yield your members as slaves to righteousness'. Yes, to righteousness, to conformity to God's standard, conformity to God's holy law, and to what man was originally. To be clean, to be pure, to be upright, to be good, to be righteous! The new life in Christ is essentially right, and upright, and honourable, and true; it is not twisted and perverted; it is upright, it is true. Righteousness!

To what does this lead if you continue practising it? The Apostle says that it leads to holiness. What is the difference between righteousness and holiness. Righteousness has reference mainly to our actions, holiness mainly to our state and condition. To be holy means to be pure within, to be pure in heart, to be pure in life, to be dedicated to God, to be more and more conformed to the divine image and character. What the Apostle says is that as you yield your members slaves to righteousness, and as you go on living this righteous life, and practising it with all your might and energy, and all your time, and everything else, you will find that the process that went on before, in which you went from bad to worse and became viler and viler, is entirely reversed. You will become cleaner and cleaner, and purer and purer, and holier and holier, and more and more conformed unto the image of the Son of God. There is an intimate relationship between theory and practice; each affects the other. So that as we control our minds and hearts, and as we put into practice what we claim to believe, and live as we should as the sons of God, we grow in holiness. We must say to ourselves, 'Noblesse oblige'. That is what the man of the world says. He is an aristocrat, and he lets all see it. He cannot forget it, and he behaves as an aristocrat. The nobility! In the same way we Christians are to remind ourselves of who and what we are. We are 'children of the Heavenly King'. We are 'members of the household of God'. We are the children of God. It is only as we remember this, and live accordingly, proud of our name and of our calling, that we shall not only live the righteous life, but we shall be advancing 'unto holiness'. Our hearts will become cleaner and cleaner, and purer and purer, and so will our lives.

> *O for a heart to praise my God,*
> *A heart from sin set free,*
> *A heart that always feels Thy blood,*
> *So freely spilt for me.*

Those are the principles! It is in this way that the Apostle teaches holiness and sanctification here and everywhere else. It is thus the New Testament teaches it everywhere. The blood has been shed for me – 'Therefore' with all I am and all I have, as I used to go in the old evil direction, I must now rise up and go in this holy direction. I must do it. 'But', you ask, 'where do I get the power to do it?' You have already received 'all things that pertain unto a life of godliness'. You do not need another experience. You do not need some new gift. You have been given everything in Christ, you are 'in Him' from the beginning of your Christian life. You are just a slacker and a cad, just lazy and indolent, indeed 'a liar', if you are not living this life. That is the New Testament way of preaching holiness and sanctification.

Twenty

*

For when ye were the servants of sin, ye were free from righteousness.
What fruit had ye then in those things whereof ye are now ashamed? for the end of those things is death.

Romans 6 : 20, 21

In these two verses the Apostle gives us reasons to support the exhortation or the command which he has given in the nineteenth verse. That exhortation, as we have seen, follows directly and of necessity from the statement of verse 18, and is parallel to that made in verses 12 and 13. Now, having given the exhortation in general, he supports it, as it were, by supplying us with further reasons for seeing and understanding that such an exhortation is most reasonable in view of what he has just been telling us about ourselves as Christian people. So from verse 20 to the end of the chapter he supplies us with these arguments or reasons. They can be divided roughly into three main parts.

First he gives us some negative reasons for doing what he has told us to do in verse 19. These are given in terms of what we once were in our old life. That is a very good reason for deciding to 'yield our members as servants to righteousness unto holiness'. Then in verse 22 he gives us the positive reason, namely, our present state and condition, and its possibilities. In verse 23 he winds it all up in a sentfor the whole truth before us both negatively and positively. Such is the analysis of this little section from verse 20 to the end of the chapter. But let us not forget this – because it is the whole object and purpose of his writing in this way – that what he is really doing is to refute the suggestion mentioned in verse 15, 'What then? Shall we sin because we are not under the law, but under grace? God forbid.'

He shows not only that that is an utterly monstrous and impossible suggestion, but that a Christian is one who has such an understanding of his present state and condition that that suggestion is to him utterly unthinkable. Here, then, we are given some of the reasons why we should live the holy or the sanctified life. I remind you, once more, that it is obviously something that we have to reason out. It is an argument. Holiness and sanctification are always the result of an argument, the result of deductions, the result of a process of reasoning. That is the New Testament way, as we have seen, of presenting Christian doctrine with regard to this vital matter.

Let us look at the Apostle's arguments, his reasons. We must comment once more on the way in which he is always ready to help us. He never stops at merely giving us a command; he always couples a doctrine with it. Invariably he gives us some reasons for it, some explanations of it. A very good example of this is found in the fourth chapter of the Epistle to the Ephesians where we see the Apostle alternating between an emphasis on doctrine and on practice, two things that are always indissolubly linked together. There is no holiness teaching in the New Testament apart from this direct association with doctrine; it is a deduction from the doctrine.

In verses 20 and 21 we are told the truth about the non-Christian, that is to say, about the life of sin. Observe the way in which Paul handles his argument. 'Is it possible', he seems to be asking, 'that anybody should say, "Shall we sin because we are not under the law, but under grace?"' It is a monstrous suggestion to any man who realizes what he was, and remembers the kind of life he lived while he was yet 'under the law' and before he came 'under grace'.

The matter divides itself into two sections. Paul first reminds us of what our state and condition was in the old life; and then in verse 21 he considers the detailed character of that life. In verse 20, then, we have a reminder once more of the state and the condition of the man who is not a Christian. Once more he says two things about it. One is that such a man is a servant, or slave, of sin. We have already dealt with that several times. It is the concept he uses right through this particular section from verse 15 onwards. Let us never forget that the real truth about any man who is not a Christian is that he is the slave of sin. The Apostle

has emphasized that repeatedly from the end of chapter 5:
'Sin hath reigned unto death.' That lies at the heart of the tragedy
of the man who is not a Christian. He does not realize it, of course,
but that does not make any difference. Slaves often do not realize
that they are slaves. That is one of the greatest tragedies in connection with sin – and sinners are always slaves of sin.

But not only were they slaves of sin, they were also 'free from
righteousness'. This is a very striking phrase, and one that can
be easily misunderstood. Some have interpreted it to mean that
during all the time of their bondage to sin they had liberty to do
anything they liked; there were no restraints at all upon them;
they were free agents who could do anything they pleased, being
absolutely free from all law and all restraints and prohibitions.
But we can dismiss that at once, because the Apostle has already
said that such people are 'under the law'. So it cannot mean that.
Others think that it is the Apostle's way of saying that before they
became Christians these people were altogether bad. But we must
reject that interpretation also, because, as we have been showing
in earlier verses, this expression 'free from' has a very definite
and particular connotation in this sixth chapter of the Epistle
to the Romans.

Indeed the very analogy the Apostle is using at this point compels us to reject both those expositions of the meaning of this
phrase, because the analogy, as you remember, is that of slavery.
Paul has put it very plainly in verse 16, where we have the basic
argument, 'Know ye not that to whom ye yield yourselves servants to obey, his servants ye are to whom ye obey, whether of
sin unto death, or of obedience unto righteousness'? You are
either a slave of sin or a slave unto righteousness. Take, for instance, verse 7, 'He that is dead is freed from sin'. In expounding that verse we defended the Authorized Version as against
another translation which would have us read, 'He that is dead is
justified from sin'. We showed that it not only means justification but that it really does mean that the man is 'freed' from sin.
Similarly in verse 11 we have the same idea, 'Likewise reckon
ye yourselves also to be dead indeed unto sin'. That means that
you are truly free from it, because when you are dead you are
free. Then again in verse 14, 'Sin shall not have dominion over
you'. Also in verse 17, 'But God be thanked that ye were the
slaves of sin' – you are no longer that – 'but you have obeyed from

the heart the form of doctrine which was delivered you', or 'unto which you were delivered', or 'enslaved, or 'entrusted'. It is explicit in verse 18, 'Being then made free from sin, ye became the slaves of righteousness'.

But even if we had not got all those examples in previous verses our explanation of this statement here would have to be determined by the next two verses, and especially by verse 22, 'But now being made free from sin and become slaves to God'. This clearly means that when you were the slaves of sin you were not the slaves of righteousness. To be 'free from righteousness' here means precisely that; you were not, in that condition, the slaves of righteousness; you were not being governed and controlled and directed by righteousness. Why not? Because you were being governed and directed and controlled and dominated by sin.

In other words the Apostle is saying again what he has been saying so many times. We are always slaves, we are either slaves of sin, or else we are the slaves of righteousness. And you cannot be slaves to two masters who are opposed to each other, at one and the same time. You cannot serve God and mammon; it is either one or the other. That is exactly what is said here – when you were the servants of sin you were not the servants of righteousness; you were quite free from the governing power which righteousness exercises over certain people.

This throws light upon a matter which is very much under discussion at this present time. The Apostle makes the statement that this is true of all people who are not Christians, irrespective of how good or how moral they may be. It is a universal statement about all who do not believe on the Lord Jesus Christ and who are not Christian. He says categorically that all such are 'free from righteousness'. This troubles many, and they ask, 'How can that be true, because every non-Christian does not live in the gutters of life? There are very good moral men, and there are unbelievers who do excellent things.' The Apostle's assertion therefore becomes one of the best ways of differentiating between morality and a merely ethical religion on the one hand, and Christianity on the other hand. I sometimes think that this is one of the most vital distinctions at the present time, for the reason that there is no question at all but that the greatest enemies of the Christian truth today are the so-called good, moral, ethical, religious people who are not Christians. They are the people to whom I have referred who say, 'Yes, I believe in the Christian ethic but am not interested in the doctrine'. They are ultimately the greatest enemies of the Christian faith and they are to be exposed as such.

Here, I say, we see very clearly the difference between such people and Christians. I grant that they are 'good' people, and if they happen to be well-spoken, good-mannered, good-looking people they cause many ill-taught Christian people to say, 'Surely it is not right to say about such folk that they are free from righteousness?' But it is so. A man who rejects Christ and Him crucified, and who does not believe in the atonement and its absolute necessity, is of all unbelievers the most dangerous, and needs to be most severely denounced, as our Lord denounced the Pharisees of old.

This 20th verse helps us to see the difference. You can look at it in this way: the non-Christian is in no relationship at all to righteousness. I am not talking about what men call justice and righteousness and equity in a human sense. He is in relationship to that, but he is not in relationship to what the Bible means by 'righteousness'. He is not governed by righteousness, he is not controlled by righteousness. What controls him is himself, his own ideas, his own thoughts, his own philosophy; indeed he is ultimately controlled, as we have seen, by sin and by Satan. The point the Apostle is emphasizing here is that the Christian, on the contrary, is a man who is governed and controlled and dominated by righteousness.

Paul puts this explicitly in chapter 10, particularly in the first three verses. 'Brethren', he says, 'my heart's desire and prayer to God for Israel is, that they might be saved. For I bear them record that they have a zeal of God, but not according to knowledge.' Then especially in verse 3, 'For they being ignorant of God's righteousness, and going about to establish their own righteousness, have not submitted themselves unto the righteousness of God'. There it is clearly defined. The righteousness that they were establishing was their own righteousness; it was not God's righteousness – 'being ignorant of God's righteousness, and going about to establish their own righteousness'. That is precisely what these good, moral men are doing, these gentlemen who like to talk about ethics. All they have is their own righteousness; it is not God's righteousness. They have nothing

to do with God's righteousness; they have not 'submitted themselves to the righteousness of God'. Note the word 'submit'.
That is the very opposite of being 'free from righteousness'.
Righteousness was not controlling those Jews. But as a Christian
you have submitted to this righteousness of God and it is controlling you. So the word 'free' means that it does not reign over
us, it is not controlling us; it is not the guiding principle of our
lives.

The second thing we say about this so-called good moral
man who is not a Christian is that all he possesses is nothing but
his own goodness and his own morality. But that is not God's
righteousness. The Bible states plainly and clearly that that is
not true righteousness. It puts it strikingly in the words, 'All
our righteousnesses are as filthy rags'. That is its true value;
that is the truth about these fine men of the world. 'Fine' is the
term that is generally used to describe them. 'What a fine man!',
people say, 'doesn't he speak delightfully, and isn't he such a
fair-minded man?' This is the man who claims that he can take
the ethic but does not want the doctrine. 'Fine man', says the
World. 'Filthy rags' says the Bible. Such men have no true
righteousness at all.

Again, take the way in which the Apostle Paul speaks about
his old life. He was once a man of that 'fine' type, you remember;
and he thought that he was doing remarkably well. But when he
comes to write that bit of autobiography in the third chapter of
the Epistle to the Philippians, this is how he puts it: 'What things
were gain to me, those I counted loss for Christ. Yea doubtless,
and I count all things but loss for the excellency of the knowledge of Christ Jesus my Lord: for whom I have suffered the
loss of all things, and do count them but dung, that I may win
Christ' [verses 7 and 8]. That is the way in which he describes the
marvellous rectitude, goodness and moralism of these people
who can do without Christ and His atoning death. It is 'dung',
it is 'refuse', it is 'complete loss'.

But lest anyone should think that this is but extreme language
as used by the Apostle Paul, let me quote the words of the Lord
Jesus Christ Himself. He turned to the Pharisees on one occasion
and said, 'You are they that justify yourselves before men'.
The people watching these good moral men on the television
screen and hearing the interviews with them, and their clever

discussions with each other and their facile speeches, say 'What fine people, what a wonderful standard they have!' But our Lord says of them, 'Ye are they that justify yourselves before men'. The people who spend their time looking at the television programmes say, 'There is no need to go to church any longer. Look at these men. They do not believe the doctrines of the Christian faith, but look at their lives and their philanthropy.' But to such men our Lord says, 'Ye are they that justify yourselves before men; but God knoweth your hearts; for that which is highly esteemed among men is abomination in the sight of God' [*Luke* 16 : 15]. It is 'abomination'. All their goodness and their morality is abomination, it stinks in the nostrils of the almighty God.

That is what the Apostle means by saying here that these people were formerly 'free from righteousness'. Righteousness is not in control of the life of such a man, and therefore his best efforts, his highest achievements are of no value whatsoever in the sight of God. Indeed the trouble with such a man is that he has no true conception of what righteousness is. What is righteousness? We shall be looking at it again, but, in essence, it means to be servants or slaves to God. These good moral people have no conception of that, they are simply living up to their own standard. They decide on the standard, and then live up to it. But they are not righteous, they are strangers to righteousness, they have nothing to do with it. There is a very simple way of proving that that type of man is a complete stranger to righteousness. It is this. A man who knows anything at all about righteousness, God's righteousness, is a man who is acutely aware of his own unworthiness, his own lack, his own desperate need. But that is never true of these people. They are well satisfied with themselves; they are like the Pharisee in our Lord's parable, who thanks God that he is not as other men, who fasts twice in the week, and gives tithes of all that he possesses [*Luke* 18 : 9–14]. How marvellous he thinks he is! And ignorant people applaud him and say, 'How wonderful'! That is the self-satisfaction, the smugness of the man who thinks that his own little ethical standard is adequate, and who has no need of Christian doctrine.

But, secondly, a man who has any conception at all of the righteousness of God, is a man who is not only acutely aware of his own lack, he is a man who begins to 'hunger and thirst after righteousness.' So our Lord puts it in His beatitude, 'Blessed are they that do hunger and thirst after righteousness, for they shall be filled' [*Matthew* 5 : 6]. Do these good moral people give any evidence of hungering and thirsting in that way? Listen to them, observe their glibness, and their smugness. They ooze out self-satisfaction and there is no humility or meekness about them. They do not hunger and thirst after righteousness; they feel they are living up to their own standard, they are obeying and honouring their own little moral code. Such men are indeed complete strangers to righteousness, or as the Apostle puts it here, they are 'free from righteousness'. They are not in its realm at all. There is nothing more terrible than to be outside the realm of the righteousness of God. It means to be outside the life of God; and there is nothing more appalling than that. It is to be living a life which is an abomination in the sight of God, though it makes a great impression upon sinful men and women. That, then, is the first statement in verse 20.

In verse 21 we have an account in detail of the type of life which is lived by such persons. The Apostle says three things about it. What a devastating analysis and exposure is it! How true it is at the present time of the life of most people in this country! What are the characteristics of this non-Christian life? First and foremost it is a fruitless life – 'What fruit had ye then?' It is an utterly profitless life; there is no value in it. That is what the Bible says about this non-Christian life everywhere from beginning to end. There is one book in the Old Testament – Ecclesiastes – which has this as its major theme. Here are typical statements. In chapter 1, 'What profit hath a man of all his labour which he taketh under the sun'? [verse 3]. Then in chapter 2, verse 11, 'Then I looked on all the works that my hands had wrought, and on the labour that I had laboured to do: and, behold, all was vanity and vexation of spirit, and there was no profit under the sun'. None at all! In chapter 3, verse 9, 'What profit hath he that worketh in that wherein he laboureth?' And again in chapter 5, verse 16, 'And this also is a sore evil, that in all points as he came, so shall he go; and what profit hath he that hath laboured for the wind?' The conclusion at which he arrives is stated at the beginning, 'Vanity of vanities; all is vanity' [1 : 2]. He had arrived at that verdict on life after much trial and experimentation. He tried wisdom, he tried learning, he tried pleasure, he tried building great palaces, he gave attention to architecture and art, he had tried everything. He had got untold wealth, he could do anything he liked. He was looking for satisfaction, so he experimented with the whole gamut of possibilities; but that is his verdict having tried it all – 'Vanity of vanities; all is vanity. What profit hath a man of all his labour which he taketh under the sun?' 'What profit', says Paul here, 'had ye then, in those things?'

But is this true? asks someone. Is that still true? Of course it is! How do you estimate the value, or the fruit, or the profit of a life? What are the tests that one applies? Let us look at them, and let us turn to the negative side first of all. The test to apply is not that of pleasure nor that of happiness. There is no doubt that, up to a point, the life of sin can give pleasure; people would not indulge in it otherwise. It also gives them a kind of happiness. That is why they go in for it – a kind of pleasure and a kind of happiness. The world believes that it is enjoying itself, it is having what it calls 'a good time'. But even granting so much, let us never forget that illuminating word in Hebrews 11, '. . . the pleasures of sin for a season'. Such pleasure does not continue; it is evanescent. There is a kind of temporary pleasure and happiness, but it is only temporary.

So if you are going to judge the value or the profit of a way of life you do not stop merely at pleasure and at happiness. For the time being the case may seem unanswerable against the Christian. The non-Christians say that they are having a marvellous time. All you can say to them at this point is, 'That is not the real test. And in any case you had better not speak too loudly, too soon. We can take up the discussion again, perhaps, in a year's time, or five years' time, or ten years' time, or perhaps twenty years' time, or thirty years' time. Then you may begin to realize that it is "the pleasures of sin for a season".' That, then, is not the real way to test the profit or the value of a life.

What then is the way? You must test it in terms of real satisfactions. We are all confronted by the two calls, the call of the world and the call of Christianity; and the question is, which is the more profitable? The valid test is, Does the call yield satisfaction – satisfaction to mind, satisfaction to heart, satisfaction to spirit? Certain great statements that have been made in the past help us to settle this matter once and for ever. Look at a man like St. Augustine before his conversion. He was a brilliant philosopher who tried to find pleasure and satisfaction while living a life of immorality. But while thus resisting the call of God he eventually came to this conclusion: 'Thou hast made us for Thyself, and our hearts are restless until they find their rest in Thee.' He could not find rest in his worldly life, he could not find it in his intellectual pursuits, he could not find it in his immoralities. He tried eagerly but he could not find it; there was no satisfaction.

There is surely nothing that is more obvious about the world today, apart from Christ, than the fact that this is still true. The world is restless, and the men and women who belong to it are restless. They get tired of one thing and they take up another. Is it not, from our standpoint, amusing to read in the newspapers of the problem confronting the cinema and the cinema owners? They are losing money; they are having to shut down their cinemas or turn them into something else. The cinema! The very places that took people from the churches, we are told, about twenty or thirty years ago. But now people are leaving the cinemas to look at television programmes or other attractions. That is but a symptom of this terrible restlessness. People get tired of everything. They have to change or mix their drinks, and their forms of sin; everything palls on them and they have to turn from one excitement to another. They are always rushing after the latest craze, the newest thing; and so you get your fashions. What makes it finally idiotic is, of course, that the latest fashion is probably something that was discarded thirty or forty years ago. They go round and round in circles because they have no real satisfaction. The test of satisfactions is indeed a valid one.

Another test of the profit or the value of a life can be expressed in a series of questions: Is there anything upbuilding in it? Does it give substance and sustenance and food? Does it help me to grow? Does it help me to develop as a human being? Does it help me to develop my faculties? Does it exercise my mind, my understanding? Does it really fill my heart and move it? Does it give me something to do that is of real value? Does it build me up, is it edifying? I have only to ask such questions for every Christian to know the answer immediately. No, there is nothing edifying in a life lived outside God and outside Christ.

Another test to apply is this – Does my manner of life help me to prepare for the latter end? What has it to give me that will help me when I am old? When I am young I seem to find satisfaction in gyrating round dance halls, but what will happen to me when I am too old to do that? Does it help me to lay by in store something for the days that are coming? What if I should lose my health, what if I should lose my work, what if I should lose my money, what will happen to me when I am on my deathbed? Does it give me some kind of reserve on which I can fall back in the crises of life? The answer quite plainly is that the worldly life gives nothing of value – nothing whatsoever.

After all the expenditure of time and money and energy, what does this non-Christian life really give? The Apostle's answer is that it yields no good fruit at all. The way to test it is to imagine what position you would be in if you were suddenly cut off from all these things. What happens to the man of the world who lives for his pleasures, who is not happy unless he is out every night, or unless the pleasure and entertainment come into his house, who has his drink and perhaps his drugs – what happens to him when suddenly his pleasures are cut off? That is the way to test the profit or the value of a life. That sinful, godless life is like a drug. It is like alcohol which only gives the sensation of pleasure and of happiness and of satisfaction as long as you are under its influence. The moment you stop taking it you have an awful reaction, and feel utterly desperate and half dead; and you are not recovered until you take more. That is true of drugs, and of alcohol; they give an illusion of satisfaction, but they only do so by drugging us and by knocking out of control our higher senses of discrimination and of understanding. It is an utterly profitless life, without value, without substance.

The Apostle's second statement concerning the non-Christian life is that it is a life of shame. 'What fruit had ye then in those things whereof ye are now ashamed?' This is appalling. Look at the things worldly people do. Unfortunately there is no need to take time over this, for we are all so terribly familiar with it as it is lived round and about us. It is a shameful life in and of itself. There are certain expressions in the Scripture that really tell us all about the shame. These things are done, says the Scripture, in the night, in the dark. 'You are no longer children of the night', says Paul to the Thessalonians, 'you are children of the day'. He talks about 'the hidden things of darkness'. Hypocrisy, it has been said, is the tribute that vice pays to virtue. Evil things are done under cover of night and of darkness. There is an inherent shamefulness about the very things the worldly do, so they wait until it becomes dark. We read about the night life of London, 'night clubs'. The very term 'night' tells us all about them, and the shame which belongs to them.

Then think of the deceit that is involved, the lying, the unhappiness that is produced. Think of the uncleanness and the shame of unworthy and evil thoughts. Think of what are described as 'jokes' about the very sanctities of life, about the most noble things in life. Is it not a shameful thing that infidelity in marriage should be regarded as a matter for jokes and for laughter, that a man who is not loyal to his wife should be regarded as a subject for jesting. Evil is regarded as entertaining. What a shameful thing! Look at the way in which men and women, in order to have their supposed pleasure, have, as I have just been saying, to drug their minds, deliberately to knock out their very highest powers in order that they may enjoy conviviality. It is shameful. It is a shameful thing that men cannot really be happy until they have more or less reduced themselves to the level of an animal. Is it not a shame to think of the many ways in which the body is being misused – the perversions, and the foulness that characterize modern life?

If you would see what the Apostle has in mind here, turn to what he has given us already in the second half of the first chapter of this epistle, or in the Epistle to the Ephesians, chapters 4 and 5. But you can read similar things in almost any morning newspaper. I did so the other morning. I happened to be reading a newspaper and my eye was arrested by a caption. The film critic was giving an account of the films he had seen during that week. I was appalled. The point the critic was making – he was evidently a man who had some decency in him – was that these things were being shown even to children; and it was nothing but filth and foulness.

There is something about this kind of life that brings into being a sense of shame. 'What fruit had ye then in those things whereof ye are now ashamed?' This is a point I am anxious to emphasize, this sense of shame with respect to these things as partly felt at the present time. That is the meaning of remorse.

The man who has got drunk overnight feels the next morning that he has been a fool, that it is a shame that he should have behaved in such a way. He can scarcely forgive himself. He feels remorse and a sense of revulsion. That is a manifestation, up to a point, of the sense of shame.

But there is something even worse than that; it is that there are so many people living that kind of life who have even lost their sense of shame. The Apostle says 'What fruit had ye then in those things whereof ye are now ashamed?' Many of them were not ashamed at the time. That, one gathers, was the truth about the immoralities of these pagan Gentiles at that particular time. They had sunk so low in sin that they had lost the very sense of shame; they were virtually saying 'Evil, be thou my good'. There are some very striking statements about this elsewhere in the Scriptures. Do you remember that illuminating statement by the prophet Jeremiah which asks whether the people who lived that evil kind of life were ashamed? 'No', he says, 'they were not at all ashamed, neither could they blush' [*Jeremiah* 8 : 12]. There is nothing worse than that; they had reached a stage in which they could no longer blush. There is hope for men and women as long as they can still blush; there is still something of moral sensibility left in them. But when they reach the stage in which they cannot even blush, it represents the very depth of iniquity. They have reached a stage in which they have lost the very sense of good and evil. They gloat over that which is wrong, they boast in iniquity. The shamefulness of it all! This is one of the most appalling things, surely, about life as we are witnessing it at the present time, that the sense of decency and of shame is disappearing, and men and women do not seem to recognize any moral standard at all. That had been true of the people to whom Paul was writing; but now, he says, you are ashamed of your sin as you look back. You were not ashamed at the time, you were so steeped in it, you were so lost in it.

That brings us to the closing statement of verse 21. Paul says, 'The end of those things is death'. Death is always the end of sin. You remember how the Apostle put it in verse 12 of chapter 5: 'Wherefore, as by one man sin entered into the world, and death by sin'. Sin came into the world, and because sin came in, death came in. Death would not have come in if sin had not come in. Sin always leads to death. We have already looked at this in detail, so I simply summarize the teaching. It includes physical death, but it is not only that. It includes spiritual death also, but it is not only that. It really means separation from the life of God in every way. It means the death of the spiritual faculty, which was man's most distinguishing and most glorious possession in his original creation. The moment man sinned he lost his contact with God, he became dead to God – 'dead in trespasses and sins'. Physical death came in also. However it is the separation from God that chiefly matters. And finally and ultimately, says the Apostle, a life of sin will be an everlasting separation from God. There is nothing more terrible and horrible to contemplate than that – eternity outside the life of God, left to ourselves. That is what the Apostle calls 'everlasting destruction from the presence of the Lord, and from the glory of his power' [2 *Thessalonians* 1 : 9].

That is the argument. We are to keep these things always before our minds as an argument for holy living. This is the way to mortify sin. You have to say to yourself, 'No, I cannot possibly do that. If I do that, I am going back to where I was, I am going back to the kind of life out of which I have been delivered, that fruitless life, that shameful life, that life which leads to death. I cannot.' We must ever keep this as an argument before our minds.

Let me ask a question as I conclude. Christian people, do you constantly keep these things before your minds; or are you just seeking for some magic formula or method by which you can be delivered from sin and temptation? Do you regard this analysis of sin, its ways and its results, which I have been making as entirely negative? Do you say, 'I cannot be bothered about this analysis of sin, I believe in just looking to the Lord Jesus Christ?' If you say that, you are denying the Scripture, you are denying this inspired Apostle's teaching. He has set before us the way to fight the world, the flesh, and the devil. You must remind yourself constantly of the nature of the old sinful life, and as you do so, you will see that to continue in it is quite unthinkable. You must so look at that life that you feel ashamed of it, and ashamed of yourself for ever having lived it in any shape or form. You must so look at it that you will feel ashamed of yourself for even desiring it for a moment. That is the way to avoid it. 'Shall we continue in sin, that grace may abound?' How can I continue in sin when it means a life that is utterly profitless, valueless, fruitless? How can I continue in sin when it is a life of shame and ugliness and foulness? How can I continue in sin when I know that it always leads to death, as it led to death in respects of the first man and woman, Adam and Eve? That is the Apostle's way of teaching sanctification and holiness. It is not just, 'Look to the Lord and abide in Him'. No, when the temptation comes, look at that old life of sin, and analyse it, and then ask, 'What is this? What is it asking me to do? Should this appeal to me at all? It is impossible, it is unthinkable, "God forbid!" I cannot even consider doing anything that belongs to a life that was without any fruit while I lived in it, that was always shameful, and is terribly shameful to me now, and which ends in nothing but death to God and death to the life of the Spirit.'

That is the Apostle's great negative argument, which should help us no longer 'to yield our members as instruments of iniquity unto iniquity', but 'to yield them as instruments of righteousness unto holiness'.

Twenty-one

*

But now being made free from sin and become servants to God, ye have your fruit unto holiness, and the end everlasting life.

Romans 6 : 22

This is one of those magnificent statements in which the Apostle sums up the truth about all who are Christians, all who are in Christ Jesus. It comes in the midst of this piece of argumentation we are considering. This verse, like the two previous verses, 20 and 21, is part of his exhortation, his command to us to 'yield our members as servants of righteousness unto holiness'. That is the command, that is the exhortation, but as part of the super-abundance, the over-plus, the 'much more abounding' character-istic of the Gospel, he not only tells us what to do, but also gives us reasons for doing it. The command is enough because it is the command of God, but such is the grace of God that He never leaves us with the bare command, he supplies us with reasons for listening to it and for obeying it.

Why should I do this? We have already seen in verses 20 and 21 that the old life was an unworthy life. Our whole position was unworthy; we were 'free from righteousness', outside its realm. There is nothing worse than that. Then we have found that it was a useless life, a fruitless life, a vain life, a life that is non-productive, and finally, that it leads to nothing and ends in noth-ing but death, final eternal separation from God and His life. But all that is negative. Yet it is very important, and we should never forget it.

But the Apostle does not stop at the negative; as usual he goes on to the positive. We have the positive reasons in this 22nd verse. Here, in a sense, he is simply repeating what he has already told us several times in this chapter. In verse 11 we have a nega-

[285]

tive, 'Reckon yourselves to be dead indeed unto sin'. But he does not stop there, he goes on to the positive, 'but alive unto God through Jesus Christ our Lord'. In verse 13 he is not content with saying that we must not only refuse to 'yield our members as instruments of unrighteousness unto sin', but that we should 'yield ourselves unto God as those that are alive from the dead, and our members as instruments of righteousness unto God'. We saw the same in verse 17: 'You were the slaves of sin, but you have obeyed from the heart that form of doctrine to which you were delivered.' We have seen it again in verse 18, 'But now being made free from sin ye became the servants of righteousness'. The great Apostle delights in repeating these things, and our delight in repeating them also is the measure of our understanding of the faith. People who do not like these repetitions are very poor Christians, if they are Christians at all!

One of the signs of the true Christian is that he never tires of these things. That is why I can never understand the type of Christian who feels that an evangelistic service has nothing for him. 'Ah, that is evangelistic' some say. 'Of course we are already saved, so we only go to church every Sunday morning, not to the "Gospel meeting".' They do not like to hear the Gospel again! What a terrible state to get into, to feel and to say, 'Ah, I know all about that; there is nothing there now for me, of course'. How unlike the great Apostle who delights in repeating these things! The true Christian cannot hear these things too often, he likes to hear the gospel, even in its simplest form, because of its central glory and because of its essential wonder. So the Apostle repeats what he has said, and yet it is not mere repetition. Whenever he repeats something like this he always adds something to it; and he does so in the verse we are considering. There is an additional thought here, as we shall see.

Let us look then at this great pronouncement, this magnificent description of the Christian, this thrilling depiction of what it means to be 'in Christ'. There are certain headings which suggest themselves to us at once and almost inevitably. The first is, that a Christian is a man who has undergone a profound change. We have heard this before, of course; in fact several times in this chapter. But let me say it again; the Christian is a man who has undergone a profound change. 'But now.' Those are the great words of the Christian – 'But', and 'Now'. What has happened?

Oh, the 'then' of verse 21 has become the 'now' of the Christian.
A Christian is a man who can talk about 'then' and 'now. 'Ye
were' – 'Ye are'. This is essential Christianity. 'What fruit had ye
then in those things whereof ye are now ashamed? for the end
of those things is death.' 'But now . . .' – complete transformation,
no longer 'then', it is 'now', it is new. Or, to express it in another
way, the 'ye were' of verse 20 has been changed and it has become this new thing, the 'Ye are' of verse 21. 'For when ye were
the servants of sin, ye were free from righteousness.' Now it is
something quite different – you have 'become'. You were this
and that, now you have 'become slaves, or servants, to God'.
That is another way of emphasizing this great change. Then you
remember how we saw in verse 21 that there is an implied word
which Paul does not actually state. He asks a question, 'What
fruit had ye then in those things whereof ye are now ashamed?'
The answer, of course, is 'None'. 'Nothing.' 'But now ye have
your fruit.' You did not have it then, but you have it now.

We are reminded immediately of the fact that the Christian
has undergone this profound change – 'But now'. It is the same
'But now' exactly as we had in chapter 3, verse 21: 'But now the
righteousness of God has been revealed' – after the appalling
description of man under the Law – 'But now . . .'. You find him
frequently using the same expression in exactly the same way
in his epistles elsewhere. This is indeed the Good News of salvation – 'But now'. This is what makes us Christian. We can say
that, and we can appreciate the value of it. Nobody but a Christian can say 'But now . . .'. The life of the other man is always the
same, there is no difference, no change. He changes his pleasures,
he changes his company, changes his sin, but his life is the same.
But the Christian's is not the same; he has left his old life, and
now he has something entirely new, something quite different.

That is the difference which the coming of the Lord Jesus
Christ into this world has made; that is the difference His glorious work has made. It is He who divides time not only into B.C.
and A.D. but also into 'then' and 'now'. 'Ye were' – 'Ye are'.
He comes in, He is the dividing line, He makes all things new.
Nothing is the same again. I therefore ask once more, Do you
glory in this 'But now?'

The Christian is meant to glory in this 'But now'. He asserts it.
That is why I maintain, and maintain stoutly, that a man who

understands this truth cannot merely lecture on it. A man who can lecture on this does not really appreciate what it means. If you know anything about this you are bound to preach! A man who can say 'But now' coldly, and merely regard them as two words, just a part of the construction of a sentence, a part of the syntax, has never seen their real meaning. No, the Christian cannot look at these words without being moved to the depth of his being. He worships, he praises God, he must shout 'But now'. This is in many ways the best test of our profession of the Christian faith. If these words do not thrill us and move us, then I think we had better re-examine our whole position.

I want to emphasize two things about this great change. I have done it all before in verse 17, but I am doing it again, and nothing can stop me. The first thing I must emphasize is the completeness of the change. It is not a slight modification, it is not a slight alteration, it is not just some mere addition. Nothing is the same! This 'Then' and 'Now' are complete contrasts. Let me put it in this way once more. There is nothing in common between the non-Christian and the Christian, and there are no gradations between not being a Christian and being a Christian. You are either a Christian or else you are not. The difference between the 'Then' and the 'Now' is an absolute one. That can never be emphasized too much. That is the Apostle's whole point here, it is the very nerve of his argument. That is how he gives us his reasons. 'Realize what you are' he says, 'You are no longer there where you were, but now you are something entirely different, and therefore you cannot possibly go on living as you lived before.' That is the essence of the argument, the absolute character of the change.

The second thing that he emphasizes in connection with this great change is that it is something that is done to us, something that happens to us; we do not decide to change. 'Can the Ethiopian change his skin, or the leopard his spots?' [*Jeremiah* 13 : 23]. The whole point, he says, is that this has happened to you. Notice the way in which he puts it, 'But now, being made free'. And even that does not put it strongly enough; the better translation is, 'Having been freed'. We have been freed, we have been set free. Then take the second phrase which reads in the Authorized Version, 'and become servants to God'. A better translation is this, 'having been enslaved to God'. We saw in verse 17 that it is all in the passive sense. This is passive, it is not something that we have done, it is something that has been done to us. We have been freed, we have become 'enslaved to God'. We are 'his work-manship', 'You hath he quickened, who were dead in trespasses and in sins'. It is God who 'hath delivered us from the power of darkness, and hath translated us into the kingdom of his dear Son'. It is His action, it is His activity, and it is His alone. You have been freed from sin, you have been enslaved to God.

That is something which we must never forget when we are considering this profound change. We cannot give birth to our-selves, we are 'born again'. It is something that happens to us. It is God who 'regenerates' us, He creates us anew. We cannot do it; He does it to us. And here you notice that in the very language, in the very words used, all this is brought immediately to the surface. That is the first thing; the Christian is a man who has undergone this profound change.

Secondly, look for a moment at the nature of the change. Here we come to the first phrase, 'Being made free from sin', or as I have said, 'Having been freed from sin'. The Apostle has said this several times, he has been saying it right through this chapter. But let us look at it once more to make certain that we really have got hold of this truth. This is 'the truth that sets us free'. That is what our Lord said to certain men, is it not? 'If you continue in my word, then are ye my disciples indeed, and ye shall know the truth, and the truth shall make you free.' As it is the truth that makes us free, let us be certain that we have really got hold of it, as we look at it here for the last time in this chapter.

I emphasize again that this is something that is already true of us; we have been freed. Paul is not saying that if we do certain things we shall be set free. He is not saying, 'Look here, you Christians, it is possible for you to be free; you must seek the experience that will give it you'. He is saying that it is something that has happened to us, is already true of us. That is the whole point of his argument. He is not talking about some new, some possible experience which we may yet have; this, he says, is true, by definition, of all who are Christians. You cannot be a Christian at all without its being true of you that you have been set free, or have been freed, from sin. That is true of every Christian; that is the argument of the whole chapter.

A Christian is one who is 'in Christ'; and because he is in Christ he has died with Him, he has been buried with Him, he has risen with Him, he is alive unto God in Him. And because of that he is freed from sin. It has already happened; it is already true of everyone who is a Christian. We must never lose sight of that. There are those who would teach you that you can be a Christian, that you can be justified, but that you are not yet 'free from sin'; that that is something at which you arrive later, that that is some further experience. Not at all! Every Christian by definition has already been set free from sin.

Once more, what does the Apostle mean? We have been giving the answer to that question ever since we looked at verse 2, 'How shall we that died to sin, live any longer therein?' That was the first time we met it, and we have been going back to it repeatedly, and working it out, and reminding ourselves of it. It means freedom from the rule and the reign and the tyranny and the whole domain of sin. The key to the understanding of this is in verse 21 of chapter 5, 'That as sin hath reigned unto death, even so might grace reign through righteousness unto eternal life by Jesus Christ our Lord'. The whole of this chapter is a commentary on that verse. So being 'dead to sin' and 'freed from sin' means that we are no longer under its rule, no longer in its realm or under its tyranny. We are entirely set free from that in the Lord Jesus Christ, into whose death we are baptized, and all that follows. It means not only that we are justified from sin, and free from its guilt; it includes that, but it means much more than that. We are entirely outside the realm of sin; it has no reign, no power over us any longer; we are out of its jurisdiction. Our Lord, we are told, 'died unto sin once', and we are to reckon the same thing to be true of ourselves. That is the argument of those verses leading up to verse 11.

Here then we are out of the territory and the jurisdiction of sin; we have left for ever its rule and its reign. But that, of course, as we have seen, and as I have emphasized time and again, does not mean sinless perfection. Of course it does not! It does not mean that we have no further fight or struggle against sin; for we have seen that sin is left in our mortal body. Unless we are careful it will reign there; not in ourselves, but there! That is why we are not to yield, not to allow it to reign in our mortal body. We are eternally delivered. I am as much saved tonight as

I shall be in the glory; but I am not as perfect as I shall be in the glory. My body is still the body of my humiliation, it is my sinful body, it is not yet the glorified body. That is to come.

We must be clear about this. Shall I dare to put it in this form? Sin in the Christian is no longer our master, it is just a nuisance. In the non-Christian it is master, it is lord, it remains; but sin is no longer my master, it is only a nuisance, it is only an annoyance, and nothing more than that. To put it in yet another way, to the non-Christian sin is on top and he is underneath. The Christian's position is that he is on top, and sin is underneath trying to get hold of him. What a glorious difference! But that is the position of the Christian. Sin is no longer his master, no longer the tyrant; and he is no longer the slave of sin. He has been freed from that tyranny. Sin now simply becomes a nuisance, an annoyance in his life, and in his living. Before, we were helpless, and slaves to sin – but no longer!

I also like to explain it in this way. When the Christian sins, he sins because he has just been foolish enough to listen to a voice to which he does not need to listen at all. He has been 'delivered from the kingdom of darkness and translated into the kingdom of God's dear Son', but there is the devil shouting at him, as it were across the road, and he is foolish enough to listen. That is the position now. The Christian is no longer the slave of sin, he has been set free from it; so he is now in the position to be able to 'resist the devil' who will 'flee from him'. You cannot say that about a non-Christian. The non-Christian cannot resist the devil, he cannot cause the devil to flee from him. The devil is master; the man is under the dominion of sin and of Satan. The devil is 'the strong man armed that keepeth his goods at peace'. How can such a man resist him and cause him to flee? But the Christian can resist the devil and he will flee from him. Though he be 'your adversary the devil who as a roaring lion roameth about seeking whom he may devour', we can resist him 'steadfast in the faith' and defeat him and cause him to disappear [1 *Peter* 5 : 8, 9]. 'The whole world lieth in the wicked one' says John in his First Epistle, chapter 5. But he also says, 'that wicked one toucheth us not'. He cannot touch Christians. He can shout at us, he can frighten us, he can entice us; but he cannot touch us! Thank God, we are out of his territory. He 'toucheth us not', he cannot, he is not allowed to, because we belong to another kingdom. He is outside as far as we are concerned; we 'have been freed from sin'.

This, I say, is the most liberating thought that we can ever encounter and grasp, this is the truth that sets us free. 'Stand fast, therefore, in the liberty wherewith Christ hath made us free' [*Galatians* 5 : 1]. As a Christian you can do that; as a Christian you must do that; as a Christian you are free to do that. You cannot address words like that to an unbeliever. What is the use of going to him and saying 'Stand fast therefore'. He cannot stand fast because he is a slave. But because we are no longer the slaves of sin but slaves of God, such an exhortation can be addressed to us. 'Stand fast, therefore, in the liberty wherewith Christ hath made us free.'

But secondly, we have become servants to God, or better, we have been 'enslaved' to God. We belong to a new Master, we are in a new territory, we are in a new kingdom. This great translation has taken place, this transference, this complete removal from an old realm, 'Enslaved to God'. The idea, obviously, is that of being purchased. Slaves were bought from one master and became the property of another; and the Apostle is reminding us that as Christians we belong to God. He frequently uses that comparison. For instance, in dealing with the question of fornication in 1 Corinthians 6, he says, 'You are not your own, you have been bought with a price' – your body is not your own, it is the temple of the Holy Ghost; you must realize this. He has already told us in verse 17 of this chapter that it is a 'willing' slavery, we have 'obeyed from the heart the form of doctrine which was delivered to us', or 'to which we were delivered'.

It is interesting to notice the series of gradations in the Apostle's use of this analogy of slavery. In verse 16 he said that we are either slaves of 'sin unto death', or slaves of 'obedience unto righteousness'. The full argument was, 'Know ye not that to whom ye yield yourselves servants to obey [slaves to obey] his servants [slaves] ye are to whom ye obey, whether it be of sin unto death or of obedience . . . '. The Christian is a slave to obedience. Then in verse 17 we are told that we have become 'slaves to the form of doctrine to which we were delivered'. 'But God be thanked that ye were the servants of sin, but ye have obeyed from the heart that form of doctrine.' We are slaves first to 'obedience', then to the 'form of doctrine'. In verses 18 and 19 he puts

it in terms of righteousness. 'Being made free from sin, you became the slaves of righteousness'; and his appeal is that we should
'yield our members slaves to righteousness'. You notice the steps
– 'obedience', 'form of doctrine', 'righteousness'. But now in this
statement we arrive at the top of the mountain, we have reached
the summit – 'But now, having been freed from sin and having
become enslaved to God'. Not obedience only, not form of doctrine only, not righteousness only – wonderful as they are – but
'slaves to God'. That is the real truth about a Christian, he is
enslaved to God. That is the secret of holiness. To realize this
is the secret of holiness and of sanctification. What we need is
not an experience, but rather to understand what is true of us,
to understand who we are and what we are. That is the key to
holiness and sanctification.

In other words the teaching is that we have no right to live
to ourselves, we have no right to please ouselves. I will go further; we have no right to sin. To sin means that we are doing
something of which our Master and our Owner disapproves,
something He hates. For a Christian to sin is like a man in an
army fraternizing with the enemy. That is what sin is; and we
have no right to do it, it is most reprehensible. Because we are
slaves of God, because we belong to Him, we are meant to serve
Him, we are meant to minister to His glory. 'The chief end of
man' – What is it? 'To glorify God and to enjoy Him for ever'.
What is the first and the great commandment? It is, 'Thou shalt
love the Lord thy God with all thy heart, and with all thy soul,
and with all thy mind, and with all thy strength' [*Matthew* 22 : 37–
38]. It is a totalitarian demand; we are to be absolutely His, and
to live for Him. We must be like our Lord and say, 'The zeal of
thine house hath eaten me up' [*John* 2 : 17]. There should be
nothing left of me, I should be consumed by that zeal. If we
thought of that, if we thought of God and our relationship to
Him, and our consequent duty, instead of thinking so much about
ourselves and our problems, our moods and states, our temptations and battles and difficulties, our whole attitude and practice
would be changed. But we tend to say, 'I do like to hear sermons
on sanctification and holiness. I am having such a hard time, and
my difficulties are great.' We talk about ourselves and outline
our symptoms as patients always tend to do. We are eloquent
about all this, and talk at great length about ourselves, our

moods and states and conditions. We crave for sympathy and for some sudden way of deliverance and healing.

What a travesty of the Apostle's teaching! What you need to be told is that you are a slave of God, that you belong to God. You must talk less about yourself and more about Him. Your business is to do what you know He wants you to do. He has bought you, bought you at such a price, such a cost, in order that you may do so. That is how the Apostle Paul preaches holiness. It is not a sentimental teaching which offers us some marvellous experience. It is a manly, almost a military exhortation: Remember who you are. You have been set free from that old slavery; you are now a slave of God. Pull yourself together; and realize who your Owner is, who your Master is.

What is holiness? It is to be like Jesus Christ. What did He say of Himself? 'I came not to do my own will, but the will of Him that sent me.' He did not consider Himself. He said 'Here am I, send me'. Though He was the Son of God He humbled Himself, He volunteered, He gave Himself utterly and absolutely. 'The words I speak, I speak not of myself', he says. 'The works that I do are the works that the Father hath given me to do.' 'And being found in fashion as a man, he humbled himself, and became obedient unto death, even the death of the cross' [*Philippians* 2 : 8]. That was the way in which He lived in this world.

Such behaviour is the absolute perfection of holiness and sanctification. And you and I are to be like that. What we need is not an experience, but the realization that we are slaves of God, and utterly and absolutely at His disposal. Whatever the demand may be, we must face it in the same way as He did. We must follow our Lord and say, 'Father, if it be possible, let this cup pass by; nevertheless, not as I will but as thou wilt'. That is the way! That is the acme of obedience! He is the One we are to follow. That is the example, that is the pattern, that is the analogy! 'Enslaved to God.'

You are not your own. Do not talk so much about the weakness of the flesh, or about the strength of temptation. Realize who and what you are, realize that your very body is the temple of the Holy Ghost. You have no right to abuse it or to mis-use it. 'You are not your own, you have been bought with a price.' The New Testament pattern of teaching and preaching about sanctification is to bring us to realize that we have been set free, that we have become enslaved unto God. Stop feeling your spiritual pulse, and commiserating with yourself. Stop waiting for some marvellous deliverance that will put everything right without your doing anything at all. We read, 'The truth shall make you free'; and the truth that makes you free is the realization of who you are and what you are.

But over and above that is the realization that, as slaves, our position is so secure. 'They shall never perish, neither shall any man be able to pluck them out of my hand' [*John* 10 : 28]. The devil thought that we could never be taken out of his hands; he was very confident. The great patriarchs had tried to free themselves from him; but they could not; he defeated them all. The Law was given by God through Moses, but it could not bring deliverance, because it was 'weak through the flesh', as Paul says in chapter 8, verse 3. But suddenly One comes into the fight, suddenly One enters the lists, and He conquers the devil and defeats him and sets us free from his tyranny. Because that has happened we can say with confidence and with certainty that the devil with all his might and the marshalling of all his forces, shall never be able to 'separate us from the love of God which is in Christ Jesus our Lord'. This means that as the slaves of God we can never be taken back into the old slavery; it is impossible. God does not and will not allow His slaves to be taken from Him by any manner of means. We are slaves of God now, and forever and forever. What an encouragement!

That brings us to the next point. We have seen that the Christian is a man who has undergone a profound change, and we have seen something of the character of the change. Let us now look at the result of the change. The first result is that 'ye have your fruit unto holiness'. What an immediate contrast with the old life! We have fruit now; we had none before. 'What fruit had ye then in those things of which ye are now ashamed?' None! Nothing! But as Christians we produce fruit. Let us never forget to observe this, that the fruit is the result of our changed condition. You cannot produce this fruit without being freed from sin and enslaved unto God. It is impossible to produce this fruit without being born again, without being regenerate. Our Lord states that quite clearly. 'Do men gather grapes of thorns, or figs of thistles?', He asks in the Sermon on the Mount. He goes on to say, 'Every good tree bringeth good fruit: but a corrupt tree bringeth forth evil fruit. A good tree cannot bring forth evil fruit, neither can a corrupt tree bring forth good fruit' [*Matthew* 7 : 16–18]. It is impossible. Before you can have the fruit you must have the tree. It is the nature of the tree that determines the nature of the fruit. So it is impossible to produce this fruit unless the great process of regeneration has taken place in us. It is only as God takes hold of us, and transplants us from that old stock to the new that we are capable of producing the fruit at all. It is only because we are 'in Christ' that we can bear this fruit. As He puts it again, 'I am the vine, ye are the branches'; and 'Without me ye can do nothing' [*John* 15 : 1 and 5].

The Apostle will repeat this again in chapter 7 in verses 4 and 5. 'Wherefore' he says, 'my brethren, ye also are become dead to the law by the body of Christ; that ye should be married to another, even to him who is raised from the dead, that we should bring forth fruit unto God.' The old husband, as it were, could not impregnate us, and we could not bear any fruit. But we are married to a new Husband, and now we can bear fruit; and we do. That is another way of stating the same truth, the point being that it is the changed condition, the changed relationship, and the fact of our being joined to Christ, and 'receiving of his fulness' that enables us to bear the fruit.

I must emphasize the words 'You have'. 'Being made free from sin and having become enslaved to God, you have your fruit.' You have got it! This is true of every Christian. There is no such thing as a Christian who does not bear fruit; you cannot be a Christian without bearing fruit. Our Lord, you remember, in that great picture in John 15 speaks of 'fruit', 'more fruit' and 'much fruit'. What I am asserting is that unless there is some fruit you are not a Christian. This is not merely my opinion. The Apostle Paul says so: 'Be not deceived, God is not mocked; neither fornicators, nor adulterers, nor effeminate, nor abusers of themselves with mankind, nor thieves, nor drunkards, nor covetous, nor revilers shall inherit the kingdom of God. [1 *Corinthians* 6 : 6–10]. It is impossible – 'be not deceived" You may say, 'Lord, Lord'; you may say 'I believe the Gospel', but if there is no fruit in your life it is vain. It is only a profession, it is only a form of 'believism'. It matters not how many 'decisions' a man has taken, if there is no change in his life he is just not a Christian. You cannot be a Christian and remain exactly as you were before. Every Christian produces fruit: 'faith without works is dead' [*James* 2 : 26].

'But now' – and he is talking about every Christian – 'being made free from sin and become servants to God, you have your fruit'. What is the fruit? He says that it is 'unto holiness'. Be careful about this. He does not say 'Ye have your fruit unto everlasting life'. No, because everlasting life is the end, not the fruit. If he had said, 'Ye have your fruit unto life everlasting', he would be teaching justification by works. But that is the exact opposite of what he is teaching. We do not have our fruit unto everlasting life, we have our fruit unto holiness. What is the fruit? It is holiness, it is sanctification.

What is holiness? We have already seen something of the answer. It means that we become further and further removed from sins such as adultery, fornication, murders, revellings, drunkenness, and all the other items in the list in Galatians 5. Those are 'the works of the flesh'. To be holy means that we no longer do things like these. But it does not stop at that. The essential thing about holiness is that we are devoted to God. Think of the 'holy vessels' in the temple. They were called 'holy' because they were set apart for that service only, for the service of God. Men no longer drank out of them in the ordinary way; they were the holy vessels of God, sanctified, set apart, used only in the temple service and in connection with the temple ritual. The mountain on which the Law was given is called 'the holy mount'. It had been barricaded off; a fence was put round it so that neither man nor beast could approach it and touch it. The 'holy mount' was the mountain that was set apart for God and for His service – devoted, dedicated to God.

That is what is meant by holiness. Holiness is not a feeling, holiness is not an experience; holiness is to be devoted to God, to be at His service. As Paul puts it again in Ephesians 2: 10, 'We are his workmanship, created in Christ Jesus unto good works, which God hath before ordained that we should walk in them'. In many passages in the New Testament we are told what these works are. In Galatians 5, from which I have just quoted, we are given by way of contrast to that list of the works of the flesh another similar list in which we are told about 'the fruit of the Spirit'. We find it again in Ephesians 4 verse 17 and following. It is the 'new walk', the new life that is pleasing to God. It is keeping the Law, manifesting the Moral Law in our lives. The Apostle will tell us in chapter 8 that, 'What the law could not do, in that it was weak through the flesh, God sending his own Son in the likeness of sinful flesh, and for sin, condemned sin in the flesh: that the righteousness of the law might be fulfilled in us, who walk not after the flesh but after the Spirit' [*Romans* 8 : 3, 4]. It means living a righteous and a holy life, even such as the Lord Jesus Christ lived when He was here.

What else does it mean? It means that we manifest the fruit of the Spirit: 'The fruit of the Spirit is love, joy, peace, long-suffering, gentleness, goodness, faith, meekness, temperance' [*Galatians* 5 : 22–23]. Such qualities become more and more manifest in our lives and daily living. I emphasize 'more and more'; because holiness is progressive, its manifestations should increase in us. Ultimately our Lord is my sanctification – 'Of him are ye in Christ Jesus, who of God is made unto us wisdom and righteousness and sanctification and redemption'. He is the 'all and in all', and 'we are complete in him'. That is true, but He also imparts it to us; that is why we should become progressively more and more holy.

There are many who do not believe this; some even teach that we remain exactly the same at the end as we were at the beginning, that our holiness and sanctification are entirely in the Lord Jesus Christ. That was the teaching of Charles G. Finney, for instance. That seems to me to be a complete denial of the Apostle's teaching here. There are others who put it in terms of 'abiding in Christ'. They teach that while you are in Him you are holy, but if you fail to abide, you will be back where you were before. But, surely, that is impossible. The truth is as the Apostle puts it in 2 Corinthians 3, verse 18: 'We all, with open face beholding as in a glass the glory of the Lord, are changed into the same image from glory to glory.' It is progressive, advancing, becoming more and more like Him. 'But' you say, 'what if such a person sins, does he not go back to the beginning?' Of course he does not! Let me use an analogy. Think of a man who is going to climb a mountain. There he is, walking along at the foot of the mountain. Suddenly he may stumble and fall. There he is, he has fallen at the foot of the mountain. Then he begins to climb the mountain. After he has gone half way up, or two-thirds of the way up, he suddenly misses his foothold and falls. But that does not mean that he slithers all the way down to the very foot of the mountain once more. Of course he does not. You can fall within a foot of the top of the mountain; but that does not mean that you are down at the foot of the mountain again. You are still within a foot of the top! So the fact that a man may still occasionally fall into sin does not mean that he goes right back to the beginning. Sanctification is a progressive process and the truth about it is, 'changed into the image from glory to glory'. We become more and more 'conformed to the image of his dear Son'. The saint matures, the saint grows, the saint becomes increasingly conformed to the image of God's dear Son.

> *Changed from glory into glory*
> *Till in heaven we take our place;*
> *Till we cast our crowns before Him,*
> *Lost in wonder, love and praise.*

That is the first result of this great change. The end is everlasting life.

Twenty-two

*

For the wages of sin is death, but the gift of God is eternal life through Jesus Christ our Lord.   Romans 6 : 23

This verse comes as a fitting end to this great chapter. It is, as we have seen, one of the pivotal chapters in this epistle and vital from the standpoint of Christian doctrine and the Christian way of salvation. The measure and the extent to which we have been able to follow it and understand it, is the measure of our rejoicing in Christ Jesus, and in the liberty wherewith He has made us free. Having studied it no one should still be in bondage, for this is the chapter of all chapters that shows us the way to true liberty.

The word 'for' at the beginning of the verse links it with what has gone before. It is indeed the conclusion of the argument which the Apostle has been conducting. The argument began in verse 20, in which he began to give reasons for paying heed to the exhortation of verse 19, which is, 'As ye have yielded your members servants to uncleanness and to iniquity unto iniquity, even so now yield your members servants to righteousness unto holiness'. He gives us the reasons in verses 20–23 in the form of an argument, and here he sums it up by emphasizing the 'end' to which the two types of life lead.

This verse closes the immediate argument. But it does more than that, it also sums up and ends the argument of the entire chapter. As we have seen, this chapter is an argument from beginning to end. We indicated at the beginning that it is part of a parenthesis. The Apostle interrupts his main statement at the end of chapter 5. He will resume it again in the first verse of the eighth chapter. Chapters 6 and 7 constitute a parenthesis in which he takes up two arguments. This verse is in many ways a summary of the argument he had been deploying and developing throughout this sixth chapter in order to refute the monstrous suggestion stated in verses 1 and 15: 'What then? Shall we continue in sin, that grace may abound?' 'What then? Shall we sin because we are not under the law, but under grace?' He refutes that, and shows how utterly monstrous it is, and how inconceivable for anyone who truly understands the doctrine of justification by faith only. This verse, I repeat, sums up the argument of the whole chapter. It is interesting to notice that it is virtually a repetition of the last verse of chapter 5, where he says, 'That as sin hath reigned unto death, even so might grace reign through righteousness unto eternal life by Jesus Christ our Lord'.

It is good that we should observe the Apostle's method. The best comparison we can use to show his method is that of the musical composer. There is something about great minds which is similar, irrespective of their particular realm. I remember hearing the late Sir Walford Davies once describe Beethoven as 'the Shakespeare of music'; and there was a good deal to be said for his definition. He meant by that, that they had the same sort of mind. The Apostle Paul certainly had a similar mind, I would say a very much greater one. But it is the same type of mind, the same order of mind, and he seems to use the same method. It is seen in Beethoven in his Sonatas and his Symphonies. He makes a general statement; then he takes up a subsidiary theme in that general theme, and works it out for a while. Then he takes up another subsidiary one and works that out for a while. You sometimes feel that he has forgotten his first original statement. But that is never the case, he always comes back to it, always returns to the point of departure. The Apostle does that very selfsame thing here. He has made his basic statement in chapter 5, verse 21. He then takes up the objection to his teaching along two main lines. He follows each out in turn; but he sees to it that in summing up his argument he returns to the exact point from which he originally set out. So this verse is in many ways a repetition of the last verse of chapter 5, and it is like it even in details.

One thing we can say in general about this verse is that it is one of the great statements of the Gospel of salvation. The Apostle clearly enjoyed stating the whole of the Gospel in one verse. He summarizes it, or puts it in a nutshell. He evidently delighted in doing so; and I trust that that finds an echo in our hearts.

What then does he say here? There are some three things which stand out on the very surface of the statement before we come to analyse it in detail.

The first is that there are two possibilities facing every individual who comes into this world, and there are only two. They are shown in this verse. 'The wages of sin is death; but the gift of God is eternal life through Jesus Christ our Lord.' The message of the Gospel is often put in this way. You have either your 'house on the sand' or your 'house on the rock'. You have either passed through the 'wide gate' or the 'strait or narrow gate'. You are either on the 'broad way 'or the 'narrow way'. You serve either mammon or God. Inevitably, it is one or the other – there are only two possibilities.

All the non-Christian views confronting mankind belong to the one category. The world makes a great deal, of course, of the minor differences; but from the standpoint of the Bible, and of salvation, they are all one. Unbelievers are divided up into nationalities; divided by iron curtains or bamboo curtains; divided politically, socially, and in many other respects; but all such divisions are irrelevant. Such divisions do not count at all in the light of eternity. This division made by the Bible is the only division. There are only two possibilities – no more!

Secondly, these two possibilities are completely different from each other. I emphasize the word 'completely'. They are altogether and entirely different, as we have already seen many times in working our way through this chapter. There is nothing in common between these two views. They do not gradually shade off from one to the other; there are no shades in the spiritual realm. Everything is black or white, and you do not gradually pass from one to the other. There is nothing like a spectrum here, but stark differences, absolute contrasts. We must never cease to emphasize this truth. There is nothing in common between the Christian and the non-Christian in a spiritual sense – nothing at all! They are absolutely different. The Christian has a new life and it is altogether different from being 'dead in trespasses and sins'.

That brings us to the third and last general point, which is that each of these two positions, which are so essentially different, has its own internal consistency; each one is consistent with itself. Different from the other, but consistent within itself. In other words, each one of these two leads by an inexorable law to ends which are quite inevitable. Start on the one road and you are bound to arrive at a given destination; start on the other road and you are bound to arrive at an entirely different destination. There is this inward consistency within the two, though they are so essentially different. Here, the Apostle is particularly concerned to emphasize the difference in the 'end'. He has stressed other differences in verses 20, 21 and 22, but emphasized the 'end' at the close of verse 22. 'Now being made free from sin, and become servants to God, you have your fruit unto holiness, and the end everlasting life.' He had mentioned in verse 21 that the end of the other way was death. He seems to say, 'I must say that again, I must underline it and re-emphasize it'. So this verse is particularly concerned with the different ends of these two ways of living.

In the light of all these matters let us look at the Apostle's contrasts. I have classified the contrasts under three headings. First, the master we serve. The analogy he has been using is one of slavery, so the first contrast between these two possibilities confronting every soul that is born into this world concerns the master whom we serve. Here again, it is a matter of two possibilities – it is either sin or else it is God. 'The wages of sin' – there is the one master. 'The gift of God' – there is the other Master. Paul had mentioned that before. 'But now being made free from sin, and become slaves to God'. It is either sin, or God. Every individual in the world at this moment is either a slave to sin, or else a slave of God. There is no neutrality in the spiritual realm. 'No man's land' does not exist in the spiritual realm. 'You cannot serve God and mammon.' We have seen that repeatedly.

The one thing that matters is, Whom are we serving? who is our master? This is the point at which we see once more that all the talk about morality and ethics, and conduct, and doing good, and all the rest, is completely irrelevant. The one thing to know about a man is this – not, how much good does he do? not, what are his ideals? not, how philanthropic is he? Those are not the vital questions to ask. The only question you need ask about any man is, Who is his master? To whom is he a slave? Though he may be apparently a 'paragon of all the virtues', though he may be a man who does a great deal of good, though he may be a most moral and ethical man, though he may appear at first sight to be very much better than most people who are members of the Christian churches, that does not tell us the real truth about him.

The one question the Bible asks about every one of us is, Whom do you serve? for whom are you living? who is your master? Is it sin, or is it God?

This is the crucial point in the fight for the Christian Gospel and faith at the present time. This is the very nerve and centre of the great fight for the Christian faith today. People are so impressed by these wonderful men, who speak so nicely and with so much culture on the television, who do so much good and talk so learnedly about doing good, and about ethics. These 'fine' men! That is the word! The Apostle's reply to all this is that it does not matter how 'fine' a man may be; if he does not do all for God and His glory, he is a slave of sin.

The Apostle gives us this truth in a most interesting manner in the Second Epistle to the Corinthians, chapter 11. He says that there were teachers who were troubling the Corinthians. He was concerned to deliver them from those 'false apostles', those specious teachers. He says, 'What I do, that I will do, that I may cut off occasion from them which desire occasion; that wherein they glory, they may be found even as we. For such are false apostles, deceitful workers, transforming themselves into the apostles of Christ. And no marvel; for Satan himself is transformed into an angel of light. Therefore it is no great thing if his ministers also be transformed as the ministers of righteousness' [2 *Corinthians* 11 : 12–15]. There it is stated clearly once and for ever. These people appeared to be 'the ministers of righteousness'; but the Apostle says that the Corinthians should not be deluded by these men, nor be deceived by them as Eve was deceived by the serpent in the Garden of Eden [verse 3]. They should realize that such men are able to transform themselves into 'angels of light', to appear to be Christians, even the apostles of Christ; but it is all false, and they are serving the devil. They should not be surprised at this, says the Apostle, because, as their master does this, it is not very surprising that they should imitate him and try to do the same.

The upshot of all this is that we must not judge men by the good they do, nor by the good and nice things they say. There is only one question, Is it all done for the glory of God?, because if it is not, it is all done in slavery to sin and to Satan. As Christian people you should not be frightened when you hear such men being praised and followed by the masses. You should say, rather: 'That is quite irrelevant, that is not the thing I am concerned about.

If they are not living to the glory of God and the Lord Jesus Christ, they are in exactly the same category as the vilest and the foulest sinners in the world at this moment; and all their "righteousness" is but as "filthy rags".' Let us say that, let us assert that; and let us not be deceived by this mere appearance of goodness. It is the master whom you serve that determines what you are. The Apostle has said all that in verse 16, but he says it again here.

That enables us to go on to the second point. Having seen the complete contrast in the masters, observe now the complete contrasts between the contract or the conditions under which we serve the two masters. They are also entirely different and have nothing in common. On the one hand it is 'wages', on the other 'a gift'.

'The wages of sin is death.' It is generally agreed that a better translation of 'wages' might be 'rations'. The word the Apostle used was the word that was used of the rations that were given to the soldiers and the slaves in Imperial Rome. They were made to work as slaves, and then they were given a 'ration' of food, and perhaps a certain amount of money. That is what the Apostle says – 'the rations of sin'. It is something earned, something that you deserve; it is something that you merit, something for which you have rendered service. But the question arises as to who decides, or what decides, the rations that are to be given to these slaves of sin? The answer, of course, is 'The Law'. It is the Law that decides the wages. The Law has laid down plainly and clearly what the result of such a life and conduct is to be. In other words, the Apostle reminds us here of something he has been saying ever since verse 20 in chapter 5 – that sin and Law always go together. Here it is, 'Moreover the law entered, that the offence might abound. But where sin abounded, grace did much more abound'. We had actually met the same idea in chapter 4, verse 15: 'Because the law worketh wrath.' Law and sin go together. In chapter 8 we shall find that Paul puts it like this in verse 2: 'For the law of the Spirit of life in Christ Jesus hath made me free from the law of sin and death.' There it is explicitly: 'the law of sin and death'. Law, sin, death all go together.

This teaching is found elsewhere in Paul's teaching. At the end of 1 Corinthians 15, for instance, 'The sting of death is sin; and the strength of sin is the law' (verse 56). These are against us. It is the Law, then, that decides that the rations paid to the man who has been a slave of sin is death. There is a very clear statement of this principle in the Epistle to the Hebrews in the second chapter: 'For if the word spoken by angels was steadfast, and every transgression and disobedience received a just recompence of reward. . . .' 'The word spoken by angels', of course, was the word of the Law. He is referring to the Law as given to Moses, and mediated by angels; and what the Law says is that every transgression and disobedience should receive 'a just recompence of reward', a reward for services rendered. That is the just recompence of reward, and, as Paul tells us, it is death.

So on the one hand you have wages, rations, determined by the Law in a strictly legal manner. 'The soul that sinneth it shall die': that is the prescription of the Law, that is the ration that will be given; and it is given.

But on the other hand we have 'a gift'; and it means 'a free gift'. This is not earned, this is not merited, this is not a just recompence; it is altogether different; it is the complete antithesis. This is solely the result of God's goodness and God's grace. Grace is unmerited favour, kindness shown to someone who does not deserve any kindness at all. It is the free gift of God to people who are utterly undeserving of it. This is the principle that works in the Christian life from beginning to end. It is the most glorious aspect of the great contrast between sin and grace which has been before us since chapter 5, verse 21: 'That as sin hath reigned unto death, even so might grace reign through righteousness unto eternal life.' It controls the whole of the Christian life from the beginning to the end; it is true of the entire method of salvation. It is what made the Apostle say in verse 16 of chapter 1, 'I am not ashamed of the gospel of Christ'. Why? Because 'it is the power of God unto salvation to every one that believeth, to the Jew first and also to the Greek. For therein a righteousness of God [from God] is revealed by faith'. It is God's free gift, entirely of grace. The Apostle bursts out in this same way when he comes to the twenty-first verse of chapter 3, and especially in verse 24: 'Being justified freely by his grace through the redemption that is in Christ Jesus.' How he rejoices to repeat these wonderful statements! The two masters are different, and the terms of service in the two cases are also a complete contrast, and altogether different.

Thirdly and lastly, the end to which each leads is altogether

[306]

different. And as I have already said, this verse is particularly concerned to emphasize the difference in the ends. The Apostle is not concerned here to tell us how to arrive at that end, for he has already done so. In the case of sin he says that the steps are, disobedience, unrighteousness, uncleanness, iniquity. The servant, the slave of sin is always led along that line. Did it not happen in the Garden of Eden? Adam and Eve had been living a life of obedience to God; but when the devil came, what was his first suggestion? That they should disobey, that they should do what God had told them not to do. Disobedience was the first step. The moment you disobey you also become guilty of unrighteousness. That, in turn, leads to uncleanness, as we saw in verse 19; and that in turn leads to 'iniquity unto iniquity'. Those are the steps.

The steps on the other side we have also seen described in verse 16. Under the Gospel we are led first of all to obedience; and obedience leads to righteousness; and righteousness leads to holiness. Once more, what a wonderful difference!

But the Apostle's chief concern here is to emphasize the difference in the ends at which we arrive in the two slaveries along those differing lines. The end to which sin leads is death. If you are a slave to sin you will be led by sin along those horrible steps which end in death. What does Paul mean by saying that 'the wages of sin is death?' He means death in every form. The moment man disobeyed he died spiritually, which meant separation from God. But it also included physical death. Man was never meant to die either spiritually or physically; but as the result of disobedience and sin he has died spiritually and physically. But, here, the Apostle is looking, not so much at the proximate results of slavery to sin, as at the final result, its final outworking, the ultimate destiny. In the meantime, as he has been telling us, it leads to 'uncleanness and to iniquity unto iniquity', and so on. But, he says, the final end of it all is death.

The best explanation of the Apostle's meaning is found in the term that is used more than once in the twentieth chapter of the Book of Revelation – 'the second death'. The wages of sin, the end to which sin leads, is the second death. In that chapter the Apostle draws a distinction. Those whose names are written in the Lamb's book of life have no part in the second death; but all others do. In other words, the wages of sin is the second death.

This means a final and irreversible separation from God, and from 'the face of God', and from the life of God. It means to be eternally outside God's life, with all the consequent misery and suffering. That is the ultimate fate of the ungodly, to be eternally outside the life of God, and all its beneficent and loving and noble and holy and pure influences; it is to be left in your uncleanness, and your iniquity unto iniquity, with that, furthermore, getting worse and worse without relief. It is to be altogether shut off, and cut off finally from God. It is to be cast into what the imagery used at the end of that twentieth chapter of the Book of Revelation describes as 'the lake of fire and brimstone', into which death and hades are cast, and also the beast and the devil himself. It is to be there everlastingly outside the life of God. That is the end to which sin leads its slaves.

But what is the end of those who are the slaves of God? What a contrast! 'The wages of sin is death, but the gift of God is eternal life.' What is 'eternal life?' It does not merely mean everlasting existence. It does mean that you continue everlastingly, as the other does; but it not only means that. Indeed that is the least significant thing about it. Eternal life means especially the knowledge of God and of the Lord Jesus Christ. It is our Lord Himself who defines it in that way in John's Gospel, chapter 17, verse 3: 'This is life eternal, that they might know thee the only true God, and Jesus Christ, whom thou hast sent.' That is eternal life – the knowledge of God! That is true life. Death means not to know Him, and to be shut out from His presence and His glory and all His blessings; eternal life is the exact opposite. It is to know God; not merely to know about God, but to know Him, and to know Him in an ever-increasing degree of fulness. It means therefore all blessedness, unalterable and spotless holiness, and imperishable glory. It means not only that we shall continue to exist, but that we shall go on living in the presence of God, we shall 'see God', we shall live in 'the light of the Lamb', and we shall be perfectly holy. We shall also be glorified; we shall be like our blessed Lord [1 *John* 3 : 1, 2].

The Apostle says elsewhere that it means that we shall 'receive a crown'. That is how he puts it in the last letter he ever wrote, the second letter to Timothy, in chapter 4, verse 8: 'Henceforth' – he is looking to the end – 'there is laid up for me a crown of righteousness, which the Lord, the righteous Judge, shall give me in that day: and not to me only.' Thank God, he went on to say, 'and not to me only'; otherwise we might feel, 'Ah yes, he was a great man, an exceptional saint'. But the Apostle says 'not to me only, but unto all them also that love his appearing'. You and I will receive this 'crown of righteousness'. In other words, it is perfection. We shall be 'without spot or wrinkle or any such thing'. We shall enjoy 'the beatific vision', we shall be enjoying the glory which God will have given us. The glory that He gave to His Son, the Son will give to us [*John* 17 : 22]. We shall be glorified, completely saved in every respect.

That is what eternal life means, sharing and enjoying the life of God to all eternity, without the slightest suspicion of an admixture of sin and evil. There will be no sin there, there will be no sighing, there will be no sorrow, there will be no tears, there will be no partings. It will be glory unmixed, absolute glory, enjoying the perfection of God Himself with all the holy angels. It means full life in every respect – body, mind, and spirit – the whole person entirely delivered from every vestige and relic of sin, and completely glorified. It will be something that even Adam did not enjoy. Before the Fall Adam was perfect, Adam was innocent, but he did not have eternal life. If you have eternal life you cannot lose it, you cannot die; but Adam died. No, 'In Him [in Christ] the tribes of Adam boast, more blessings than their father lost', as Isaac Watts puts it. Adam would have gone on to this had he continued in obedience; but he failed and fell. If he had continued in obedience he would have been granted this eternal life, which the Lord gives us as the end of our salvation. Peter in his First Epistle, chapter 1, verse 9, describes it as 'Receiving the end of your faith, even the salvation of your souls'. That is the same thing.

This eternal life begins here in this world. We have eternal life the moment we believe in the Lord Jesus Christ; but the Apostle is concerned here about the ultimate end of it. We have it, but in another sense we are going to receive it. Have you noticed an apparent contradiction in the Scripture concerning this? We are already saved, but the Apostle Peter says that we are going to receive salvation as an end. There is no contradiction at this point. We are only given a foretaste of salvation here, a first instalment, a little sample; but the fulness itself awaits us. 'Henceforth', as Paul says, 'there is laid up for me a crown of righteousness.' That is the end; 'The crowning day is coming by and by'. He is going to give us this 'crown of righteousness' ultimately; and in the meantime we are –

> *Changed from glory into glory*
> *Till in heaven we take our place*

There, then, are the three contrasts – the two masters, the two terms of service, the two ends at which we arrive. That completes the account of the contrasts, but it is not the end of the verse. The Apostle never leaves it just like that. Having described the contrasts – masters, terms of service, ends – he seems to ask, How has this become possible? How can this have happened? He tells us, and once more brings in the blessed Name – 'through Jesus Christ our Lord'. He could not leave that out; he never does so. Do you remember how he ended chapter 5? 'That as sin hath reigned unto death, even so might grace reign through righteousness unto eternal life by Jesus Christ our Lord.' Take verse 11 in this sixth chapter: 'Likewise reckon ye yourselves also to be dead indeed unto sin, but alive unto God.' That is what he set out to say. But he cannot stop at that – 'through Jesus Christ our Lord'. He never fails to go on to add that, never fails to remind us of the way in which all has come to us, all has been made possible.

Are we like the great Apostle? Or do we stop with our classifications, and forget the Lord who has brought it all to us, and without whom we would have nothing at all? The whole of our life is in Christ, it is 'through'' or 'in' 'Jesus Christ our Lord'. Everything is from Him, and without Him there is nothing at all. This blessed future which is offered us and promised us is all 'through Jesus Christ our Lord'. It is in Him and because of Him that we are justified freely by God. We receive our justification as the result of His work, His spotless life of obedience, His atoning sacrificial death where He received our punishment. 'We are justified', says Paul in chapter 5, verse 9, 'by his blood'. 'He was delivered for our offences, and raised again for our justification.' It is all in Jesus Christ – His incarnation, life, obedience, agony, death, burial, grave, resurrection, ascension, return, session at the right hand of God in the glory everlasting. It is 'through Jesus Christ our Lord'; and without Him we have nothing. It is because of Him that God declares us to be righteous. He imputes to us the righteousness of Jesus Christ. But He does not leave it at that;

[310]

He joins us to Him. That has been the great theme of this chapter. 'Know ye not', he says, 'that so many of us as were baptized into Jesus Christ, were baptized into his death? Therefore we are buried with him by baptism into death: that like as Christ was raised up from the dead by the glory of the Father, even so we also should walk in newness of life.' 'Planted together in the likeness of his death, we shall also be in the likeness of his resurrection.' We are joined to him, we are 'in him'. And because of that Paul has drawn these various deductions.

Because we are in Christ and joined to Him we have been set free from sin, we are dead to sin; it has no more power or authority or rule or reign over us. Secondly, we are 'alive unto God', and know 'the exceeding greatness of his power to us-ward that believe'. I am open to that. I am in the plan and purpose of God. He has set his affection upon me, He has known me 'before the foundation of the world'. I am in this great plan and scheme of redemption. Christ's life is in me, and I am in Him. He is the Vine, and I am a branch; He is the Head, and we are the members of the body. And because of Him we have received the Spirit. The Spirit that dwelt in Him dwells in us, and it is this Holy Spirit who leads us and guides us and directs us. He brings us to the Scripture, opens our understanding, and opens the Word to us. It is the Spirit that produces our sanctification; His work is progressive. Sanctification goes on and on. But we have received the Spirit through Jesus Christ, because we are in Him and joined to Him.

To close, we can put it like this. God's purpose is to bring us to glory. 'It behoved him'. says Hebrews 2:10, 'of whom are all things, and for whom are all things, in bringing many sons to glory to make the Captain of their salvation perfect through sufferings.' The object is to 'bring many sons to glory', the glory we have been trying to describe. That is God's purpose. The whole object of salvation is to bring us to that glory where we shall be perfect and spotless and sinless, without wrinkle or any such thing, holy and perfect in the presence of God. That is God's purpose. Is there anything, therefore, which can be so monstrous and foolish and irrational as to suggest that such preaching leads people to say 'Shall we continue in sin that grace may abound?' Or, 'Shall we sin because we are not under the law, but under grace?' The Apostle scoffs at such a suggestion. 'Can you not see', he says in effect, 'that the whole object of justification by faith is to bring us to glory, that the end is eternal life? How can such a programme, such a purpose, ever be any kind of encouragement to sin?'

That is how the Apostle finally ridicules it. The purpose of God is the exact opposite of sin and all it represents, and to which it leads. God is 'of purer eyes than to behold evil, and cannot look on iniquity' [*Habakkuk* 1 : 13]. Christ, to whom we are joined, is the exact opposite of sin. He was 'that Holy One', perfect in all His ways, 'tempted in all points like as we are, yet without sin'. He was 'holy, harmless and undefiled', and we are joined to Him. All this is the antithesis, the exact opposite of sin. What a foolish suggestion, therefore, that such preaching should encourage people to go on sinning!

That leaves us with a final question. What is it in any man that can ever make him understand such a Gospel? What was it that made these critics of Paul say that his preaching of justification by faith was an incitement and an encouragement to sin? How can men say such a thing face to face with such statements, and such a Gospel? But there is a further question: What causes men and women who have heard the Gospel deliberately prefer to live a life of sin, with all its uncleanness and its iniquity, and its unprofitable character, and in spite of the fact that they are told that it will certainly lead to that 'second death' of endless suffering? What is it in man that makes him, when he hears this, deliberately reject it, and think that he is clever in doing so? What is it that causes any man who has ever heard the Gospel and its offers of the free gift of salvation to refuse it? There is only one explanation. Such people are spiritually dead, they are slaves of Satan, they have been 'blinded by the god of this world'.

Can there be any other explanation? As you look at the two types of life, in every respect, from beginning to end – the masters, the types of life lived, the ends to which they lead – and see people rejecting the glory and deliberately choosing the way which leads to death, and boasting of it and delighting in it, one must ask: What explains it? There is only one explanation, they are 'dead in trespasses and sins'.

What then explains that any one of us is a Christian? For we are all like that by nature, by natural birth. What makes any man a Christian? Oh, it is grace, it is wondrous grace! There is no other explanation.

Romans 6 : 23

A debtor to mercy alone,
Of covenant mercy I sing

Nothing else! Nothing of which we can boast! It is all due to God's infinite kindness and compassion, it is because of 'the exceeding riches of his grace', it is because of His 'abundant mercy', it is because 'God is love'. May this love, this grace, possess us whole, and so deal with us that we shall feel that the exhortations of verses 12 and 13, and verse 19 in the sixth chapter of Romans are the height of reasonableness, and inevitable. We must not yield our bodies to sin, we must not allow sin to reign in our mortal flesh, or yield our members as servants and instruments of unrighteousness and sin. Seeing this, we must gladly obey the exhortation, and yield our every faculty, and all we have and are, as instruments and servants and vehicles and implements of righteousness unto holiness, and to the praise of our glorious God. 'The wages of sin is death, but the gift of God is eternal life through Jesus Christ our Lord.' Do you already possess the first instalment? Do you feel the first stirrings within you? Do you look with eager anticipation for the glory which is coming, and 'the crown of righteousness' which God Himself will place upon your brow? Do you meditate upon this bliss, this glory that is awaiting us – to be 'with Christ', and basking in the sunshine of God's glory; to be glorified ourselves and to spend our eternity in that glorious condition?